KEEP CALM
AND
Understand Society

An Introduction to Sociology

Calvin Henry Easterling

"Have a happy day!"

Ph.D., University of North Texas

M.Th., Southern Methodist University

M.A., Stephen F. Austin State University

B.A., McMurry University

Alpha Kappa Delta

Eta Epsilon Iota

Kendall Hunt
publishing company

Cover image © Shutterstock.com

Kendall Hunt
publishing company

www.kendallhunt.com
Send all inquiries to:
4050 Westmark Drive
Dubuque, IA 52004-1840

Published in the United States of America

Table of Contents

Preface

"Keep Calm and Carry On" was a poster produced by Great Britain in 1939, in response to threats from Nazi Germany to heavily bomb and eventually invade England. Many people thought it was ludicrous and impossible, but isn't it always better to calmly and rationally consider your surroundings before flying off in different directions out of fear and ignorance?

The study of sociology is one of the most exciting, interesting, and absorbing enterprises in which it is possible for humans to engage. It can serve the purpose of teaching us to become life-long learners with skills of knowing how to interpret statistics and current events in the light of history and social science.

This volume makes the assumption that transmission of the calming influence of sociology is within the realm of possibility. It aims toward fostering an appreciation of theory as well as the various substantive areas of sociology, which are sometimes said to have more "real world significance." The so-called empirical study which is not informed or inspired by a theoretical rationale of any kind (such as the kind of research encouraged by the eminent anthropologist Franz Boas) is nothing more than the gathering and dissemination of data—in Biblical terms, tinkling brass and sounding cymbal. My sincere prayer is that this volume will help in the process of assisting the reader in her move toward a "considered consideration" of the proliferation of sociological data available for thoughtful study.

This book should further serve to assist the reader in the formulation of her own social orientation. One may choose from among all the various perspectives presented herein. An individual may experience a "paradigm shift" when the revelation of a particular perspective becomes obvious. For others, bits and pieces of various social models may be incorporated in such a way as to modify already-held positions. There is always the possibility of the eclectic approach, in which no particular paradigm is adopted carte-blanche as one's "own," but different models are considered appropriate in particular contexts.

The reader may, of course, remain unimpressed with any attempt at engaging in the sociological enterprise as presented herein. This could be due to the reader's complete reservation of judgment until some indeterminate future time when the "right" theory makes an indelible impression on her, or a convincing argument is made in defense of a particular position. There could be a simple lack of interest in the subject matter, in which case, no apology need be attempted. The remaining logical reason for any failure of this volume in helping the reader assess the range of sociological models would be either:

1. A fundamental void of meaningful social thought available

   or

2. A fundamental flaw in this particular presentation of the sociological adventure

The author wishes to acknowledge the following for their roles in the publishing of this book: the infinite Covenant God of the Bible who is the source of all that exists; Gail Lynn Easterling for her encouragement and love; and my many outstanding students for their challenging questions and zest for life. Noteworthy, also are the Honors Research Group members Anna Bailey and Alex Mills; Behavioral Sciences administrative assistant Sandy Turnbow; and the staff of Kendall Hunt Publishers, Reveilee Lanning and Kim Schmidt.

—*Calvin Henry Easterling, Tulsa, Oklahoma*

Chapter 1

Thinking About Things Social

© Lot_is_studio/Shutterstock.com

From the earliest times, humans have thought about their social predicaments. Social analysis has been done in kitchens, pubs, churches, truck stops, and occasionally in the halls of academe. Anyone who thinks about social relationships is in some sense a sociologist, just as anyone who thinks about God is doing theology, however limited and uninformed such thought may be. The purpose of this book is to provide assistance for those who are interested in things social and desire some historical perspective and guidance for the grand task of social analysis. The assumption is that this volume will help make the experience more enjoyable and of a higher caliber.

Whether stated explicitly or implicitly, every sociological activity is ultimately based on some view of human nature. For Karl Marx, this was the tendency for conflict, for George Herbert Mead, the affinity toward

1

acting out roles, and for Emile Durkheim, human nature was the "longing for belonging." Nisbet (1990) called it the "quest for community." Most theories are concerned with describing and explaining social processes.

A social theory is really nothing more than a model of social interaction, whether at the macrolevel or the microlevel or both. It is a proposition or a set of propositions that relate in some way to our empirical observations in the experiential realm. A theory is a construction of the mind of the theorist and has no "reality" outside the thoughts of the theorist and possibly of those who attempt to comprehend it although some, most notably Levi-Strauss (1947), have proposed that the order we ascribe to the external universe is simply a reflection of the patterns of the human brain. Even if that is true, it would still be a constructed entity.

A theory is always contingent and hypothetical. It can never be conclusively "proven." Even if the results of observation seem to agree with the theory on a fairly consistent basis, one cannot be absolutely certain that some subsequent event will not counter the theory. Conversely, a theory can be effectively debunked (or "deconstructed," in Jacques Derrida's parlance) by locating even a single observation that conflicts with the prediction of the theory, and it must be abandoned or modified. Each time empirical observations seem to agree with the theory, our confidence in it is bolstered. Of course, one can always cast doubt on the competence of the particular individual making, reporting, or interpreting the observation, thus attempting to deconstruct—not the phenomenon, but its potency.

The Search for Patterns

What the theorists are always searching for, just as Easter egg hunters scrutinize every nook and cranny for their precious treasures, are PATTERNS of behavior. There are fewer than 100 naturally occurring elements that make up the entire physical universe around us. Galaxies, football stars, detergents, and spiders are comprised of the same basic stuff. It is how that stuff is arranged, or patterned, that makes the difference. We are told that every fingerprint of every person ever born is unique, yet each contains only three patterns—whorls, loops, and arches. Cole (1985) said, "Nature seems to be built on patterns, and looking for those patterns is the primary occupation of artists and scientists alike." The primary question of theoretical sociology is "What patterns occur in every society, in every culture?" More pragmatic-prone theorists are willing to discuss the practical implications of their theories, whereas others are content to conceptualize only on abstract levels.

The Search for Understanding

There is something about the study of sociology that is truly exhilarating, lifting one above the mundane facts and statistics of other substantive areas of study. The electrifying element involved may be the sensation that one is on the very cusp of uncovering the real nature of humanity, society, and social interaction, or that insightful understanding (Weber's *verstehen*), may actually be possible. In Sartrean terms, this is the project of "possessing the world through knowledge (Sartre, 1943)."

When the author was an undergraduate college student trying to decide on a major, he analyzed himself to determine just what it was that he wanted in life. He could have chosen the pursuit of money, self-expression through art, or any of a hundred other directions. He decided upon the study of sociology because what he desired above all else was to understand human society—why things are the way they are and why we do things we do. The appeal of attempting to discover answers to the compelling "why" questions of existence was acutely alluring. The author attests that the adventure of this quest for such social and behavioral insight has been a most rewarding one.

Grand Theory Versus Midrange Theorizing

Building a comprehensive sociological theory of the entire "social system," including the micro and macrolevels of analysis, is undoubtedly an extremely difficult and perilous enterprise. It has been attempted, most notably by Parsons (1951) and the economist Alfred Marshall, but we usually divide the problem into pieces or sections and devise a number of what Robert Merton referred to as "midrange" theories. Each of these fragmentary theories characterizes and predicts a certain narrow array of observations, either disregarding the effects of other such arrays or scientifically evading them by holding them "constant." It is conceivable that this approach is utterly inappropriate, erroneous, and unsatisfying in terms of achieving any grand overarching enlightenment regarding the essential nature of society. It is, on the other hand, certainly the way in which sociology has made what headway it has achieved up to the present.

We may thus be doomed to arrive at theories no more comprehensive than the various midrange theories. Perhaps someday someone will string together several limited theories into a grand scheme that will offer the utmost in explanatory and predictive power. If this should happen, it would possibly be the case that the theory itself had predicted itself!

One factor that reduces the likelihood of the discovery of such a grand theory when dealing with human societies is the phenomenon of the existential free will of human beings. When physicists and cosmologists concoct their "theories of everything," they do not have the limitation of the conscious decision-making ability of human individuals because atoms, photons, and neutrinos cannot choose their responses when acted upon by physical laws, quantum-level phenomena notwithstanding.

When weighing, contrasting, and assessing theories, it is advisable to keep in mind several criteria by which they may be evaluated. There are several such criteria to consider.

1. **Lucidity**—A good theory will "eschew obfuscation." A theory that is unclear is incapable of being fully understood. One problem might be that of failure to operationally define one's terms. Padding a theory with technical language and jargon may lend it an aura of authenticity and arbitrary authority, but only serves to obscure its insights, if, indeed, it contains any. Ideas that are not intelligibly articulated are objectionable candidates for clearheaded appraisal.

2. **Consistency**—The essence of the sociological enterprise is to depict a social model which holds together. The theory must, first of all, not contradict itself by making contentions in one section and then repudiating them elsewhere. It is indisputable, of course, that one's suppositions may become modified with time, but recurring inconsistencies can weaken even a promising theory. For example, Hobbes appeared to conjecture that certain early humans had particular notions and behavior in what he referred to as "the state of nature," that is, at the very time at which the "social contract" was made. This is contrary to Hobbes' own hypothesis, which states that the social contract cannot appear until society has been created by the contract! Similarly, there is the obvious inconsistency in Marx's insistence that the essence of human nature is conflict, but conflict will no longer take place in

the eschatologically inevitable harmonious state of communism. It is essential, then, that a theory's most serious internal contradictions be effectively averted, because to a great extent its worth will eventually be rated on the basis of how cogently its mutually supporting parts all hang together.

3. **Realism**—Need it be said that no theory can endure which is grounded on claims of empirical reality which are patently untrue? No social theory has ever succumbed because of an insignificant inaccuracy in a factual detail, but the chronic failure to furnish empirical assertions which conform to actual social occurrences in areas of chief importance to a theory can sabotage the credibility of the entire enterprise. No social conflict theory, for example, could persist in the face of unequivocal proof of the absence of conflict in social relations.

4. **Logical Coherence**—Some of the more typical flaws in social theories stem from the reckless practice of generalizing from scant or incomplete empirical data. The situation is particularly difficult because so much of what is assumed by many social theories, particularly those that are phenomenological, cannot always be seen in the molecular motions of humans, but must necessarily be deduced or attributed as a result of careful scrutiny of observed data. It is not normally feasible to carry out social experiments to check theoretical hypotheses, particularly when they appertain to considerable social transformations over prolonged intervals. Should any theory's hypothetical propositions be regularly disputed by empirical documentation, it must be discredited.

Each social theory presents a perspective of human interaction and makes some basic assumption concerning human nature. A social theory is, in the broadest sense, a paradigm, a model, a perspective, a way of looking at the world. At the very least, it is a proposition about some aspect of social reality, whether at the macro, midrange, or microlevel. The search for social patterns and understanding of why society is the way it is comprises the underlying motivation for the vast majority of sociological theorizing. In summary, there have been repeated bold attempts at building grand theories encompassing the entire "social system" or that are universally applicable in all social settings, but the bread-and-butter of sociology has been the various "midrange" theories.

Paradigm Shift

The study of sociology and social theory has proven to be life-changing for many people. By their own testimonies, countless students have told me that "their eyes were opened" when they began to think in terms of "the big picture" that sociology provides. This is the primary reason why sociology was banned in Communist China for 26 years, during the early years of the Soviet Union, and in Hitler's Germany. Müller (2016) compiled a list of 361 Austrian sociological authors exiled between 1933 and 1945. The list can be found on the website of The Archive for the History of Sociology in Austria at the Institute for Sociology at Karl Franzens University Graz. All authors listed have published at least one book or several journal articles in the field of sociology. The list includes the eminent figures Alfred Adler, Georgy Lukacs, and Karl Mannheim.

Such a change in one's way of looking at the world is sometimes referred to as a "paradigm shift." This is a term introduced by Thomas Kuhn, the outstanding philosopher of science. An example of a paradigm shift on a personal level is provided by Covey (1990).

I remember a mini-paradigm shift I experienced one Sunday morning on a subway in New York. People were sitting quietly—some reading newspapers, some lost in thought, some resting with their eyes closed. It was a calm, peaceful scene.

Then suddenly, a man and his children entered the subway car. The children were so loud and rambunctious that instantly the whole climate changed.

The man sat down next to me and closed his eyes, apparently oblivious to the situation. The children were yelling back and forth, throwing things, even grabbing people's papers. It was very disturbing. And yet, the man sitting next to me did nothing.

It was difficult not to feel irritated. I could not believe that he could be so insensitive as to let his children run wild like that and do nothing about it, taking no responsibility at all. It was easy to see that everyone else on the subway felt irritated, too. So finally, with what I felt was unusual patience and restraint, I turned to him and said, "Sir, your children are really disturbing a lot of people. I wonder if you couldn't control them a little more?"

The man lifted his gaze as if to come to a consciousness of the situation for the first time and said softly, "Oh, you're right. I guess I should do something about it. We just came from the hospital where their mother died about an hour ago. I don't know what to think, and I guess they don't know how to handle it either."

Can you imagine what I felt at that moment? My paradigm shifted. Suddenly, I <u>saw</u> things differently, and because I <u>saw</u> differently, I <u>thought</u> differently, I <u>felt</u> differently, I <u>behaved</u> differently. My irritation vanished. I didn't have to worry about controlling my attitude or my behavior; my heart was filled with the man's pain. Feelings of sympathy and compassion flowed freely. "Your wife just died? Oh, I'm so sorry! Can you tell me about it? What can I do to help?" Everything changed in an instant.

At its very best, sociology teaches you how to think. At its very worst, sociology teaches you what to think. It is not as important to learn facts as it is to learn principles.

When I read Bobby Fischer's book on how to play chess, the major point I gleaned was that one should not memorize specific moves, plays, and sequences of moves. One should, rather, adopt certain attitudes, general strategies, and principles of the game.

In sociology, though we live, breathe, eat, and sleep statistics, parameters, and detailed accounts of actual occurrences, what we are ultimately looking for are patterns of behavior. These patterns will hopefully apply from society to society and from generation to generation. A pattern may seem to ostensibly recede for a time, only to reoccur at some future juncture.

Definition of Sociology

Sociology is the scientific study of social interaction and the products of social interaction. By "scientific study" is meant the logical and systematic investigation of subject matter.

Science is more precisely defined as a systematically accumulated body of organized knowledge including a set of logically connected propositions concerning the behavior of certain phenomena as they repeatedly occur under certain conditions. For example, water—H_2O—is the result every time hydrogen and oxygen combine under similar conditions.

It is the goal of sociology to document and illustrate the occurrence of social phenomena. This is accomplished no differently from any other scientific discipline. The scientific method is—or should be—adhered to rigidly. The steps in the scientific method are fourfold:

1.   **The recognition and formulation of a problem**. Here the choice is made concerning the object or phenomenon(a) to be studied.
2.   **The collection of data** through observation and/or experiment. For the social sciences, much of the data are retrieved from the Bureau of the Census and other records, surveys, polls, and so on.
3.   **The testing of hypotheses** or research questions.
4.   **Dissemination of the results** through publication in journals or monographs or through presentation to professional gatherings, thus adding to the general body of knowledge.

"**Social interaction**" refers to the interaction of two or more persons. When, for instance, Dennis passes by Margaret on the sidewalk and they both say "Hi," has social interaction occurred? The answer is yes, but not at a very significant level. Marriage is social interaction at a much more intensive level. Teacher–student interaction is social interaction, as are church worship services, protest marches, sales pitches, gang fights, and employment interviews.

The "**products**" **of social interaction** refers to whatever is produced as the result of the interaction of two or more persons. An automobile is a product of social interaction. A shirt is a product of social interaction, as are a pen, an office building, a tennis ball, and—yes—you, yourself! Nonmaterial things can be the products of social interaction, as well, such as a university, a church, a club, patriotism, truth, culture, and so on. Society itself is the product of social interaction, along with all of its institutions, such as the family, the military, government, religion, education, health care, business, sport, and entertainment.

The Easterling Decalogue Model

When thinking about the discipline of sociology, it is helpful to utilize the Decalogue Model, based on the passage from Exodus 20:1-17, in which Moses received the Ten Commandments from the finger of Yahweh. An analysis of this passage reveals a major distinction between theology and sociology.

Theology is the study of the vertical relationship between hominids and God. Anyone who thinks about God is, in some sense, "doing theology." The first four commandments relate, therefore, to theology.

Sociology, on the other hand, is the study of our horizontal relationships with one another. The other six commandments relate to sociology.

THEOLOGY: 40%

1. Thou shalt have no other gods before me.
2. Thou shalt not make and worship any graven image.
3. Thou shalt not take the name of the Lord thy God in vain.
4. Remember the Sabbath day, to keep it holy.

SOCIOLOGY: 60%

1. Honor thy father and mother, that thy days may be long on the earth.
2. Thou shalt not kill.
3. Thou shalt not commit adultery.
4. Thou shalt not bear false witness against thy neighbor.
5. Thou shalt not covet anything that is thy neighbor's.
6. Thou shalt not steal.

Theology quite properly comes first, since for believers, one's relationship with the Almighty supersedes all other relationships in priority. Notice, however, that the majority of the law pertains to social relationships. This model should serve to underline both the preeminence of theology and the relative importance of sociology.

Similarly, the Jewish founder of Christianity, Jesus of Nazareth, highlighted repeatedly the relative importance of horizontal human relationships. One example is His answer to a question in Matthew 22:36-40.

THEOLOGY:

1. Master, which is the great commandment in the law?
2. Jesus said unto him, Thou shalt love the Lord thy God with all thy heart, and with all thy soul, and with all thy mind.
3. This is the first and great commandment.

SOCIOLOGY:

1. And the second is like unto it, Thou shalt love thy neighbor as thyself.
2. On these two commandments hang all the law and the prophets.

Name _____   Date _____

Chapter 1   Thinking About Things Social

Chapter Exercise

(This assignment is to be carefully torn out and completed at the direction of the instructor. The answers are to be legibly handwritten directly on the sheets. Do not photocopy these pages, as such action would constitute a blatant violation of the copyright laws of the United States of America. Thoroughly read the assigned text before attempting to complete a tear-out assignment. It is obvious when a student has tried to fill-in an assignment without reading the background material.)

Describe a "paradigm shift" that has occurred in your life. It might be related to your conversion experience, your choice of a major or minor subject, or to your theological orientation. Describe your perspective both before and after the shift took place.

Lines for writing front and back of this page:

_____

_____

_____

_____

_____

_____

_____

_____

_____

_____

_____

Chapter 2

The Dead Giants

A number of sociologists are commonly referred to as the "dead giants" of sociology. This is so for two reasons. First, they are dead; and secondly, their work has had such a profound effect upon the discipline.

Harriet Martineau

Harriet Martineau (1802–1876) was a prominent English novelist and sociologist. She descended from a paternal line of medical practitioners, ending with the death of her elder brother at less than 30 years of age. Her father was not a surgeon, but a manufacturer. She was born the sixth child in a family of eight on June 12, 1802.

© Bettmann/Contributor/Getty Images

She reports her childhood as having been an unhappy one. Her mother is said to have lacked tenderness with children.

Harriet suffered ill health as a child. She almost died in infancy due to a dishonest wet-nurse who concealed the fact that she had lost her milk. She had a serious hearing problem, a severe vision disorder, had no sense of smell, and reported an inability to digest her food. She also suffered from severe nightmares and "causeless apprehensions" during the daylight hours. She was in constant terror of her environment. Her mother is reported to have been a dominating woman who "ruled" the home and her family. Harriet resided in Norwich, where her French ancestors had settled in an attempt to escape persecution in their homeland.

A Productive Career

In 1820, Martineau's father died, leaving Harriet to support herself in a patriarchal society. Her fiancé also died, and she never married. She successfully supported herself as an author in numerous genres. She published essays, tracts, reviews, novels, travelogues, biographies, how-to manuals, journal articles, newspaper columns, histories, children's stories, and sociologically informed nonfiction. She was known in England as a successful writer.

Martineau was brought up as a devout Unitarian, which is evident in her first writings, reflecting strong religious direction. She adopted "Necessarianism," which provided her with an intellectual bridge to a social scientific perspective. She published *Illustrations of Political Economy* in 1834. In this writing, Martineau used fiction to explain the principles of the new science of political economy, and her effort was very successful. She lived in London during this time, and she was associated with Charles Babbage, Thomas Carlyle, George Eliot, Florence Nightingale, Charles Dickens, Thomas Malthus, William Wordsworth, Charlotte Bronte, Charles Lyell, and Charles Darwin. *Illustrations of Political Economy* aided her entrance into British literary society and helped her establish financial independence.

In 1834, Martineau visited the United States for a 2-year study. She toured the United States and wrote her observations in two books, *Society in America* and *Retrospect of Western Travel*. In 1838, she wrote *How to Observe Morals and Manners*, in which she articulated the principles and methods of empirical social research.

In 1848, Martineau made a trip to the Middle East, and reported on her trip in *Eastern Life, Present and Past*. In Auguste Comte's *Cours de Philosophie Positive*, she is credited with the facilitation and introduction of positive philosophical ideas into the United States, primarily as a result of her famous translation of Comte's most influential sociological work from French into English.

Impact of Martineau

Before Karl Marx, and decades before Emile Durkheim and Max Weber, Harriet Martineau sociologically examined social class, forms of religion, types of suicide, national character, domestic relations, the status of women, delinquency, and criminology. She further investigated the intricate interrelations between repressive social institutions and the individual.

Harriet Martineau was a pioneer in sociology. Alice Rossi justly celebrates her as "the first woman sociologist."

Martineau lived her last years in the Lake District, where she built a house at Ambleside. Her final years were spent in failing health. She died at age 74 in 1876. She had lived her life with a deep sense of personal and social mission. She exemplifies this in the following statement: "Authorship has never been for me a matter of choice. I have not done it for amusement, or for money, for fame, or for any other reason but because I could not help it. Things were pressing to be said; and there was more or less evidence that I was the person to say them." (Martineau, 1883a, p. 155)

Auguste Comte

The individual who is known as the "Parent of Sociology" is the Frenchman Auguste Comte (1798–1857). This is so despite the fact that Martineau was his contemporary and in some respects his intellectual superior.

Born into a Catholic family in Montpellier, France, Comte studied at the *Ecole Polytechnique* for a time, but was expelled as a subversive because of his republican views. He served as secretary to another social theorist, Saint-Simon, from 1817 to 1823. In 1830, he founded a group determined to enhance the education of young people from the working class. Later in life, he founded the "*Societe Positiviste*," a religion similar to the Catholic Church but without reference to God. He taught the humanistic idea that man was the highest form of life and humanity would solve all its own problems through science.

Social Physics—Comte actually coined the term "*sociologie*" (sociology) in 1838. At first, he called the new discipline "social physics," because he wanted it to be associated with the so-called physical sciences, the oldest of which is probably astronomy.

Comte maintained that society had both **social statics**, or a tendency to maintain equilibrium, and **social dynamics**, corresponding to what is today called social change. These two ideas have become the bases for later theoretical constructs of the social system, social conflict, and social change.

N+1 Factor—Central to Comte's thought and to sociology itself is the idea of the "N+1 Factor." This refers to the notion that society is more than just the sum of its parts. Society or any group within society is not just a collection of individuals, but is a social reality and has a "life" or identity of its own.

Three major stages in the history of social thought—Comte taught that there have been three major stages in the history of social thought. The first stage was the **theological stage**. In this stage, it was believed that the social order was set up and ordained by supernatural personalities. The gods of Greece, Rome, and other societies ruled the world and determined what happened among humans.

During the second stage—the **metaphysical stage**—equally mystical but more abstract explanations were made concerning the existence of societies. During the metaphysical stage, it was thought that there were impersonal forces at work (such as the forces of god and evil) that determined social outcomes.

The third and final stage in the evolution of social thought, according to Comte, is the **scientific stage**. This refers to the application of the scientific method to the ways in which reality is conceived. The hope is that science will save the world.

Positivism—Comte stretched the idea of the third stage into what became known as positivism, the idea that science is the path to knowledge. He actually founded a religion—complete with priests and "temples" in several European locations—predicated upon the humanistic belief in science as the "savior" of humanity.

Science will provide us, it was asserted, with the solutions to all human problems such as disease, famine, and war. Positivism was an extreme form of belief in the idea of progress: "every day, in every way, the world is getting better and better." The application of science was to be the antidote to the many ills of society.

Of course, since Comte's time, there have been many major wars—including two world wars—droughts, floods, and famines. Science has flourished through the years, but so have poverty, disease, pollution, starvation, nuclear proliferation, racism, sexism, ageism, crime, drug abuse, child abuse, woman-battering, and political corruption. Certain political regimes have even attempted to completely annihilate entire categories of people.

Where was science through all this? Quietly going about its business, providing many benefits for humanity. It is incorrect to expect science to be something it cannot be, as Comte expected; namely, the salvation of the planet. There is no doubt, however, that science has made great contributions to the quality of life, life expectancy, and material comfort of billions of persons.

Herbert Spencer

Another "dead giant" of the discipline of sociology is the Englishman Herbert Spencer (1820–1903). Spencer was a close friend of Charles Darwin and a firm believer in and an outspoken advocate of the theory of macro-evolution. He wrote textbooks on biology (Spencer, 1867) used at Oxford and Cambridge. It was, in fact, Spencer, not Darwin, who coined the phrase **"the survival of the fittest**." Spencer did not only believe in biological evolution, but also in the evolution of human societies (the word "evolution" simply means change in a particular direction). This idea was adapted in various forms by Marx and many other social theorists.

© Michael Nicholson/Contributor/Getty Images

Spencer carried his idea of the survival of the fittest to such an extreme that he openly opposed all governmental welfare programs to help the poor (Spencer, 1898). Those who were poor did not deserve to survive because they were "less fit." It was up to the process of evolution to naturally "weed out" the weaker members of society. This notion became known as **"Social Darwinism."**

Spencer's ideas provided justification for laissez-faire capitalism. He opposed immigration and his views are known today to have been fairly racist. He wrote letters to the Queen and to Parliament urging them to remove at once all lighthouses from the seacoasts of the British Empire around the globe. His reasoning was that only those ships whose navigators were the "fittest"—those who could navigate safely along rocky coastlines at night or in stormy weather—should survive. He was convinced that this would force navigators to develop better techniques. Spencer argued against "racial" intermarriage, for he saw it as a deterioration of the human species. He debated against public schooling, for only those who could afford an education should receive instruction. By the same logic, he argued against the postal service and the public library system. He also championed the idea that "the less government the better," which became the cardinal principle of libertarianism.

Spencer's Influence

Though he never held an academic post at any college or university (for a time, he edited the British journal, *The Economist*), Spencer's ideas had a broad distribution. He wrote in a popular journalistic style that caught the attention of many people worldwide. Industrial leaders of the time warmly supported and received him. His views were particularly widely accepted in the United States because they fit neatly the concept of laissez-faire capitalism and downplayed the importance of government intervention in the business world.

John D. Rockefeller is said to have been an ardent admirer of Herbert Spencer and a proponent of his ideas, and even to have taught some of these principles in his Baptist Sunday School class in Cleveland, Ohio. This is undoubtedly because Social Darwinism tended to validate Rockefeller's practice of eliminating his competition in the oil production business by means of rebates, kickbacks, bribes, and price-fixing.

Spencer had a great influence on E. A. Ross and other American sociologists early on. William Graham Sumner at Yale University was particularly enamored with Spencer's ideas. Spencer was heavily influenced by British market theory, but Sumner was naive about economics. Lester Ward, of Brown University, was better read than Sumner, but pretty well followed Spencer.

Herbert Spencer was one of the popularizers of agnosticism. He observed accurately that a bird has never been able to fly into outer space. He concluded by analogy that it is impossible for the finite to penetrate the infinite. He missed an alternative possibility that the infinite could penetrate the finite. This is what Christians claim that God has done through the incarnation of Jesus, the Christ (Little, 1968).

Emile Durkheim

Emile Durkheim (1858–1917), a French sociologist, must be included in our list of "dead giants." He was born in Epinal, near Strasbourg, the son of a Jewish rabbi, and was educated in France and Germany. He studied law, philosophy, and social science, and was the first professor of sociology at the University of Bordeaux. In 1902, Durkheim became a lecturer in sociology and education until his death in 1917.

Durkheim's work is fundamental to the discipline of sociology. He was mostly concerned with the impact of the large-scale structures of society—and society itself—on the thoughts and actions of individuals. He was rather influential in shaping structural-functional theory with its emphasis on social structure and culture. He further insisted that sociology must be a comparative science which makes comparisons between and among societies at comparable levels of development.

The Study of Suicide

Durkheim is perhaps best known for his study of suicide. He studied suicide statistics in various nations of the world. Although some of his data were necessarily unreliable, he nevertheless was able to draw some general conclusions. He saw that suicide rates were somewhat higher in more industrialized countries. Within the societies he studied, Durkheim found suicide to be more common among men than among women, among Protestants rather than Catholics and Jews, and among the wealthy and single persons than among the poor and those who were married.

Durkheim believed that suicide was related to what he called "social solidarity." **Social solidarity** is cohesiveness or the extent to which people feel bonded to others or integrated into society. Married people tend to have more social solidarity than single persons. Wealthy people and men tend to have greater personal autonomy or freedom than the poor or women; hence, less social solidarity or "sense of belonging." Protestantism tends to be more individualistic than most other forms of religious belief. Protestant theology tends toward belief that salvation is dependent upon an individual's personal relationship with God, rather than upon one's group membership in a church or denomination. Certain ethnic groups experience greater social solidarity than do others; hence, there are ethnic variations in suicide rates.

Durkheim's book *Suicide* was published in 1897. About a century later, his concepts and theoretical hypotheses concerning suicide still hold water. In the United States today, suicide tends to be largely a White male phenomenon. The **suicide rate** (Macionis, 2016) for White males (26.9 per 100,000) is almost three times that for African American males (9.5). White males are three times more likely to commit suicide than are White females (7.9). African American females (2.1) are the least likely candidates for suicide, though the rate for Hispanic females is only 2.2.

Durkheim operationally defined **suicide** as all deaths that result from an active or passive act by the victim herself which she knows will result in her death. Before he could develop any general ideas of causation, he first had to search for similarities among the various modes of suicide. Five of these he attributed to what he referred to as "a psychopathic state of mind." These were:

1. *Maniacal*—a result of hallucinations or delirium.
2. *Melancholy*—extreme depression.
3. *Obsessive*—a preoccupation with one's own death.
4. *Impulsive*—without cognitive reasoning.
5. *Suggestion*—descendants of suicide victims may be more likely to commit suicide, but Durkheim insisted that this is due to "the power of suggestion" rather than to heredity. (Durkheim, 1897)

While exploring the possibility that climatic conditions may affect suicide rates, he found that one factor was the length of daylight, which varied directly with the rate of suicide. He concluded that this was due to the increased number of interactions during daylight hours. There are contemporary researchers who have made similar findings and who suggest more lighting for suicidal persons. Durkheim spoke of four types of suicide.

1. In **egoistic suicide** the individual lacks concern for the community with which she is inadequately involved. The

individual is not well integrated into a social unit. It has been claimed that loneliness is more deadly than obesity or smoking (Olien, 2013).

2. **Altruistic suicide** is due to an excessive sense of duty to the community. An example would be the Japanese *kamikaze* pilots who flew their bomb-laden aircraft directly into U.S. Navy ships during World War II or contemporary so-called "suicide bombers" performing terrorist attacks on. Durkheim said that when there is a great deal of altruistic suicide, it is an indicator that social integration is too strong.

3. **Fatalistic suicide** occurs when the individual's future looks bleak. It is the product of one possible response to hopelessness, the feeling that "nothing matters, nobody cares." Fatalistic suicides occurred in large numbers during the U.S. stock market crash of 1929. Durkheim attributed this type of suicide to excessive regulation (e.g., slavery, or prison populations; there may be only 12/100,000 suicides in the general population, but 135/100,000 in county and city jails).

4. **Anomic suicide** is quite the opposite of fatalistic suicide. It occurs, according to Durkheim, due to society's failure to control and regulate the behavior of individuals. Anomie means a state of "normlessness" and indicates a general weakness in society's provision of guidelines for the expected behavior of individuals. Anomie means that social boundaries are not clearly drawn; individuals are confused concerning what behaviors are expected of them. It occurs when individuals do not have a clear concept of what is and is not acceptable behavior due to lack of sufficient moral constraint.

The Sociology of Religion

Durkheim's interests were not limited to the study of suicide. He was interested, as well, in religion in all its forms. His foundational work in the sociology of religion is *The Elementary Forms of Religious Life*, published in 1912. Durkheim's other major works are *The Division of Labor in Society*, published in 1893, and *The Rules of the Sociological Method*, published in 1895, in which he laid the groundwork for most of the research that has been done in the social sciences.

In *The Elementary Forms of Religious Life* (1912), Durkheim focused on nonmaterial social facts, particularly religion. Religion has a **"dynamogenic" quality**—the capacity to both dominate individuals and raise them above ordinary abilities and capacities. Using secondary data, Durkheim studied the Arunta Aborigines of Australia. He believed that, in contrast to modern, developed religions, the primitive setting provided:

1. Clearer forms of the essential nature of religion.
2. More basic ideological systems.
3. More intellectual and moral conformity (Ritzer, 1988).

Primitive religion also gave insight into modern religion. In primitive societies, religion is equated with the collective conscience, but as society develops, religion becomes merely one of a number of collective representations (such as law, education, the family, the state, and science); these later collective representations, however, have their origins in primitive religion.

A key question to Durkheim is the source of primitive and modern religions. Durkheim's definition of **religion** goes like this: "A religion is a unified system of beliefs and practices relative to sacred things; that is to say, things set apart and forbidden—beliefs and practices which unite into one single moral community called a church, all those who adhere to them (Durkheim, 1912)." He assumes that only one social fact can cause another social fact; thus, society is the source of all religion. Some conditions for the development of religion are:

1. Society creates religion by separating phenomena into the sacred or the profane. The sacred is that which set apart and forbidden, causing awe, reverence, mystery, or respect. The profane includes the ordinary elements of everyday life—the commonplace and mundane.
2. A set of religious beliefs about the nature of religious things.
3. A set of religious rites or rules of religious conduct.
4. A church or overarching moral community.

Durkheim believed totemism was the simplest and most primitive form of religion. **Totemism** is a religious system in which such things as animals and plants are regarded as sacred and as emblems of a clan (a primitive form of social organization). The plant or animal is a material representation of the immaterial forces or the collective conscience of society.

According to Durkheim, the collective conscience is derived from society; that is, the clan is the ultimate source of religion. The clan creates totemism through what Durkheim describes as "collective effervescence"—moments in history in which new and increased levels of collective exaltation change social structures. Examples of this phenomenon include the Renaissance and the Reformation. Totemism is the symbolic representation of the collective conscience. Society, according to Durkheim, is the source of the collective conscience, religion, and, therefore, God; hence, for Durkheim, God and society are the same. The collective conscience can be differentiated on four dimensions:

1. **Volume**—the number of people enveloped by the collective conscience.
2. **Intensity**—how deeply the people feel about it.
3. **Rigidity**—how clearly it is defined.
4. **Content**—the form which the collective conscience takes.

Durkheim's approach to social problems was to treat them as pathological. He thought they could eventually be "cured" by "social physicians," who were actually reformist in orientation. In this regard, Durkheim is rather positivistic, believing structural reform would alleviate social maladies.

Social Facts

Durkheim is also remembered for his use and development of the concept of "social fact." **Social facts** are the social structure and cultural norms and values that are external to, and coercive of, actors. He delineates between material and nonmaterial social facts. **Material social facts** include society, the structural components of society, and the morphological components of society. **Nonmaterial social facts** are such things as morality, the collective conscience (equal to "religion" in more primitive societies), collective representations (such as law and science), and social currents (nonmaterial social facts which have the same objectivity and ascendancy over the individual, but without such crystallized form).

The Division of Labor

In *The Division of Labor in Society* (1893), Durkheim provides an analysis of the development of the modern world which is based on two ideal types of society. He taught that the division of labor in a society determines the kind of society.

The **division of labor** refers to the separation of work into distinct parts, each of which is completed by an individual or group of individuals. The primitive type has a relatively undifferentiated social structure. This type is characterized as having **mechanical solidarity**, which means the norms of the society bear directly upon the individual and exercise social restraint on her. The modern type leaves individual behavior unregulated. This type is characterized by Durkheim as having **organic solidarity**, which is based on the interdependence of highly individuated members. **Dynamic density** is a social fact which is a causal factor in Durkheim's theory of the transition from mechanical to organic solidarity. This concept refers to the number of people in a society and the amount of interaction that occurs among them.

Max Weber

© Hulton Archive/Staff/Getty Images

Another of the "dead giants" of sociology who rose to eminence after Calvin and Hobbes is Max Weber (pronounced "Mocks Vay-burr"), a German sociologist (1864–1920). This dead giant has greatly influenced sociological thought and method.

Weber was the oldest of seven children in a prosperous bourgeois family. His grandparents on both sides were fairly wealthy. His mother was pietistic. His father was a lawyer who was active in politics and favored Bismarck, who unified the German states. Weber was authoritarian and Max's mother was browbeaten. They lived in Berlin during most of Weber's youth.

Max began studying law at the University of Heidelberg at the age of 18. He did military service in 1883, which he took very seriously. He joined the Association for Social Policy and worked with them throughout most of his life. His brother Alfred was an important German economist who is best known to sociologists for his study of the relationship between culture and the growth of knowledge.

Weber occupied a chair in political science at the University of Heidelberg. His first lecture was on agricultural economics. Marianne, his wife, became well-known for her writings about Weber and other sociologists, such as Simmel, Michels, and Toennies.

In 1897, Weber had a severe argument with his father, who died soon afterward. Max subsequently had a mental breakdown and became academically inactive for 4 years. Though he eventually recovered somewhat, his health was poor for the remainder of his life.

After his recovery, Weber worked hard and developed a good reputation for serious scholarship among the senior professors at his university. He began a grand effort to categorize everything sociological. *Economy and Society* (1922) was his major work. It was not finished at the time of his death.

In 1910, Weber was in very close contact with every German social scientist and organized the German Sociological Society with Georg Simmel and Ferdinand Toennies. Along with Marianne, he maintained correspondence with those who were in dispute with each other, including Robert Michels, who felt so bitterly toward the other German sociologists that he changed his residence to Italy.

During World War I, Weber was an enthusiastic German patriot and was involved in establishing German war hospitals. He served on the German delegation at the conclusion of World War I, and he helped write the Weimar Republic Constitution. Very committed to modern democratic ideas, Weber was a "republican." He did not think that everyone's ideas were equal. He was class-conscious, an anglophile, and had a deep sense of honor and obligation. He believed that a class system was helpful in reducing tyranny.

Verstehen

Weber emphasized substantive sociology over methodology. He wanted to show causal analysis of phenomena and viewed the task of sociology as that of supplying concepts useful for the causal analysis of history. Weber emphasized the importance of *verstehen*, "sympathetic understanding," trying to understand the author and not just the text. This is also known as hermeneutics, looking at what a person has written in comparison with its context and with her other works as well as with her *sitz im leben* (situation in life).

Defining one's terms was a major concern of Weber's, as was **causality**— the probability that an event will be followed by another event. He believed that sociology is a probabilistic science and ought to make predictive causal statements, since there is no single scientific model, there are only potential sciences.

The Protestant Ethic

Weber is perhaps best known for his monumental book *The Protestant Ethic and the Spirit of Capitalism* (1905/1920). In this work he theorizes about the causes for the phenomenal growth of capitalism in the Western World. Unlike Marx, who, in his insistence upon the preeminence of the economic variable, was unidimensionally deterministic, Weber attempted to illustrate that other factors, including ideas and beliefs, could be equally as influential.

When Weber talks about Protestantism, he means primarily fundamentalistic Calvinism. The major tenet of Calvinism upon which Weber focuses is the idea of predestination. **Predestination** means that God has already—from the foundation of the world; that is, before anyone was born—determined each individual's eternal destiny. There is nothing anyone can do to change her eternal destiny. Prayer will not help, nor will repentance, nor good works. Whether one is going to Heaven or Hell; that is, whether a person is one of the **"elect"** or one of the **"condemned,"** is predestined by God.

According to Calvin (1509–1564), however, even though it is not known at birth whether a person is one of the elect, God does provide **signs** which give indications of an individual's destiny. For instance, if a person lives a "holy" life, works hard, is not lazy, and becomes prosperous in business or a profession, it is obvious that the "blessing of God" is upon her life and she is probably one of the chosen elect. On the other hand, if one is a drunkard or a scoundrel or even simply unfortunate in business, it is obvious that she is among those whom God has condemned.

Weber's stroke of genius lay in his ability to relate this theology, which had become predominant throughout much of Europe and the American colonies by 1750, to the rise of capitalism and the industrial revolution. He reasoned that the desire to prove oneself to be among the elect led to what has been called the **"Protestant work ethic."** This work ethic, in which one's diligence showed her eternal destiny to be Heaven, dove-tailed very nicely with the needs of capitalism.

People worked hard to build factories, farms, textile mills, mercantile enterprises, and so on. In the process, they built a vast and complex economy. In time, the religious elements of the work ethic diminished, but it remains as a powerful cultural force today, still fueling the world's capitalistic economy with drive, ambition, and willpower.

Ideal Types

The **ideal type** is a conceptual tool sociologists developed for historians. It is a heuristic device (a way to explain something) which may be static or dynamic, but with a tendency to change over time. Ideal types are revised continuously to incrementally improve their "fit" with reality. An ideal type is at the extreme end of a continuum, and may not actually exist in reality, but is used solely for the purpose of classification and comparison.

Profane   Sacred

Rationalization and Bureaucracy

Weber is heralded for his extensive writings about bureaucracy (Weber, 1922). He was the first person to write academically about bureaucracies. His concept of "ideal types" of formal organizations is still accepted today. He insisted that bureaucracy has the highest level of efficiency and that capitalism probably provides the best-known historical setting for the rise of bureaucracy. Capitalism requires rational calculations of productivity and the coordinated efforts of large organizations. **Rationalization** refers to the substitution of explicit formal rules and procedures for spontaneous methods and attitudes. The ultimate result of this substitution process is rationalized institutions and the paramount archetype of these is the bureaucracy.

Power, for Weber, refers to the probability that a command will be followed. Rational authority (sometimes referred to as rational-legal) is grounded on belief in the legality of the constitution and statutes. If an individual's leadership position has been legally obtained, then that person's authority is legitimate. If power follows illogical but shared understandings, it is traditional. Traditional authority tends to produce arbitrariness. Any leader can destroy her credibility by breaking too much tradition. **Charismatic authority** is ascribed to the leader by the people. It is leadership which cannot be defined as traditional or rational.

Value Free Sociology

Weber further contributed to sociology by his insistence upon being "value free" in sociological research (Weber, 1922). Though it is probably impossible to prevent one's own personal beliefs, prejudices, and values from entering into one's work, Weber believed it was possible and urged sociologists to diligently endeavor to do so. This is because there are so many special interests that would like to skew sociological research in their favor. Such interest groups might include the alt left, conservatives, Marxists, feminists, ethnic groups, religious groups, political parties, and so on.

It is acceptable for one's values to be influential in the choice of what to study. It is not acceptable, however, according to Weber, to allow those values to affect the collection, manipulation, and presentation of the data. This part of the research process must be conducted strictly scientifically, fairly, and completely without any bias. The sociologist's values may reenter the process when drawing conclusions based on the data, but not to the extent that the results are misrepresented.

Name _____   Date _____

Chapter 2   The Dead Giants

Chapter Exercise

(This assignment is to be carefully torn out and completed at the direction of the instructor. The answers are to be legibly handwritten directly on the sheets. *Do not* photocopy these pages, as such action would constitute a blatant violation of the copyright laws of the United States. Thoroughly read the assigned text before attempting to complete a tear-out assignment. It is obvious when a student has tried to fill-in an assignment without reading the background material.)

Based on your readings, select any one "dead giant" and comment on the influence of his or her contributions to modern society.

_____

_____

_____

_____

_____

_____

_____

_____

_____

_____

_____

_____

_____

Chapter 3

The Three Major Paradigms of Sociology

The Structural–Functional Paradigm

A model is a paradigm or a way of thinking about something. In sociology, a **theoretical paradigm** is a fundamental image of society that guides sociological thinking. This same concept is sometimes referred to as a **theoretical perspective** or a way of looking at—viewing—the world.

There are countless theoretical perspectives used by sociologists to explain the varieties of social phenomena around us. These are generally thought to revolve around three major paradigms which have provided the bases for the majority of social thought: structural functionalism, social conflict theory, and symbolic interactionism.

According to Dahrendorf, there are several basic assumptions of structural functionalism (Dahrendorf, 1959):

1. Every society is a relatively persistent, stable structure of elements.
2. Every society is a well-integrated structure of elements.
3. Every element in a society has a function, that is, renders a contribution to its maintenance as a system.
4. Every functioning social structure is based on a consensus of values among its members.

Talcott Parsons

The sociologist most commonly associated with the structural–functional paradigm is Talcott Parsons (1902–1979), although much of the theory was originally formulated by Emile Durkheim and Herbert Spencer. Parsons graduated from Amherst College and studied at the London School of Economics and Heidelberg University. In 1946, he became the first chairperson of Harvard University's Department of Social Relations. The structural–functional paradigm views society as a social system made up of many different parts that work together to generate relative stability, or "equilibrium."

Durkheim framed the **organic model** of society, in which it is thought that each of the various parts of society has a **function** for the good of the whole, just as parts of the human body have individual functions which further the continuation of that organism. Just as the parts of the organism are arranged in a certain order, with the head in a particular position, as well as the heart, lungs, limbs, and so on, so does society have structure. The **structure** of society consists in the arrangement of its institutions, customs, beliefs, and other patterns of behavior.

The idea of "function" is very important in sociology. It provides a vehicle for the analysis of the various forms of behavior. For instance, some people denigrate the custom of having a funeral for a person who is deceased. "Just bury me in a pine box when I go. I don't want no preacher sayin' fancy words over me." The sociologist, however, will point out that the funeral service is functional. It may do nothing, in fact, for the deceased, since she has already departed, but the service is directed toward those who are still living. It provides the theological or philosophical explanations of death and the circumstances surrounding the death of this person. It helps alleviate the fear of death, which may pervade survivors when one among them departs this life. The funeral service commemorates the life of the deceased in terms that may renew the survivors' commitments to their nation, society, family, or religion. Not the least among the functions of the funeral is that it serves as a rite of passage. It is a ritual that makes it clear that this individual has passed from one status (in this case, life) to another (death, or some state beyond ordinary life).

In addition to the organic model, there is also the **mechanistic model** of society. In this framework, the society is likened to a machine; for example, an automobile. The automobile has structure and most cars have a basic structure that is similar. The various parts of the automobile are functional for the operation of the whole machine. The engine, tires, transmission, steering wheel, and so on, each is structured in a particular position and plays a role in the safe or enjoyable operation of the vehicle. Those structural functionalists who subscribe to the mechanistic model point out its analogical parallels to the social realities around us.

Parsons suggested that just as a machine has needs (e.g., oil, fuel, maintenance, an operator, and streets) in order to function and an organism has needs (e.g., food, water, air, proper temperature, and protection from the elements), so does the "social system" have needs. These needs, called by Parsons (1951) "functional imperatives," or "**functional requisites**," include:

1. **Adaptation**—The problem of securing from the environment sufficient facilities (such as food and shelter) and then distributing

these facilities throughout the system. This is achieved through the economy.

2. **Goal attainment**—The problem of establishing priorities among system goals and mobilizing system resources for their attainment. This is achieved through the political process.

3. **Integration**—The problem of coordinating and maintaining viable interrelationships among system units. This is achieved through the educational and legal institutions.

4. **Latency**—Includes both

   a. **Pattern Maintenance**—The problem of how to ensure that actors in the social system display the appropriate characteristics (motives, needs, role-playing skills, etc.), which is achieved through religion and the family

   b. **Tension Management**—The problem of dealing with the internal tensions and strains of actors in the social system. This is achieved through the civil and criminal justice systems.

As can be seen in this list of functional requisites, the various needs of society are met by the various social institutions. These institutions work to maintain the "**equilibrium**" of society; that is, to keep society as it is. Structural functionalism is, therefore, a somewhat "conservative" paradigm, in that it defines as functional the social mechanisms which function to avert social change.

The typical questions asked by structural functionalists include:

1. "What social patterns tend to persist in human societies?"
2. "How does each pattern function to keep society going as it is?"

Robert K. Merton

Robert K. Merton was a student of Talcott Parsons at Harvard University and later taught at Columbia University. He elaborated the structural–functional paradigm with a typology of functions. Merton introduced the concepts of manifest and latent functions.

© Pictorial Parade/Staff/Getty Images

1. **Manifest functions** are consequences that are recognized and intended by the actors.

2. **Latent functions**, conversely, are consequences that are unrecognized and unintended.

   To exemplify the concepts of manifest and latent functions, let us use the analogy of the automobile. The manifest function of an automobile is to provide basic transportation from point A to point B. This is the obvious and intended consequence. If this was the only function, everyone would be content to drive an old ugly car. This is, however, not the case; therefore, we can conclude that a latent function of the automobile is that of a status symbol. A sleek prestigious vehicle is more desirable to many persons than the perhaps more reliable and fuel-efficient cheap car.

3. Merton further introduced the idea of **dysfunction**. He proposed that there may be some elements of society, which are not functional. In fact, certain phenomena may be harmful to the smooth operation of the social system. Examples would include alcoholism, child abuse, crime, poverty, and so on.

The term "dysfunctional family" refers to a family that is neglectful of its children or perhaps even negatively socializing its children, so as to be expensive to society in terms of producing young people who are dependent upon social services and welfare when they reach adulthood, prone to criminality, unhealthy, and who may, in turn, abuse their own children. To continue the analogy of the automobile, it could be considered dysfunctional in a number of respects, not the least of which is air pollution.

The Functions of Poverty

Herbert Gans is a structural functionalist who has taken a novel and ingenious approach in the consideration of poverty as actually being functional for society. According to the Bible, Jesus stated that the poor would be with us always in our earthly predicament (St. Matthew 26:11). Gans (1971) has made a well-known sociological attempt at explaining why this is so.

1. The existence of poverty ensures that society's "dirty work" will be done. In America, poverty functions to provide a low-wage labor pool that is willing—or, rather, unable to be unwilling—to perform society's dirty work at low cost.

2. Because the poor are required to work at low wages, they subsidize a variety of economic activities that benefit the affluent. Because the poor pay a higher proportion of their income in property and sales taxes, among others, they subsidize many state and local governmental services that benefit more affluent groups.

3. Poverty creates jobs for a number of occupations and professions that serve or "service" the poor, or protect the rest of society from them. Many activities and groups flourish because of the existence of poverty such as the numbers game, the sale of heroin and cheap wines and liquors, prostitutes, pawn shops, the police, the criminal justice system, and the peacetime army, which recruits its enlisted personnel mainly from among the poor.

4. The poor buy goods others do not want and thus prolong the economic usefulness of such goods as day-old bread, fruit and vegetables that would otherwise have to be thrown out, secondhand clothes, and deteriorating automobiles and buildings.

5. The poor lack the political and cultural power to correct the stereotypes that other people hold of them and thus continue to be thought of as lazy, spendthrift, and so on, by those who need living proof that moral deviance does not pay.

6. The poor offer vicarious participation to the rest of the population in the uninhibited sexual, alcoholic, and narcotic behavior in which they are alleged to participate and which, being freed from the constraints of affluence, they are often thought to enjoy more than the middle classes.

7. Culture created by or for the poor is often adopted by the more affluent. The rich often collect artifacts from extinct folk cultures of poor people; and almost all Americans listen to the blues, African American spirituals, and country music, which originated among the poor.

8. People need to know where they stand, and the poor function as a reliable and relatively permanent measuring rod for status comparisons.

9. A goodly number of Americans have entered the middle class through the profits earned from the provision of goods and services in the slums, including illegal or unrespectable ones that upper-class and upper middle-class business people shun because of their low prestige.

10. The aristocracy who are active in charity must have the poor to demonstrate their superiority over other elites who devote themselves to earning money.

11. The poor, being powerless, can be made to absorb the costs of change and growth in American society; for instance, they did the backbreaking work that built the massive infrastructure of the United States, in which the wealthy take such pride.

12. The poor facilitate and stabilize the American political process, because they can rarely support Republicans, they often supply the Democrats with a captive constituency that has no other place to go.

13. An economy based on the ideology of laissez-faire requires a deprived population that is allegedly unwilling to work or that can be considered inferior because it must accept charity or welfare in order to survive.

Herbert Gans made a great explanation of why poverty is important in society today. Another problem that society seems to always drag on and complain over is the constant presence of crime. Often criticized and always scrutinized, the correctional industry has long been seen as a negative force, but there may be positive logic behind the function of that perceived dilemma as well, as stated by Scoggin in a personal correspondence to Easterling:

1. Crime provides boundaries and a code for rights and wrongs, which engages, shapes, and grows our society.

2. Crime provides jobs to a variety of mid-level occupations. Without people to chase, deputies, detectives, forensic analysts, jail workers, and security camera developers would be out of a job in their field.

3. Without people breaking the rules, average citizens would have no definitive answer for "How far is too far?" When driving or shopping, and if there was no such thing as "too far" there would be a terrible absence or order and everything would be a lot more dangerous.

4. The power of authority increases when they show their power within good reason, and crime is a way for federal agencies to show that they have control, thus keeping order and assuring people of the hierarchy in society.

5. It is proven that having people locked up behind bars boosts the moral of the people who are not behind bars, no matter how bad the economy is.

6. High incarceration rates provide topic matter to major talk shows and political media channels. Without which they would not have much to talk about on some days, forcing good people to watch lesser things like sports or Game of Thrones.

7. The donut industry provides quality confections to all citizens and relies on public safety officials for most of their income during regular hours. Without crime, losses would trickle down from the officers to the donut shops and change not only breakfast time but the world as we know it.

8. Crime gives us an example of what not to do, without which children would have much less of an example and much less of a reason to act well and strive to achieve things honestly. Without reasons or rewards to be good, many may be lead to grow up to be irresponsible hooligans and overall detriments to society.

Is it now clear why the so-called "War on Poverty" has been declared but never fought? What about the "War on drugs?" Regardless of your answer, Gans' ideas (and Chast's) serve to illustrate the sociological concept of "function."

Social Conflict Theory: Marx, Veblen, and Simmel

Karl Marx

There is yet another "dead giant" of sociology whose views, with the possible exception of those of Spencer, have most impacted the larger world community. He is Karl Marx (1818–1883), an economist, a historian, a philosopher, and social activist, but more than anything else, a brilliant sociologist. Marx's brilliance lay not in his unrealistic utopian yearning for the ultimate communist state, but in his stingingly pertinent social analysis.

© Everett Historical/Shutterstock.com

Sociologists have largely dismissed Marx's eschatology, but his sociology has had a global influence. The term "**Marxist**" is applied to those who seek to achieve Marx's ideal goal of world communism. Those theorists who simply utilize portions of his analytical method are referred to as "**Marxian**" scholars.

The social conflict paradigm views society as a system characterized by:

a. Social inequality
and
b. Social conflict

Social inequality and social conflict together generate **social change**. Whereas structural functionalism focuses upon how the social system maintains its equilibrium, social conflict theory is first and foremost a theory of social change.

The major question that the social conflict paradigm seeks to answer is: "Who benefits from a particular social arrangement and who loses out?" It becomes obvious that social conflict seems almost the exact antithesis of the structural–functional perspective when one considers the basic assumptions of the social conflict paradigm, which are as follows:

1. Every society is at every point subject to change; social change is ubiquitous.
2. Every society displays at every point dissensus and conflict; social conflict is ubiquitous.
3. Every element in a society renders a contribution to its disintegration and change.
4. Every society is based on the coercion of some of its members by others.

The sociologist most responsible for developing this perspective is Karl Marx. In this section, Marx's personal history is first discussed, focusing upon his early years, his college career, and the years immediately after college.

The Communist Manifesto (1848) was written jointly with Friedrich Engels and the circumstances surrounding its being penned are most interesting. The Manifesto is organized into three distinct sections.

Part I is a discussion of the **bourgeois** (wealthy capitalist class) and **proletarians** (workers or common laboring class, also referred to as "the *proletariat*"). Marx begins with the astounding statement that all human history is the story of class struggle. The results of the conflict will be either a revolutionary change in the whole structure of society or the common ruin of the contending classes. The evils of capitalism are many, according to Marx, including the exploitation of the masses, the alienation of the workers, and the maximization of profits.

In Part II, Marx speaks specifically of the proletarians and the communists. He proposes the abolition of private property, an intermediate period of **socialism**—that economic system in which the natural resources as well as the means of production are collectively owned. He further delineates 10 necessary steps in the Workers' Revolution, the abolition of nationality, bourgeois culture, and the family, and predicts the disappearance of the ruling elite.

The remainder of the Manifesto (Part III) is composed of attacks against various socialist heresies. Marx argued that there were "false" socialists and "true" socialists.

Early Years

Marx was born May 5, 1818, in what is now known as West Germany. He was one of seven children of Jewish parents.

Marx's father, Heinrich, was a lawyer. For business purposes, he was baptized in a Protestant church a year before Karl was born. Karl was himself baptized at age 6. Karl's mother, however, remained faithful to Judaism.

Young Marx was a witness to conflict at an early age. His parents' religious divergence is a case in point. In addition, his father was involved in political agitation for a Prussian constitution.

Marx's adolescent writings exhibited a spirit of Christian devotion. Another recurring theme was his supposed willingness for self-sacrifice on behalf of humanity. His later works are an attempt at achieving the ideal of equality for all humans.

College Career

In October of 1835, Marx entered the University of Bonn, where a politically rebellious student culture was thriving. A large group of students tried to disrupt the federal government while in session. Some were arrested and many were expelled from the University. It is not known whether Marx participated, but he was certainly involved in the cultural milieu of challenge to established authority.

Marx's bent toward conflict was given further opportunity to manifest itself as he served in the position of president of the Tavern Club which, under his leadership, was at odds with the more aristocratic student associations. He even fought a duel and was once arrested by police for being drunk and disorderly.

Marx's studies were exclusively in the humanities, such subjects as Greek and Roman mythology and the history of art. He left Bonn in October of 1836 to study law and philosophy at the University of Berlin. This is where he was first introduced to Hegel's philosophy. He even joined the Young Hegelians, a large group of students who were involved in a new literary and philosophical movement. One of their frequent speakers was a young faculty member named Bruno Bauer who taught that a new social catastrophe "more tremendous than the advent of Christianity" was about to occur. The German government opposed the Young Hegelians and undertook to drive them from the universities. Bauer was fired from his lectureship. Marx's most intimate friend of this period served a prison term for his political radicalism.

Unable to graduate from the University of Berlin, Marx submitted a doctoral dissertation to the university at Jena, and was awarded his degree in

April of 1841. His dissertation analyzed the differences in the philosophies of Democritus and Epicurus, within the Hegelian framework of thesis/antithesis.

Life After College

Marx was very much influenced by the 1841 publication of a manuscript by Ludwig Feuerbach, which criticized Hegel from the materialist standpoint. After reading Feuerbach, Marx moved toward combining Hegel's dialectic with Feuerbach's materialism.

In October of 1842, Marx became editor of the Berlin newspaper, *Rheinische Zeitung*. He became popular due to his editorials about such matters as the sorry state of housing among the poverty-stricken classes in Berlin and the raping of the forests by excessive tree cutting. He also wrote extensively about the new concept of communism. Circulation of the newspaper tripled within 1 year, but government authorities closed it down, and Marx moved to Paris.

Shortly before moving to Paris, Marx was married to Jenny von Westphalen. Jenny was no stranger to the conflict orientation. She was descended, on her mother's side, from the rebellious Scottish earls of Argyle, and her father was a fervent follower of the French socialist Saint-Simon.

In Paris, Marx began associating with communist societies of French and German working men. In 1844, he published an article entitled, "Toward the Critique of the Hegelian Philosophy of Right," which included his famous assertion that religion is the "opiate of the masses." In this article, he called for "an uprising of the *proletariat*," in order to bring the ideals of philosophy into the realm of reality. This caused such opposition from the government that Marx was expelled from France and left for Brussels on February 5, 1845.

It was in Brussels that Marx developed his lifelong friendship with Engels. Engels had also been a Young Hegelian in college and became a communist under the influence of Moses Hess. In England, he was associated with the followers of socialist Robert Owen. He was a partner in the firm of Ermen and Engels in Manchester, Great Britain, and often aided Marx financially. Engels collaborated with Marx on virtually every major literary undertaking.

In 1847, Marx and Engels were invited to compose the manifesto for a secret communist society called the League of the Just. The name was later changed to the Communist League, upon Marx's suggestion. He and Engels worked on the document from the middle of December, 1847, to the end of January, 1848. It was adopted at the annual meeting of the Communist League. Marx then moved away from Brussels just in time to avoid being expelled by the Belgian government.

The Manifesto may or may not have been the spark that ignited the flame, but history records that in the first months of 1848, following the publishing of *A Manifesto of the Communist Party*, revolution suddenly erupted in the European states of France, Italy, and Austria.

Das Kapital (1867), a much more scholarly and extensive work, was not published until 19 years later. *The Communist Manifesto*, however, has had a much greater impact on the world scene largely because of its broad distribution.

It should be obvious by examining a few of the biographical facts about Marx's life that he was not just a passive scholar writing from his ivory tower. His was a life lived in conflict—from his college years on to having his newspaper shut down and being expelled from country after country because of his call for the downtrodden of the world to unite and end their domination by the private owners of resources and the means of production.

Bourgeois and Proletarians

"The history of all human society," says Marx on the first page of the manifesto, "past and present, has been the history of class struggles." The key word is "struggles." Struggle, contrast, dialectic, and conflict are the very nature of social interaction, according to Marx, and arise as the natural result of social inequality. "Freeman and slave—patrician and plebeian, baron and serf, guild-burgess and journeyman—in a word, OPPRESSOR and OPPRESSED—stood sharply in opposition to each other (Marx and Engels, 1848)."

A paradigm may be defined as a way of looking at the world. It is the "eyeglass" through which one perceives the environment—in other words, it is a perspective. Ritzer (1988) says it is "a fundamental image of society that guides sociological thinking".

The theoretical paradigm adopted by Marx, if we were to attempt to categorize him, is that of social inequality, resulting in class conflict, the eventual consequence of which is social change. He says that the nature of social relationships is the inevitable division into conflicting opponents—master versus slave, lord versus commoner, and so on. These opposing classes have carried on perpetual warfare for centuries, sometimes masked, and sometimes open and acknowledged.

There are only two possible outcomes of the class struggle in any given setting. The invariable conclusion is either:

1. A revolutionary change in the whole structure of society
   or
2. The common ruin of the contending classes

The terms Marx usually utilizes when discussing the opposing classes are *bourgeois* and *proletariat*. "*Bourgeois*" is from the word burgher or "townsman," referring to a capitalist.

The **economy** is that social institution which organizes the production, distribution, and consumption of goods and services. **Capitalism** is the type of economic system in which the natural resources and the means of production are privately owned. The capitalists, or "*bourgeoisie*," are the owners of the natural resources and the means of production. They are the oppressors in the industrial milieu, who profit from the labor of the oppressed class.

The "*proletariat*", in contrast, are the workers who lack their own means of production and hence sell their labor to live. They are the oppressed masses, according to Marx, who are **exploited** (used, manipulated, taken advantage of unfairly, raped, pillaged, robbed, and abused) by the *bourgeois* class.

Marx insists that the *bourgeois* treat the *proletariat* as a commodity like any other article of commerce. They are consequently exposed to all the adversities and difficulties of competition and to all the fluctuations of the market.

Marx vividly laments the **alienation** (estrangement from nature, from satisfaction with one's work, from one's fellow humans, and ultimately, from one's own identity) of the workers.

"Payday" is a day of misery for the laborer, for that is when she gives up the paltry subsistence wage for which she has given a portion of her very life to the landlord, the pawnbroker, the shopkeeper, *ad infinitum*. Marx contrasts the alienated and deprived state of the *proletarian* (the French word for poverty is *misere*) with the opulent luxury of the *bourgeoisie*.

In addition to the exploitation of the masses as the means of production and the alienation of the workers, Marx expresses a third aspect of the "evil of capitalism." Unrestrained capitalism tends toward the **maximization of profits** rather than the rational pursuit of profit. The chief requisite for the existence and rule of the bourgeoisie is the accumulation of wealth in the hands of private individuals: the formation and increase of capital. The chief requisite of capital is wage labor because through human reproduction it can multiply itself.

Structurally, Marx's social theory has three primary components. The base of society is the **means of production**. This would include natural resources as well as factories, machines, technology, and so on. The **infrastructure** consists of the relationships between the capitalists, who control the economic process, and the large labor pool of proletarians, who are simply a source of labor. Upon this infrastructure are built the major **social institutions**, as well as core cultural values and ideas. It

SUPERSTRUCTURE
(Institutions: Govt., Family
Religion, Education, Economy)

>>>>>

INFRASTRUCTURE
(Class System)
&
(Relations of Production)

>>>>>

BASE
(Means of Production)

Marx's Social Structure Model

is important to keep in mind that this structural system is moving through history, and constantly changing as it does so.

Marx saw most of the proletariat as thinking in terms of a pattern he called "**false consciousness**." This is the belief that the shortcomings of individuals themselves, rather than society, are responsible for the personal problems that people experience. For instance, workers tend to experience alienation as a personal problem, but Marx maintained that it is really a consequence of industrial capitalism. Workers can overcome their alienation by uniting and throwing off the chains of their slavery. This can only come about once they have changed their perspective to "class consciousness." **Class consciousness** refers to awareness on the part of the workers of their shared oppression within the framework of the infrastructure and the necessity of their united opposition to the capitalists and capitalism itself.

Proletarians and Communists

For Marx, the eschatological end of all class struggles will come at some time in the future when history has run its course and the proletariat will ultimately prevail over the bourgeoisie and establish a classless society, free of inequality, with the means of production owned collectively. This ultimate social structure, called

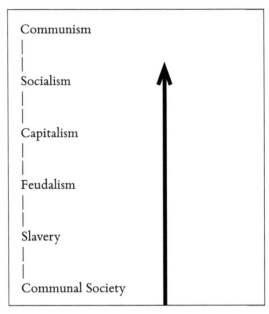

Historical Steps toward Communism

communism, Marx surely recognized as a "**utopia**" (a Greek word meaning "not a place"). That is, though he intellectually understood the unlikelihood of such a perfect society in reality, still he considered it the only goal worth pursuing, and espoused its inevitability.

In the earliest human societies, life was lived primarily in communal harmony; but eventually a ruling elite emerged, enslaving other humans. As cultures and technologies changed, so did the relations of production, from slavery to feudalism, to capitalism, but the central theme was the dominance of one group over another and this persisted through each historical period. Replacing capitalism will be socialism, an economic system in which natural resources, as well as the means of production, are collectively owned, and the state is run by a benevolent dictatorship of the **proletariat**. The state will operate with a strong hand to eliminate inequality on every level. Once this has been accomplished and a truly classless society has been established, the ruling elite of the socialist government will step down from power and there will be no further need for any humans to rule over others, as the cooperative spirit of communism will supersede any and all future conflicts that may try to surface.

A necessary historical event is to inevitably take place sooner or later in every capitalist nation, as workers unite in revolutionary force and capitalist empires capitulate, becoming socialist republics under **proletarian** leadership.

Marx lists 10 measures these new socialist states will need to take to ultimately usher in the ideals of pure communism:

1. Expropriation of landed property, and the use of land rents to defray State expenditure.
2. A vigorously graduated income tax.
3. Abolition of the right of inheritance.
4. Confiscation of the property of all emigres (political refugees) and rebels.
5. Centralization of credit in the hands of the State, by means of a national bank with State capital and an exclusive monopoly.
6. Centralization of the means of transport in the hands of the State.
7. Increase of national factories and means of production, cultivation of uncultivated land, and improvement of cultivated land in accordance with a general plan.
8. Universal and equal obligation to work; organization of industrial armies, especially for agriculture.
9. Agriculture and urban industry to work hand in hand, in such a way as, by degrees, to obliterate the distinction between town and country.
10. Public and free education of all children. Abolition of factory work for children in its present form. Education and material production to be combined.

The remainder of the *Manifesto of the Communist Party* is primarily a diatribe against all the socialist "heresies" of Marx's day. There were a number of groups calling for the end of inequality in society without a workers' revolution. This, to Marx, was an impossibility, since the *bourgeois* are quite simply not going to voluntarily forfeit their superior position of wealth through dominance.

Criticisms of Marx's Theory

Marx's analysis has had enormous influence on sociological thinking and, in fact, on political history itself. His thought has been severely criticized, however, on a number of grounds.

1. Max Weber criticized Marx's assumption that social prestige and power are almost totally derived from one's economic position. This brand of unidimensional causality is commonly referred to as **"economic determinism."** Weber hypothesized a different causal formula known today as **"socioeconomic status,"** which is a composite of several variables, namely, **class** (corresponding to

income or wealth), **status** (corresponding to prestige and related to occupation and education), and **party** (corresponding to power). Critics can thus attempt to dismiss Marx as being too simplistic and narrow in failing to take into account factors of determinism other than income alone. Still, it is generally recognized by most macrolevel social researchers that income and/or wealth is the most influential single determinant of one's social standing and access to the goods and services available in society.

2. Marx seems to have overlooked or ignored the crucial element of the **Davis-Moore hypothesis** that unequal rewards are an effective motivating force to get people to perform certain social roles. The thesis is that physicians, for example, will not be willing to undergo extensive, lengthy, and expensive training if there were not the prospects of unusually high financial reward. The question is, why would anyone in a communist state put forth such a great effort if he were to receive the same rewards as someone doing simpler work with much less effort? Perhaps, the answer lies in Marx's own work performance. Though he had an earned doctorate and could no doubt have found steady work teaching in an institutional setting, he chose instead to study, write, editorialize, and advocate his views, all with very little financial reward. His motivation was what he thought was beneficial for society. Perhaps he projected his own orientation in this regard on other humans, assuming that, given the opportunity to work in a helping capacity, nonmonetary motivation would drive them toward excellence in their work. Also, supposedly, at least in the idealized socialist state, workers will no longer feel alienated from their work and will be able to enjoy their work for its own sake.

3. A common criticism of Marx is the notion that the capitalist class has become fragmented over time. Companies that were owned by families a century ago are now owned by stockholders. This is a weak criticism, however, since much corporate stock in America is owned by a small percentage of the population, thus clearly defining themselves as an economic elite with great power.

4. Similar to the third criticism is the argument of the advent of the middle class in the United States and most other capitalist nations. The majority of the labor force today are in the tertiary sector, that is, the service and information industries. These are primarily "white-collar" occupations. These people do not identify with manual labor and tend to think of themselves not as lower class

but as middle class. The evidence, to the contrary, indicates that many white-collar workers earn less than blue-collar laborers, and much of their work is characterized by monotonous, alienating routine. Marx would say that this class is deluding itself with false consciousness, unaware at the conscious level that they are being exploited for the profits of the already wealthy.

5. A fifth weakness is Marx's prediction that workers would become progressively more and more dissatisfied with their situations in society, that is, with the relations of production, and would revolt against systems of gross inequality. He did not foresee the organization and subsequent influence of labor unions. Research suggests that labor unions have had a substantial impact on the improved economic standing and working conditions of great numbers of laborers. They have obtained retirement programs, insurance policies, and other concessions from their employers. Such gains, however, have been the result of a great amount of conflict. Each step has been opposed by the owners of the means of production, and it has been likened to the proverbial "pulling of teeth." Workers with a class consciousness perspective can see that a few economic concessions are really nothing to the capitalist owners—something akin to the tossing around of chicken feed so the chickens will stay on the farm to give their eggs and ultimately their bodies to the "owners."

There have certainly been many other criticisms of Marx's ideas and predictions. His impact has been substantial, though, and his unidimensional sociology is enduring considering the period and the circumstances in which he functioned. The *Manifesto of the Communist Party* was only one of many of his and Engels' works. It is not, by any means, the most scholarly nor the most comprehensive of their manuscripts. It certainly has been a social force in its own right, however, in fostering class consciousness within many social settings since its publication.

Marx' Personal Character

Marx was by no standard a model family man. As has been mentioned, he was married. He and his wife Jenny had six children. Three of the children starved to death in infancy due to lack of food, though Marx, himself, did not personally do without. Two of his children later committed suicide. On one occasion, he received a gift of 160 pounds (approximately $500). He did not use this money for his family's needs. Instead, they were evicted from their apartment. Marx spent all of Jenny's family inheritances and did not even attend her funeral. Marx spent much of his time writing love poems to satan (Wurmbrand, 1986).

Thorstein Veblen

Thorstein Veblen was born in Manitowoc County, Wisconsin, to Norwegian immigrants on July 30, 1857. Veblen left a provision in his will that his biography should never be written, but the request has been ignored. According to Dorfman's definitive biography of Veblen (1934), his parents had decided 10 years earlier to leave their home in Norway and move to the United States. There had been a severe economic depression in Norway, and Thomas Anderson Veblen and his wife Kari read a book that had influenced thousands of  Norwegians: Johan R. Reierson's Pathfinder for Norwegian Immigrants to the North American States and Texas.

A day before beginning their overseas voyage, the Veblens buried their firstborn child. When they had gotten as far as Hamburg, Germany, they were left stranded by their captain and it was a full month before they could continue on. They finally obtained passage on a whaling vessel, but the water supply ran out and all children under 6 years of age died. Thomas Veblen contracted a severe fever aboard ship. Four and a half months after leaving Norway, physically ailing and practically penniless, the Veblens eventually reached Milwaukee. The next day, Thomas walked 28 miles to Port Washington, Wisconsin, and went immediately to work in a factory. He sent for Kari and she obtained a job as a maid in Port Washington.

After a few weeks, Thomas Veblen started working at his trade, building and finishing houses, and saved his money until he had enough to make a down payment on some farmland. He became a leading farmer in the area, and sent to New York for the first two-horsepower thresher in Wisconsin.

The Norwegian immigrants did not get along very well with the "Yankees" of the area. Thorstein Veblen wrote later: "The Scandinavian Immigrants settled over the North Middle Region as tillers of the soil, while the American population of the East at the same time scattered over the same region in the towns; with the result that the foreign immigrants did the work necessary to the reclamation of this stretch of fertile land, and the native-born in the towns did the business. This business was prevailingly of a prehensile character, being carried on by men well at home in the common law of the land, and directed at getting something for nothing at the expense of the foreign immigrants who were unfamiliar with the common law" (Dorfman, 1934/1972).

When Thorstein was 8 years old, his family moved to Wheeling, Minnesota, where his father had purchased a farm. His father again became a leading farmer in the area and became a beekeeper and planted an orchard.

English was never spoken in the Veblen household, as Thomas and Kari had never learned it. Thorstein never spoke any English until he went to school. He spoke with an accent all of his life.

Neither his siblings nor his neighbors had a very high opinion of Thorstein. On his first Sunday in Minnesota, he was in a fistfight. He is said to have fought and bullied the boys, teased the girls, and pestered the old people with stinging sarcasms and nicknames. One of the neighboring farmers commented that he had never seen "such a lazy looking person who performed his job with so few motions (Dorfman, 1934/1972)."

College Career

At age 17, Veblen entered nearby Carleton College, a Calvinist institution from which his older brother Andrew had graduated before joining the faculty at Luther College. Although it was a small local college, Carleton was said to have been patterned after the standard of scholarship maintained by the best New England Colleges. The classics, religion, and moral philosophy were stressed. The college even possessed an observatory. The one person at the school who possessed distinctive intellectual quality was John Bates Clark. Professor Clark was a graduate of Johns Hopkins University and was officially the librarian and taught political economy, history, English, and moral philosophy. He favored a mild form of socialism and had a profound influence on Veblen's thinking.

Veblen met his future wife at Carleton College, Ellen Rolfe, whose uncle was the president of the college. She was descended from old and distinguished families. One of her uncles was president of the Atchison, Topeka, and Santa Fe Railroad. He made the racist statement denigrating Norwegians (Dorfman, 1934/1972). Thorstein traced her genealogy and proved to her that her father's family was descended from Norwegians several centuries earlier.

Veblen did so well at Carleton, despite being disliked by all the faculty except Professor Clark, that he was allowed to skip the junior year entirely.

At the end of his senior year he was chosen as what is now known as "valedictorian" of the graduating class. His graduation address was said to have been a spectacular performance. Instead of the usual topic such as "The Duty of a Christian Scholar," he spoke on "Mill's Examination of Hamilton's Philosophy of the Conditioned" (Dorfman, 1934/1972).

After his graduation in 1880, Veblen became a mathematics teacher at Monona Academy in Madison, Wisconsin. The school closed permanently at the end of a year, however, and Thorstein and his brother Andrew, partially under the influence of Professor Clark at Carleton College, both decided to attend Johns Hopkins University in Baltimore, Maryland.

His time in Baltimore was quite significant in Veblen's development, for he was for the first time in the culture of the Old South, which had a highly developed leisure class. For some time he boarded with a family which still clung to its aristocratic traditions. He was "much amused with the family's maintenance of the grand old pre-war style" (Dorfman, 1934/1972).

Veblen was unable to obtain a scholarship at Johns Hopkins and left after a year to attend Yale. His father obtained a loan back in Minnesota to enable him to continue in college.

At Yale, Veblen's two major professors were Noah Porter and William Graham Sumner. The two professors were always embroiled in bitter disputes with one another, but both considered Veblen their brightest student. Veblen won Yale's John A. Porter Prize for the best English essay. His topic was "The Cause of the Panic of 1837."

Veblen received his PhD degree from Yale in 1884. His dissertation topic was "Ethical Grounds of a Doctrine of Retribution," in other words, "why we need not believe in God" (Dorfman, 1934/1972).

Life After College

Having applied to Carleton and other colleges for a teaching position but totally without success, Veblen returned to the Norwegian farming community in Minnesota. He did essentially nothing but read everything he could get his hands on for the next 7 years.

In 1888, Veblen and Ellen Rolfe were married. Still unable to find a job, he enrolled in Cornell as a graduate student in 1891.

The University of Chicago was founded in 1892 by a grant from John D. Rockefeller. Albion Small, a student and disciple of Lester Ward, was chosen to be the chairperson of the sociology department. Veblen was hired in the economics department, not as a tenured faculty person, but as a teaching fellow, and enrolled in graduate courses in economics.

Veblen became academically prolific, despite not being on the regular faculty. He wrote two articles published in the first volume of *The Journal of Political Economy*, and wrote many book reviews of anthropological works.

Using Thomas Kirkup's *History of Socialism* as a textbook, Veblen taught a course in socialism at the University of Chicago. He attracted few students. The students criticized him for the irrelevancy of many of his discussions, the impossibility of taking notes in his classes because his lectures followed no logical order, and it was almost impossible to get from him an exact answer to any question. Only a minority of his students became his "disciples," supposedly the abler ones. "They liked his free spirit and were impressed by his vocabulary, his erudition, and his impersonal discussion" (Dorfman, 1934/1972). He seemed to the students to have "read everything," and quoted most from Chaucer, George Borrow, William Morris, and Cervantes. He drew much of his discussions from anthropology, and talked as much about the Hopi Indians, the Samurai, and the Hebrews of the Old Testament as he did of Adam Smith and Karl Marx.

Veblen finally attained the rank of Instructor of Economics in 1896. In 1898 and 1899, he published three articles in the *American Journal of Sociology*: "The Instinct of Workmanship and the Irksomeness of Labor," "The Beginnings of Ownership," and "The Barbarian Status of Women" (Dorfman, 1934/1972).

A month after the last of these articles was published, Veblen published his first and most well-known book, *The Theory of the Leisure Class: An Economic Study in the Evolution of Institutions*. He had to rewrite it a number of times before its literary style was acceptable to the publishers. They thought so little of its commercial value that they required Veblen to put up a guarantee.

The Theory of the Leisure Class launched Veblen's fame. Reviewers were either very enthusiastic about his ideas or else vitriolic in their condemnation. The idea that businessmen are really only barbaric predators in disguise shook up many quarters. Veblen never achieved the academic rank he desired. His views were more accepted in Europe than in the United States, but he did draw many loyal followers in the United States.

The remainder of Veblen's life is a flamboyant story in some ways, but it is outside the scope of this article. He subsequently taught at Stanford University, the University of Missouri, and the New School for Social Research in New York City. He also worked for a time for the Food Administration in Washington, DC. His last 3 years were spent in a cabin in the mountains of California overlooking the sea. He died August 3, 1929, near Menlo Park, California.

The Theory of the Leisure Class

Thorstein Veblen's major life's work emphasized technological evolutionism, but he is better known for his depiction of leisure class behavior and the competitive emulation of that class by most of the rest of society. *The Theory of the Leisure Class: An Economic Study of Institutions*, published in 1899, is a discussion of the conflict between the **predatory** (leisure) and the **industrious** (working) classes.

Veblen begins with a typically evolution-ridden reference to the most likely types of cultures to have highly integrated leisure classes: "The institution of a leisure class is found in its best development at the higher stages of barbarian culture; as, for instance, in feudal Europe or in feudal Japan. In such communities the distinction between classes is rigorously observed; and the feature of most striking economic significance in these class differences is the distinction maintained between the employments proper to the several classes. The upper classes are by custom exempt or excluded from industrial occupations, and are reserved for certain employments to which a degree of honour attaches" (Veblen, 1899).

The non-industrial upper-class "employments" may be categorized under government, warfare, religious observances, and sports. The employments of the inferior class are manual labor, industry, or whatever has to do directly with the everyday work of getting a livelihood. Virtually the entire range of industrial employments is an outgrowth of what is classified as woman's work in the primitive barbarian community.

Veblen theorizes that the leisure class has emerged gradually during the transition from primitive savagery to barbarism, or from a peaceable to a warlike stage. Two conditions are necessary for a leisure class to emerge:

1. The men become primarily engaged in war or the hunting of game or both; that is, the infliction of injury by force and stratagem.
2. Subsistence must be easy enough that a considerable number of people can be exempted from the routine of labor. The trophies or booty the men bring home from the raid or hunt came to be prized as evidence of their prowess, exploits, power, and esteem.

In the sequence of cultural evolution, the emergence of the leisure class coincides with the beginning of **ownership**. The earliest form of ownership, according to Veblen, was the ownership of the women by the able-bodied men of the community. The practice of seizing women from the enemy as trophies gave rise to a form of ownership-marriage, which in turn resulted in a household with a male head. Through time the concept of ownership expanded to include not only women, but also the products of their labor;

hence, the ownership of things as well as of persons. Gradually, accumulated property replaced the trophies of predatory exploit as the conventional evidence of success and esteem. There arose an inherent dissatisfaction in property ownership, however, until individuals could own as much as their neighbors, and then more than their neighbors, *ad infinitum*. Eventually, it has become the desire of everyone to exceed everyone else in the accumulation of goods.

The characteristic feature of leisure class life is the conspicuous exemption from useful employment. Veblen gives two extreme examples: "certain Polynesian chiefs, who, under the stress of good form, preferred to starve rather than carry their food to their to their mouths with their own hands . . . a certain king of France, who is said to have lost his life through an excess of moral stamina in the observance of good form. In the absence of the functionary whose office it was to shift his master's seat, the king sat uncomplaining before the fire and suffered his royal person to be toasted beyond recovery" (Veblen, 1899).

The leisure classes, in Veblen's time at least, were involved in the study of dead languages and occult sciences, correct spelling, poetry, various forms of music and art, the latest fashions in clothing and furniture, games, and sports. They were also heavily engaged in such things as fancy-bred animals, typically greyhound dogs and race horses.

Veblen's explanation of the evolution of the woman's role from that of slave to that of conspicuous consumer is quite interesting. As wealth accumulates on his hands, the gentleman-of-leisure's own consumption is not visible enough to the community to show evidence of the vast extent of his opulence. The aid of friends and competitors is therefore brought in by resorting to the giving of valuable presents and expensive feasts and entertainments. In addition, the master of the house supports artists, assistants, patrons, and so on, who also live in a leisurely manner, thus fulfilling the function for their benefactor of showing the community that he has such means as to multiply his consumption of goods through them. As we ascend the social scale, the point is reached where the duties of leisure and consumption rest upon the wife alone. In Western culture, this point is found among the middle class. The head of the middle-class household applies himself to work with the utmost diligence in order that his wife may render for him the degree of leisure and consumption that he imagines will give him esteem in the community. What we see in this is not the revolution against the leisure class, as Marx had theorized would occur, but the emulation of them by their social inferiors.

Even the most abjectly poor, according to Veblen, practice some form of **conspicuous consumption**, or at least yearn to do so. The means of communication and the mobility of the population now expose the individual to the observation of many persons who have no other means of judging his status and esteem than his display of goods (perhaps through his clothing and means of transportation). One's neighbors often are not socially one's neighbors, nor even acquaintances; still, their good opinion is highly desired.

With current economic necessity causing many wives to work and the changing mobility mentioned above, there is a definite trend in the direction of increased conspicuous consumption and less emphasis on leisure. Veblen mentions that this tendency has a deterrent effect on many families' willingness to save money. This has also caused the domestic private lives of many to become quite shabby, as compared with the overt portions of their lives carried on before the eyes of observers.

Veblen asserts that in all communities, especially where the dwellings are less expensive, the local religious sanctuary is more ornate and more conspicuously wasteful in its architecture than the dwelling-places of the congregation. This is because the sanctuary is not for the comfort of the worshippers, but for the esteem of the deity. Furthermore, the priests should not engage in industrially productive work, nor should any such work be carried on in the sanctuary, because the anthropomorphic deity is considered to be in the ultimate highest realm of the leisure class. When people come to the sanctuary, they should be clad in garments more expensive than their everyday work clothes. On certain holidays set apart in honor of the deity, no ordinary work should be done. In fact, one day out of seven should be set apart for leisure, as an extension of the deity's leisure class status.

Throughout *The Theory of the Leisure Class*, Veblen touches upon many subjects, relating them to the leisure class and cultural evolution. Sports did not escape his critical attention. He says that hunters and anglers claim their motives to be the love of nature and the need for recreation, but underlying these is the old predatory need of man to kill all living things he can overpower by violence and cunning. Athletic sports, likewise, represent a return to barbarism and accentuate the human traits which cause damage and desolation.

The human propensity for gambling is another trait of the barbarian temperament. Veblen says that the chief factor in gambling is the belief in luck. There is a sort of subconscious hope that betting on a particular person in competition or a particular horse in a race or a hand of cards will lend luck—strength, superiority—to the person or object. Furthermore, betting heightens the excitement of the contest by giving the winning side more glory and the losing side more of the pain and humiliation of defeat.

The last institution Veblen treats in the book is higher education. He says, "Even today there are such things in the usage of the learned community as the cap and gown, matriculation, initiation, and graduation ceremonies, and prerogatives in a way which suggests some sort of a scholarly apostolic succession. The usage of the priestly orders is no doubt the proximate source of all these features of learned ritual (Veblen, 1899)." These ritualistic features are more pronounced in the liberal arts and classical institutions of higher learning than in the more technological and practical branches of the educational system.

Some Criticisms of the Theory of the Leisure Class

Veblen is generally classified as a conflict theorist. In *The Theory of the Leisure Class*, he pits the leisure class against the working class. In other writings he contrasts Business (the capitalists) and Industry (the productive element of the economy, including the labor force). His social theory concerns social change and cultural lag.

1. Veblen constantly talks about process—the process of institutionalization, and so on, yet he never actually defines what is meant by "process." He tends to make vague and sweeping generalizations without operational definitions.

2. Throughout Veblen's verbiage, he seems to infer that at some undetermined point in history there was a kind of primitive communism, a vague sort of "golden age," when relationships were honest and all people were in harmony. Such a theory does not really come from empirical studies of concrete social reality—in other words, there is a real problem of historicity with some of Veblen's references to past cultures. Perhaps this reflects the influence of Rousseau's idea of the "noble savage," but still it cannot be relied upon for the foundation of a serious social theory.

3. Another weakness in *The Theory of the Leisure Class* is Veblen's use of the concept of "instinct." He probably derived this from the influence of Darwin and Spencer. He talks about the "instinct of workmanship," and the "predatory instinct." Presumably, anyone can make up whatever instincts he thinks humans have and use this concept to explain human behavior. Actually, in Easterling's opinion, "instinct" is not very useful as a social science tool, and besides, Veblen never defines what he means by the concept itself.

4. Teggert criticizes Veblen on the point of his faulty—at times seemingly functional—anthropology. Veblen tended to extract anthropological anecdotes, such as the story of the French king related earlier in this article, and fit them neatly into his theoretical scheme (Davis, 1941/1980).

5. Another problem with Veblen's work was his extreme positivism, which is somewhat incongruous with his generally critical and cynical tone. He had great admiration for the machine and for the ability of science to solve social problems. This is the attitude of Saint-Simon and Comte. Veblen went so far (in one of his later works) as to suggest a "Soviet of Technicians" to guide the future society. Not even Comte was this naive. Comte recognized the need for allocation of goods, and not simply their production. Veblen believed that the general welfare of society was directly related to the maximum production of material goods. He assumed that modern society had solved the problems of scarcity. It is not likely that such a society could be held together (Davis, 1941/1980).

The Theory of the Leisure Class became popular outside academia during Veblen's lifetime because it was considered a satire at the expense of the privileged class. In recent decades, however, social scientists have begun to recognize some of Veblen's concepts as the products of a brilliant, sophisticated, and original mind. He genuinely put his analytical finger on the pulse of the leisure class and thereby has made a significant contribution to the body of useful theoretical knowledge.

Georg Simmel

Georg Simmel (1858–1918) was a substantive analytical theorist. (His name is pronounced Gay-org Zim'l.) He was primarily interested in Form versus Content. **Forms** (social patterns) are similar in every social setting, but the **Content** (substance) of interaction is infinitely variable. The major questions Simmel asked about any social Form were:

1. What does it mean in its pure state?
2. Under what conditions does it emerge?
3. How does it develop?
4. What accelerates or retards its operation?

George Ritzer has said of Simmel that he is the "junior partner of a quartet," meaning the great German sociologists, Weber, Marx, Toennies, and Simmel. He was a popular and brilliant lecturer, the son of wealthy Jewish parents who traveled in intellectually stimulating circles.

Simmel had some amount of difficulty getting his dissertation accepted at the University of Berlin, ostensibly due to anti-Semitism. He finally received his doctorate in 1888 and took a position as a privatdocent—a teacher who was paid only by student fees—until 1900. He was given an academic appointment in 1900 and in 1914 he obtained a regular appointment at the University of Strasbourg. He was the object of a substantial amount of anti-Semitism from the faculty there.

Simmel's writing is said to show genius, yet it is remarkably readable. Several Americans visited Berlin and heard Simmel's lectures, including Albion Small. Simmel's essays were published in the *American Journal of Sociology* in its early days. His work also appealed to Robert Ezra Park, of the University of Chicago. Max Weber was a close friend, as were Toennies and Michels, although reason and meaning were not the foci of his work, as they were for Weber and Toennies. Simmel was one of the founders of the German Sociological Society.

The Philosophy of Money

One of Simmel's major works was *The Philosophy of Money* (1978). It was considered to be very successful as an accurate description of contemporary society. He emphasized that the exchange of money eventually reduces the individual to a commodity. Furthermore, money readily lends itself to rational calculation; therefore, it encourages society to downplay the emotional. He insightfully pointed out what he referred to as "A Curious Paradox:"

1. Money frees man—money is a means to get things independent from other assets.
2. Money enslaves man—if you do not have it, you are at the mercy of those who do.

Simmel's Analysis of Sociology

Simmel's book *Soziologie* (1908) was his attempt to write a treatise on sociology itself. In it he outlined what he thought sociology is and what its methods should be. He outlined three types of sociology:

1. **Philosophical Sociology**, which borders on the metaphysical, aims at understanding "society" in its broadest senses.
2. **General Sociology**, which describes social life in an historical context; a description of social structures in terms of their historical contexts (but distinct from a rigid chronology).
3. **Pure or Formal Sociology** (the best known; many of Simmel's lectures were in this area), which was a sociology of Forms, which he called Sociations; Pure Sociology deals with the Forms in social life abstracted from the content. Dyad, for example, is the same, whether a business partnership or a love relationship.

The variety of social configurations were the subjects of most of Simmel's writings. He analyzed schools, churches, families, and so on, at a high level of abstraction. In *Conflict and the Web of Group Affiliations* (1956), he asserted that social differentiation occurs in differing degrees. He made a distinction between organic and rational differentiation. He was fascinated with numbers and was an early proponent of the idea that as you increase the number in a group, you loosen the bonds between individuals, although the stability of the group increases. He talked at length about the relative strength of the bonds within and the stability of dyads, triads, and larger groups.

Simmel further believed that human nature includes something he referred to as **"the instinct to fight"**; thus, conflict is imminent. Another important idea is that conflict between groups is likely to reduce conflict within groups, but prolonged conflicts between groups are likely to increase conflict within the groups.

Simmel has been touted by some as the "exemplary micro-sociological mind." In point of fact, the content of most of his analyses is micro-oriented. He did not try to draw the line between psychological and sociological phenomena, and his work has been particularly attractive to many psychologists. Coser (1977), however, points out that Simmel is not exclusively micro-analytical, as many of his analyses were at the institutional level, and he could validly be classified as a "social conflict theorist."

Modern science is prone to accept theories of linear causation, but thanks, in part, to Simmel's influence, dialectical thinking is not dead. **Dialectical sociology** analyzes social phenomena by looking at oppositions, as in Marx's application of Hegel's system.

Symbolic Interaction

The symbolic interaction paradigm views society as a highly variable product of the continuous interaction of individuals in various settings. Since it deals primarily with individuals and small groups, it is said to be at the **"microlevel"** of social analysis. The structural–functional and social conflict paradigms, since they deal with society-wide or institutional phenomena, are said to be at the **"macrolevel."**

Symbolic interaction is precisely what the term implies: social interaction conducted at the symbolic level. A symbol is anything recognized by the members of a culture as having a particular meaning. The most commonly utilized system of symbols is language, but symbolic interactionists study many other forms, including "body language."

George Herbert Mead

George Herbert Mead (1863–1931) is the sociologist to whom is attributed the distinction of laying down the foundations of the symbolic interaction paradigm. He was a professor of philosophy at the University of Chicago, but most of what he taught became an important part of the discipline of sociology. Most of his students became sociologists. Mead emphasized the role of language, particularly in the process of socialization.

According to Mead (1934), children learn the various roles of society by taking on the roles of others. This takes place early on through play, then progressively becomes symbolic. At first, the child emulates particular others, for example, her parents. This is the remarkably human ability to take the viewpoint of another. This is analogous to the thought, "What if I were in her shoes?" Humans have an innate ability, if not the inclination, to practice the **Golden Rule**: "Do unto others as you would have them do unto you." St. Matthew 7:12; St. Luke 6:31. This eventually evolves into what Mead called the **generalized other**; that is, a notion of the general attitudes and ideas of expected behavior in the person's culture. In other words, the individual internalizes the attitudes of society and virtually modifies her personality so as to be

© Paul Fearn/Alamy Stock Photo

"adjusted" to her conception of the generalized other. The generalized other is distinct from Mead's concept of the **significant other**, which refers to any person who has a substantial impact on an individual's socialization process.

What his all leads to is the development of the "**self**." The whole point is that the self is a social product. There can be no self—no "individual"—except in relation to others. The infant has no conception of herself as an individual, no notion that she is set apart from other individuals. Only as she interacts with her mother and others, bumps up against things, finds that she has a name, is clothed and bathed, and feels the boundaries of her body, does she begin to be aware of a separate identity. Roughly at the age of 2 she begins to use the pronouns "I," "me," and "you," indicating that she is beginning to be conscious of herself and of other persons as separate individuals. This awareness grows as she acquires language and can participate in symbolic interaction. She can perceive roles and their relationships. As she observes and responds to her mother and others in the household, they become meaningful references to her, objects that bring her pleasure, frustration, security, and the like. Their reactions are important to her, and in order to win the responses she wants, she must anticipate what they are going to do by putting herself in their positions. She gradually takes on their attitudes and imagines their responses to her—that is, she "**takes the role of the other**." It is in doing this that she becomes an object to herself, first seeing herself through the eyes of others, and eventually being able to look at herself from outside herself, so to speak—to see herself from the perspective of others. Instead of experiencing only vague subjective sensations or emotions, she can be aware of, and think about, her wants, wishes, feelings, aches, pains, bad moods, and ideas, looking at them as if she were standing at some distance. She can act toward herself and guide herself.

The Myth of the Individual

Easterling has carried this theme of the individual as a social being to its ultimate conclusion. The socialization process is the process of becoming fully human, or, more formally, it is the lifelong process of learning the patterns of one's culture and realizing one's potential as a human being.

Choice-making and preference distinction together comprise a complex function of social and individual thought and sub-thought. The exterior stimuli involved in the process are so numerous as to shatter the myth of individual determination. One step further along this line of thought would lead us to a consideration of the concept of the individual as myth.

We are totally social beings, yet we have individual loci of awareness and response to environment. Perhaps, individuals may be thought of as centers of social concentration. Sometimes these centers are hostile to other such centers. All are somewhat different due to having absorbed different aspects of an infinitely variable global environment.

Rarely, if ever, do two or more centers merge completely on a merely human level. Fans at a sporting event may sometimes become "of one mind" in cheering their team on to victory. Worshippers sometimes merge as "one in the Spirit" while exalting the supernatural. This "oneness" among several centers of social concentration has seldom, if ever, endured over a long period of time. The merging may, however, recur on many occasions over time and the social centers become "bonded" or "united" by virtue of life experience. Other bonding devices, of lesser impact, may include such phenomena as like loyalties, opinions, occupations, mutual hardships, mutual enemies, kinship through blood, marriage, or adoption, intellectual thoughts, class, status, organizational memberships, and other cultural factors.

Each center of social concentration is responsible to some extent for its relationships with other centers. The "individual" is brought into existence by a social group (a sexual dyad), and is nurtured, fed, and socialized by others. Truly, if ever there were a myth, it is that of the individual: autonomous, separate form and independent of society, with a psychological self distinguished from its social life and the world around it.

Just as each leaf, blade of grass, frog, bird, or insect has its own existence yet is essentially part of a much greater ecology, so is each center of social concentration essentially tied into its social system. This is not to suggest that each such center is always in harmony with the larger social system, but certainly exists, acts, and reacts only in relation to it.

Dramaturgical Analysis

Dramaturgical analysis views the world, as did Shakespeare, as a stage, and all the people as actors. Erving Goffman asserts that we deliberately try to make particular impressions of ourselves upon the minds of others. Social interaction is the interesting result when people are constantly "on stage" with each other as the audience.

One of Mead's (1934) important concepts is the **definition of the situation**. This refers to the different ways in which various people in a particular setting interpret what is going on. When an individual is in the presence of others, her major agenda, according to Goffman (1959), becomes **impression management**, the attempt to impact the others' definitions of the situation in such a way as to put the self in a positive light; that is, to give a particular impression of oneself. According to dramaturgical analysis, a man vacationing on the beach is more likely to be concerned with the impression he makes on others than with enjoying a refreshing swim or relaxing by reading a good book. He is "on stage" as long as he thinks someone may be observing him, and his every act is influenced by his attempt to make the right impression.

The following is an excerpt from a novel (Sansom, 1956). Preedy, a vacationing Englishman, makes his first appearance on the beach of his summer hotel in Spain:

> But in any case he took pains to avoid catching anyone's eye. First of all, he had to make it clear to those potential companions of his holiday that they were of no concern to him whatsoever. He stared through them, round them, over them— eyes lost in space. The beach might have been empty. If by chance a ball was thrown his way, he looked surprised; then let a smile of amusement lighten his face (Kindly Preedy), looked around dazed to see that there were people on the beach, tossed it back with a smile to himself, and not a smile at the people, and then resumed carelessly his nonchalant survey of space.

> But it was time to institute a little parade, the parade of the Ideal Preedy. By devious handlings he gave any who wanted to look a chance to see the title of his book—a Spanish translation of Homer, classic, thus, but not daring, cosmopolitan, too— and then gathered together his beachwrap and bag into a neat sand-resistant pile (Methodical and Sensible Preedy), rose slowly to stretch at ease his huge frame (Big-Cat Preedy), and tossed aside his sandals (Carefree Preedy, after all).

> The marriage of Preedy and the sea! There were alternative rituals. The first involved the stroll that turns into a run and a dive straight into the water, thereafter smoothing into a strong splashless crawl toward the horizon. But of course not really to the horizon. Quite suddenly he would turn on to his back and thrash great white splashes with his legs, somehow thus showing that he could have swum further had he wanted to, and then would stand up a quarter out of water for all to see who it was.

The alternative course was simpler, it avoided the cold-water shock and it avoided the risk of appearing too high-spirited. The point was to appear to be so used to the sea, the Mediterranean, and this particular beach, that one might as well be in the sea as out of it. It involved a slow stroll down and into the edge of the water—not even noticing his toes were wet, land and water all the same to him!—with his eyes up at the sky gravely surveying portents, invisible to others, of the weather (Local Fisherman Preedy).

Existential Sociology

© Stacey Lynn Payne/Shutterstock.com

The realm of microlevel sociology includes existential sociology. **Existentialism** is the branch of philosophy which centers upon the problem of the reality of human existence. The existentialist fully realizes the awesome freedom which accompanies self-awareness, but is often overwhelmed by the infinite range of alternative behaviors. The existential sociologist endeavors to explain social interaction and the products of social interaction on a purely phenomenological (abstract) level of analysis.

Typical of the concerns of existentialism are:

1. Why are we here?
2. What is existence?
3. What is the meaning of existence?
4. What is the purpose of life?
5. What is the meaning of life?

In the ever-raging battle for preeminence between form and essence, existentialism usually comes down on the side of essence. This is clear in the writing of Kierkegaard (1961). Our thoughts, for instance, have both form and essence. Form refers to extrinsic existence, "what you are"; it is concerned with death because form is temporary. Essence, on the other hand, is intrinsic, concerned with "who you are," "why you are," "that you are at all," and sometimes even "whether you really are." Essence has no fear of death because the essence of a person never dies. The reality of death, however, is a major theme in much existential writing, including that of Kierkegaard, who insisted that humans are not in the process of living, but in the process of dying.

The modern "prophets" of the existential ilk include Heidegger (1927), Kierkegaard (1961), Sartre (1943, 1945), Fromm (1941), Wheelis (1958), Frankl (1962), May (1961), Tillich (1952), and a host of novelists, playwrights, and poets. Perhaps, the dean of them all was the French author Camus (1942, 1969), whose haunting *The Stranger* has been required reading in French schools since the 1960s. Kafka's (1957) *The Trial* is an exasperating example of Austrian existential art. In Easterling's opinion, the best picture of what existentialism is really about can be found in the Spanish writer Unamuno's (1931) short story, "Saint Manuel Bueno, Martyr."

In its most negative form, the existential view becomes **nihilism**, the fatalistic idea that "nothing matters, nobody cares." This philosophy sprang up in Europe following the extensive devastation and tragic destruction of World War I. Its early artistic expression was **dadaism**—art without meaning. This expressed precisely the mood of the intelligentsia at that time. It has survived through the "beat generation" of the 1950s, the "if-it-feels-good-do-it" narcissistic hedonists of the 1960s and 1970s, the "alternative rock" Generation X-ers of the 1990s, and to the varieties of punk and gothic styles that are proliferating rapidly.

Imago Dei

In its most positive form, existential thinking can open up an awareness of tremendous personal power. The realization that one has a choice of being proactive or reactive in one's life comes from the existential revelation. It is claimed that God created humankind in His image (*Imago Dei*). That means that He gave each of us a free will, just as He is free. He does not force us to do anything. We are completely liberated, if we only truly knew it.

Major themes in existential sociology include the issues of autonomy, self-sufficiency, and the idea that essence is in the self. The agenda of a practical existential sociology would include acceptance of one another in terms of each other's essence rather than form, the casting off of the bonds of determinism by external influences, and the achievement of genuine freedom regardless of one's circumstances through realization of the power of creating one's own meaning from among a virtual cornucopia-smorgasbord of available choices of alternative behaviors.

Postmodernism

© CTRLH/Shutterstock.com

The study of social theory must begin with the age-old problem of the real versus the ideal, observable phenomena versus what cannot be observed, the material versus the immaterial, and the molecular versus the ethereal. Before one becomes too hard-nosed in demanding that every statement must be empirically verifiable, she should consider the actuality of dreams, illusions, and hallucinations. In these instances, we are misled by our senses. It is undeniable that these occur at times, so how can we be certain that we are not constantly being deceived by our senses—that all we experience is in some sense illusory?

Our ability to assess and understand the world around us, according to Sapir and Whorf, depends in large measure upon the structure and mediation of our language. This notion, coupled with the (possibly) illusory nature of supposedly observable phenomena, should severely limit our boldness in making unreserved wholehearted assumptions about the essence of things social. The postmodern hesitation need not be considered a fly in the ointment of scientific progress, but it should be seriously taken as a precautionary pause—the proverbial look before one leaps into the positivistic quagmire of unchallenged presumptions.

Postmodernism is not a new paradigm from which to theorize and build models of what we supposed to be empirical reality. It represents, rather, a new wisdom by which our theorizing becomes more responsible, thoughtful, and honest. To acknowledge the tentativeness of one's ideas or conclusions is not to deny the possibility of their ultimate fundamental integrity. It simply means that all our theories, axioms, observations, and inferences will be given probationary status rather than elevated to the platform of infallibility. The simple fact is that many ideas are accepted because the individuals who stated them have themselves been hoisted into the ranks of intellectual nobility, rather than because the ideas themselves have relevancy, explanatory power, or theoretical potency. **Postmodernism** is really the result of a gradual realization that authority figures can be universally heralded but still be wrong in their assumptions and/ or conclusions. The above graphic demonstrates that Ptolemy's view, though held as truth by nearly everyone, later was shown to be incorrect by Copernicus. In time, Copernicus' view was found to be inaccurate by Isaac Newton and others. Some of Newton's findings were later corrected by Einstein, and some of Einstein's most deeply held ideas do not match with today's quantum theories. The lesson is that you cannot place your unfailing faith in any set of human facts, regardless of how greatly esteemed may be the proponents of the idea. Postmodernism is not a disregard for authority, but it is a cautionary stance of exercising critical thinking and not accepting every precept that comes from authority figures at face value.

Many scholars inadvertently serve to legitimate the authority of their disciplines by their reverent obeisance to historical precedence. They transmit this deferential attitude to their students who, for the most part, accept their "baptism" of the discipline's standard fare as unquestionably axiomatic. They make the assumption that some "intellectual tribunal" of the past possessed privileged access to infallible truth. It would be unthinkable to criticize any of the "foundational principles" which had been laid down many years before by persons of unimpeachably authoritative credentials. "After all, they may reason, who are we to question the introductory textbooks. They are in print!"

This type of academician usually fails to train (or half-heartedly trains) students in the techniques of the healthy practice of critically analyzing ideas, data, methodologies, experimentation, and so on. Perhaps the disciplinary "canon" is perfectly accurate and right-on-target in its entirety. If this is the case, there may be no harm in accepting carte blanche all the hand-me-down precepts of the "dead giants." If, on the other hand, there are errors or anachronisms in the "body of accumulated knowledge," such as the viruses of racism, greed, patriarchy, ahistoricity, or noncontextuality, or if the "facts" of the discipline do not match the *sitz im leiben* (situation-in life) of contemporary citizens, then there exists the danger of irrelevancy, or worse, potentially catastrophic cases of miseducation, malpractice, and social casualty.

This is not to say that the latest is necessarily the best (which is the tradition of modernism, in which everything must be "new and improved"). The academic tradition has proven, through time and in myriads of contexts, both its own merit and stamina. Its more enduring tenets will continue to assert themselves even under the critical gaze of the postmodern test of relevancy. That which is truly worthwhile will constantly reinterpret itself, recasting and refurbishing old motifs that had grown stale or fallen into disuse. That which is transitory, defensive, or intent on survival for the sake of self-perpetuation, however, should be discarded.

The "founding parents" of academia were created as such by their contemporaries and those who came after them, and to a certain extent, their construction is still occurring. Whether or not they intended to institutionalize the new academic enterprise, they chose to relate to the world and to possess it through knowledge and understanding. This same process is continuing among scholars today under the "postmodern" injunction from the premodern St. Paul in I Thessalonians 5:20–21: "Do not despise the words of the scholars, but test everything; hold fast to what is good."

Each time she so much as cites a source, the zealous scholar unintentionally removes attention (and therefore scrutiny) from the source itself, thereby relegitimating the source. As Lyotard (1984) has said: "Knowledge is only worthy of that name to the extent that it reduplicates itself (lifts itself up) by citing its own statements in a second-level discourse (autonomy) that functions to legitimate them." This phenomenon is similar to the process of politicians' surrounding themselves with "yes persons," thereby taking on the appearance of being authoritative without the necessity of relevance, accuracy, or accountability. The end result is to apply the rubber stamp of approval to the tedious reiteration of modernity. The "bottom line" is that the zealous scholar unintentionally dovetails into and fuels the discipline's self-perpetuating feedback loop just as succinctly as does the career professional.

Easterling has posited that the God has "approved" the educational endeavor by His warning through the prophet Hosea (751 BC): "My people perish for lack of knowledge." The emerging yet unnamed postmodern paradigm may provide some basis for optimism concerning the academic project—even as heady as the optimism of the positivistic narrative—by establishing an environment which may be hospitable for both dialectic and dialogue. The words of Tolstoy (1931 [1869]) continue to haunt the halls of academe even today: "Science is meaningless because it gives no answer to our question, the only question important for us: 'What shall we do and how shall we live?'" The author disagrees with the thought that science is meaningless, but Tolstoy's point is well taken.

It remains for the future to devise a picture of the truly postmodern academician. Postmodernism is a punctuation mark at the end of modernism.

The question is: is it a period, an exclamation point, a question mark, or only a semicolon—a pause introducing the next major social paradigm? As sociologist David Ford has said, "Perhaps Comte's three stages are now in reverse!"

Michel Foucault

The postmodern work of Michel Foucault (1926–1984) is broad and complex. It contains shifts in emphases and it reflects a variety of theoretical inputs. Aspects of Weberian theory, Marxian ideas, hermeneutics, phenomenology, and Nietschean power–knowledge relationships are found in his work as he attempts to peel away layers of truth (since for Foucault ultimate truth is not to be found).

Foucault's earlier work was influenced by structuralism. It focused on methodology or an "archeology of knowledge" involving a search for a set of rules for the formation of discourse. He abandoned the structural approach because he felt that it failed to address the issue of power and its link with knowledge. For this reason, he has been labeled as "post-structural."

His later orientation addressed the **"genealogy of power"** (a term coined by Nietzsche) or how people govern themselves and others through the production of knowledge (Foucault, 1977). Knowledge generates power by "constituting people as subjects and then governing the subjects with the knowledge." Foucault is critical of the hierarchicalization of knowledge, and of the sciences, in particular, because they are thought to rank highest in forms of knowledge and exert the greatest power. History lurches from one system of domination (based on knowledge) to another; however, knowledge is always contested.

Name _____ Date _____

Chapter 3   The Three Major Paradigms of Sociology

Chapter Exercise

(This assignment is to be carefully torn out and completed at the direction of the instructor. The answers are to be legibly handwritten directly on the sheets. Do not photocopy these pages, as such action would constitute a blatant violation of the copyright laws of the United States of America. Thoroughly read the assigned text before attempting to complete a tear-out assignment. It is obvious when a student has tried to fill-in an assignment without reading the background material.)

Try to assess just how "positivistic" you are. Do you have great hope or confidence that humanity will find solutions to all of its major problems? Why or why not?

_____

_____

_____

_____

_____

_____

_____

_____

_____

_____

_____

_____

Chapter 4

Culture

The Concept of Culture

Culture includes all the beliefs, values, artifacts, and behavior of people. It is a very broad concept. Blue jeans are an aspect of culture, as are religion, comic books, patriotism, birth control devices, and bigotry.

It is necessary to discern between things that differ but are strongly associated. Weight and mass, speed and velocity, faith and belief, prejudice and discrimination, and sex and gender are examples of phenomena that are closely related but quite distinct. "Culture" and "society" are often confused because they are so intertwined with each other. **Culture** is a shared heritage or way of life, whereas **society** is a group of people who live within particular geo-graphical boundaries and who share a culture. These concepts are easy to dis-tinguish if one will simply remember that society refers to people and culture refers to their way of life.

Culture can be reflected upon in terms of both nonmaterial culture and artifacts (material culture). **Nonmaterial culture** refers to the intangible creations of society (ideas, beliefs, etc.). **Artifacts** are the tangible products of human society—things made of molecules which are shaped, formed, or fashioned by hominids.

One of the things for which sociologists and anthropologists are constantly searching is patterns of behavior. Murdock (1945) has listed a number of patterns of such patterns. They are called **cultural universals** because they are practiced in every known culture. The form of each practice may vary widely from one society to another, but the basic pattern exists everywhere.

Examples of Cultural Universals

*Age-grading	Hairstyles
Athletic sports	Housing
Attempts to influence weather	*Incest taboos
Bodily adornment	Language
Calendars	Laws
*Cleanliness training	Marriage
Cooking	*Mealtimes
Courtship	Medicine
Dancing	*Mourning
Decorative art	Music
*Division of labor	Myths
Dream interpretation	Numerals
*Etiquette	*Patriarchy
Family	Personal names
*Firemaking	Property rights
Folklore	*Protocol
Food Habits	Religion

Food taboos	Sexual restrictions
Funeral ceremonies	Surgery
Games	Toolmaking
Gestures	Trade
★Greetings	Visiting
Gift giving	★Weaning

(Indicates cultural universals added to Murdock's list by Easterling)*

An American anthropologist spent a year and a half in the village of some so-called "primitive" Indians in the rain forests of South America. His experience on the first day of encountering the Yanomamo was so startling that Chagnon spent the next 3 days lying in a hammock. The ailment from which he suffered is known as culture shock. **Culture shock** is the cognitive disorientation which often accompanies a person's introduction to a culture radically different from one's own.

A firm grasp of the concept of culture can be of substantial value to the student and to society in a number of ways. It will help us to appreciate and understand the implications of human customs and institutions. As we gain insight into the various elements of culture, we shall become more at home in the world and better able to predict the behavior of others. We shall begin to gain an attitude toward our own culture that is more objective and less reified. A basic knowledge of culture also helps us to be more tolerant of other cultures.

Ethnocentrism and Cultural Relativism

Ethnocentrism is a concept introduced by William Graham Sumner (1840–1910), founder of the sociology department at Yale University. It refers to judging other cultures by the standards of one' own culture. Ethnocentrism is an attitude of prejudice or superiority toward other cultures. It is exemplified by the character portrayed by Marlon Brando in the film *The Ugly American*, who made a real monkey out of himself as the U.S. ambassador to an Asian country. He tried to bully the Asian officials into compliance with U.S. government objectives rather than negotiating with them as equals. To borrow an example from the real world, there is the classical image of President Lyndon Baines Johnson yelling at the Filipino legislature—at the top of his lungs—making demands upon them as a master would bark orders to inferior servants.

If ethnocentrism is carried to an extreme it can develop into such dangerous forms as racism, sexism, ageism, religious bigotry and civil religion, and even the monstrously warlike form of belligerent ethnocentrism known as jingoism. **Jingoism** is an irrational configuration of military patriotism. Examples would include Nazi Germany's attempt to exterminate the Jews. Jingoism refers directly to a song sung in British pubs in the late 1870s:

We don't want to fight but by Jingo if we do
We've got the ships, we've got the men, we've got the money too
We've fought the Bear before, and while we're Britons true
The Russians shall not have Constantinople.

Ethnocentrism is not always undesirable. It is possibly at times a healthy condition to take pride in one's school, community, family, and so on. Such a mild form of ethnocentrism tends to increase solidarity (sense of belonging), helps the individual adjust to her social environment, and promotes social stability.

Many times an analysis of our speech patterns can illustrate just how unfounded much ethnocentrism can be. For example, the use of the label "American" exclusively for a resident of the United States is itself somewhat ethnocentristic. The word "American" applies to all the inhabitants of North America, South America, and Central America, not just to the United States.

A popular cartoon depicts an American woman and her husband on vacation in the Mediterranean region. They are viewing the ruins of the Acropolis, some of which are still standing and some are in a state of rubble. The husband ehtnocentristically says, "Well, if this had been back home it would have been condemned!"

Every group is ethnocentric to some extent. It is the idea of "us versus them." It is the basis of the pre-Copernican idea that the earth is the center of the universe and all the stars and planets revolve around us. Many societies around the world, such as the Navajo, refer to themselves as "The People." The author recalls being rather startled upon seeing an Israeli map for the first time. The United States was out on the edge of the map—out on the edge of the earth! Of course, the Middle East was in the middle.

An anthropologist studying the Guajiro Indians of Colombia related an example of the universality of ethnocentrism. She remembered when she once spoke with an Indian woman of high social class about marriage, and the Indian custom of giving money and cattle to buy the wife. She had not yet come fully to understand the Indian culture, and while the woman spoke of her price this anthropologist felt terribly sad that a Colombian woman could be sold like a cow. Suddenly the Guajiro woman asked, "And you? How much did you cost your husband?" The anthropologist smugly replied, "Nothing. We Americans aren't sold." Then the picture changed completely. "Oh, what a horrible thing," the Indian woman said. "Your husband didn't even give a single cow for you. You must not be worth anything." And she lost all respect for the anthropologist, and would have nothing further to do with her, because no one had given anything for her (Foster, 1962).

The converse of ethnocentrism is called cultural relativism. **Cultural relativism** refers to the procedure of evaluating other cultures by their own standards. It means being nonjudgmental and having an attitude of respect for cultural differences.

The concept of cultural relativism involves the realization that one's own culture is but one among many. We generally prefer our own culture primarily because we were socialized within its context. We are most comfortable, therefore, in that setting.

Within the educational community, this idea is called "multiculturalism." As applied in the United States, **multiculturalism** is the recognition that there is a great deal of cultural diversity in both our past and present. Persons of non-European ethnic heritage will comprise a numerical majority of the U.S. population within the first half of the 21st century.

Traditionalists believe that it is essential to highlight what is often called the "canon" of the **great books** of Western civilization, including famous works by Shakespeare, Chaucer, Melville, Faulkner, and so on. The argument goes that works by Plato, Shakespeare, and others are of such superior intellectual and artistic quality that they have meaning for everyone, and thus transcend any consideration of gender, race, or ethnicity. The "great books" can contribute much toward a solid classical education, but the fact is that this canon overwhelmingly consists of White male authors. Educational curricula should reflect the contributions and history of African Americans, women, and non-Western peoples. Stubborn adherence to the Western canon tends to perpetuate the dominant Eurocentric ideology that serves the interests of the plutocratic elites. The movement in support of multiculturalism represents a challenge to long-standing inequalities based on gender, race, and ethnicity. It is a move in the direction of broadening our appreciation of humanity's multifaceted cultural and intellectual history.

Cultural relativism, though a desirable attitude, in general, does not mean that we should accept all behavior in every society as moral in its own context. Human rights violations are difficult to justify in any context. Infanticide and cannibalism are not in the same category of problems as what to wear, definitions of truth and beauty, or even style of government.

Some missionaries have been notorious for attempting to change the cultures in the areas where they carried out their ministries. The Great Commission, however, enjoins them only to preach the "gospel" to every creature, not American or European culture. Though it is not known for certain, it is doubtful that God is a U.S. citizen or that "Old Glory" flies over the skies of Heaven.

Xenophobia

Xenophobia refers to the fear and/or hatred of things foreign. It reflects a narrow provincialism that is slow to accept new or different ideas and resistant to change. A xenophobic individual may harbor hatred toward categories of people over events that occurred generations earlier. In contrast, **xenocentrism** is the belief that the products, styles, or ideas of one's own society are inferior to those of another. Some companies have been quick to jump on the bandwagon of foreign-sounding product names. For example, *Haagen Dazs* ice cream is made in Teaneck, New Jersey, not in the Netherlands, as many people suppose.

Afrocentrism

Afrocentrism is a perspective which allows Africans to be subjects of historical experiences rather than objects on the fringe of Europe. It is not simply the study of Africa and African people, and so on, but it is the study of anything from the African perspective. What usually occurs is Eurocentric study of African phenomena, but it is also possible to study Europe and the United States from an African perspective.

Strategies for Coping with Other Cultures

1. Try to suspend judgment and confront the unfamiliar with an open mind.
2. Try to imagine events from their perspective rather than from yours.
3. After a period of careful and critical thinking, form a judgment of the unfamiliar cultural practice.
4. Reevaluate your own culture in the light of your new experience.

What Are Americans Like?

1. They call themselves "Americans," even though the United States is only one part of North and South America.
2. They are very informal in the way they dress and in the way they treat each other, regardless of age or social standing.
3. They are generally competitive, engaging in banter—friendly joking, "getting in the last word."
4. They are achievers who love to display their business awards on office walls and their sports trophies at home.
5. They ask a lot of questions which may seem to foreigners to be pointless, elementary, and rather personal, but no impertinence is intended.
6. They value punctuality and use appointment calendars, seeming to be always in a hurry, but they get a great many things done. It is a very productive society.
7. Silence makes them nervous.

The Elements of Culture

In sociology we are always looking for patterns of behavior. There are several aspects of culture itself that are applicable to every culture—in every era and geographical location. These are the basic elements—the parts, pieces, building blocks, or components of all cultures. Five such elements have been identified.

Symbols

Every known culture has utilized symbols. A **symbol** can be anything that is recognized by the members of a society as having a particular meaning.

The raised hand, for example, will be recognized as a symbol for various phenomena depending upon the context. If you are driving a car and raise your left hand out the window, it implies that you intend to turn right. Whether it is that of a policeman in the street, a student in class, a referee at a sporting event, a charismatic in a worship service, or a farmer at a cattle auction, the raised hand serves as a symbol with a particular meaning in each instance.

Other symbols include the swastika, the cross, the dove, "X" (for Malcolm X), corporate symbols, sporting team mascots, and national flags. Most symbols are so familiar to the members of a culture that little effort is needed to interpret the meaning of a given symbol.

The shortest letters on record were between Victor Hugo and his publisher. In 1862, Hugo wrote his publisher about the sales of his book, *Les Miserables*. The letter had no words—only one symbol—the punctuation mark "?." The publisher replied with a single symbol: "!."

For millions of people, the U.S. flag brings feelings of national pride and fond thoughts of the freedom and liberty it represents. What do you suppose the people of Nagasaki and Hiroshima feel when they view the same flag? What about Native Americans, who were conquered and displaced by the bearers of that flag? The point is that a given symbol has a shared meaning within a culture but may mean something else entirely in a different culture.

Language

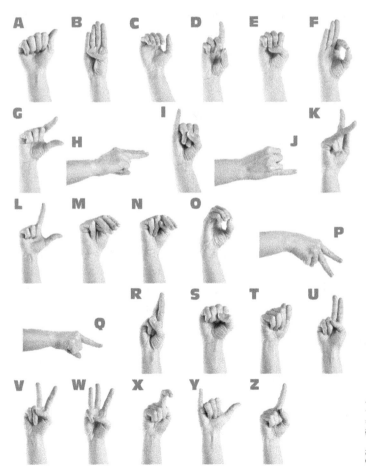

© Givaga/Shutterstock.com

Language is a system of symbols with standard meanings that allows the members of a society to communicate with each other. Language is an important element of culture because it is the primary means of cultural transmission.

Cultural transmission is the transfer of culture from generation to generation. This may take place through oral and written history, education, and socialization, but language is always the central medium.

When we say that language is a system of symbols, we do not necessarily mean audible sounds. Sign language, written language, computer language, flag signals, the Morse code, tom-toms, and even smoke signals could qualify as languages.

More than anything else, language is symbolic. This means two things. First, even when the thing being spoken about is not immediately visible or present, its meaning is communicated. Secondly, its significance is arbitrary; that is, the person receiving the message could not guess the meaning just from the sound or other symbol given (as a picture of a horse to represent a horse or a wolf howl to represent a wolf).

These two points are illustrated by the story of a storekeeper who painted the sign on his window: "We have fresh fish for sale here today." A series of customers questioned the sign. "Why say you 'have' fish? Otherwise you wouldn't put up a sign." So he erased the two words "We have." Next customer: "Would you be selling fish if it were rotten?" So he erased the word "fresh." Next customer: "Doesn't everyone know it's for sale today?" So he eliminated "today," leaving only the words "Fish for sale here." Another customer pointed out that "here" was redundant. So he chopped it to "Fish for sale." Finally, when a customer assured him that it was for sale, he removed "for sale," leaving only one word: "Fish." The next customer asked, "By the way, what does that word 'fish' mean on your window?"

Written English can be quite confusing to the uninitiated. George Bernard Shaw once suggested that the spelling of fish be changed to "ghoti." He used gh as in "tough," o as in "women," and ti as in the word "nation."

Animals in the wild communicate with warning calls (indicating the presence of a predator), mating calls, calls designating that food has been found, and so on. Sea mammals, in particular, as well as some primates, have demonstrated the use of systems of symbols in communicating with one another, though the complexity of such languages does not approach that of human language.

The gap between human and animal communication, however, may not be as wide as the student might think. A great number of animals have been taught to use language effectively. For example, a chimpanzee named Washoe was taught 150 symbols, the fundamentals of American Sign Language (ASL). One day when she was on an island with other chimpanzees, Washoe noticed that some humans across the water were having cold drinks.

She kept signing, "Roger ride come gimme sweet eat please hurry hurry you come gimme sweet you hurry you come ride Roger come give Washoe fruit drink hurry hurry fruit drink please." A plane flew over just then, and Washoe mentioned that, too. She signed, "You me ride in plane" (Hahn, 1971).

It is commonly thought that so-called primitive or preliterate societies that are not technologically advanced are characterized by simpler language systems than those of more complex societies. This is by no means the case. "The language of a technologically simple people, though lacking terminology for some of our conveniences, may have a rich vocabulary for events or phenomena that are of particular importance to that society" (Ember & Ember, 1993). Some peoples in northern climates are said to have as many as 200 different words for frozen water—not just ice, sleet, snow, and hail. Some peoples in coastal regions, furthermore, have numerous terms for the conditions of the sea—not just tempestuous, rolling, choppy, and calm.

Complex societies may have thousands of specialized technological terms, but these are by no means within the domain of the ordinary citizens of those societies. The core vocabulary excludes such technical jargon. All languages have a core vocabulary of about the same size, regardless of the complexity of the society. In addition, many so-called "primitive" languages have grammatical structures more complicated than those of "civilized societies" (Biesanz & Biesanz, 1969).

Linguistic scholars have reconstructed the ancestral languages of most of the various families of languages on the planet. A reconstructed ancestral language is known as a **protolanguage**. Three such protolanguages have been identified. One is **proto-Sino-Tibetan**, which includes all the languages of Tibet, Burma, and both northern and southern China. Another is the **proto-Niger-Congo** family of languages, of which proto-Bantu is a subfamily. Bantu languages (spoken today by about 80 million people) and other Niger-Congo languages are predominant throughout central, eastern, western, and parts of southern Africa.

The language family to which English belongs is called **Indo-European**. It includes some of the languages of India and most of the languages of Europe. Approximately half of the almost 6 billion inhabitants of planet Earth speak Indo-European languages (Akmajian, Demers, & Harnish, 1984).

The ancestral Indo-European language, which has been partially reconstructed, is called **proto-Indo-European (PIE)**. Various theories have been proposed about the original homeland of PIE. Some scholars forcefully contend that it began in the Eastern Ukraine about 3000 BCE. It makes some sense, though, that PIE developed, as other researchers insist, in the area known as Anatolia (Turkey) around 6000 or 7000 BCE. From the more central location of Anatolia, the language could have spread far to the east, west, and north.

Contact among cultures always results in the borrowing of words. For example, "siesta" has entered into English, and "weekend" has become a common word among speakers of French. Conquest and colonization usually cause a great deal of borrowing. The conquest of England by the Normans in 1066 AD introduced French as the language of the aristocracy.

It was 300 years before the educated classes began to write in English. During this time the English borrowed words from French and Latin, and the two languages—English and French—became more alike than they otherwise would have been. About 50% of the English general vocabulary has been borrowed from French (Ember & Ember, 1993).

The **color terms** of languages further illustrate the impact of culture on language. All cultures have only a few words for the basic colors. In English the basic color terms are black, red, white, blue, green, yellow, gray, orange, purple, brown, and pink. Each basic color term is a **morph** (the smallest unit of language that has a meaning). All other color terms in the language are variations or combinations of the basic color terms.

The linguists Berlin and Kay (1969) have effectively demonstrated that the number of basic color terms in the language is correlated with the complexity of a culture. Complex societies may have a greater number of decorated objects or a more complex technology of dyes and paints, necessitating additional color terms.

Edward Sapir and Benjamin Lee Whorf hypothesized that language is more than simply a vehicle for interpersonal communication. Their proposal is known as the **Sapir–Whorf Hypothesis**, which insists that humans can know the world only in terms their language provides (Sapir, 1961; Whorf, 1956). People who speak different languages, therefore, live in vastly different realities. There are as many worlds as there are languages. An individual who learns more than one language is likely to have a broader grasp of social reality and a greater propensity for understanding.

Values

Values are the standards we use to evaluate whether something or someone is desirable or undesirable, good or bad, appropriate or inappropriate, and so on. They are socially shared ideas about what is right.

Values are sometimes thought to be absolute or relative. **Absolute values** are values that are always applicable. A person who values nonviolence absolutely will not react with violence even in the face of a direct threat to herself or her loved ones. She will not support military action under any circumstances.

The converse of this is known as a **relative value**. To the person whose value of nonviolence is relative, violence will be undesirable except in certain situations. The ethic is situational and the value is a preference rather than a conviction.

Sociologist Williams (1964) has identified several major **value orientations** in the United States. These "American values" include such values as achievement and success; activity and work; moral orientation; humanitarian mores; efficiency and practicality; progress; material comfort; equality; freedom; conformity; science and rationality; nationalism–patriotism; democracy; individualism; and racism and group-superiority.

Norms

Norms are ideas of expected behavior shared by the members of a society. They are rules by which society guides our behavior. Norms are principles of behavior which are binding (to some extent) and serve as social control mechanisms to gain compliance with societal objectives.

Norms may be either positive or negative. Negative norms are called **proscriptive norms** and are the "thou shalt nots" of a culture. "Thou shalt not drive drunk" is an example of a proscriptive or prohibitive norm. Positive norms are called **prescriptive norms** and are the "thou shalts" of a culture. An example might be "Thou shalt fasten thy seat belt." Proscriptive norms prohibit certain behaviors, whereas prescriptive norms prescribe certain behaviors. Sumner, an Episcopal priest who taught the first sociology course in the United States in 1875, introduced the concepts of folkways and mores. **Mores** (pronounced "mo rays") are morally binding norms that are considered so necessary for the survival or smooth functioning of the society that they are usually enforced by law and backed up by the dominant religious system. As with norms in general, mores may be either proscriptive or prescriptive. Proscriptive mores are often called **taboos**. Examples include taboos against incest, theft, and murder. Examples of prescriptive mores might include taking care of one's children or wearing clothes in public.

According to Sumner, **folkways** are norms that have little moral significance. These norms include manners, etiquette, decorum, matters of protocol, and fashions of dress. Not spitting on the sidewalk would be a proscriptive folkway. An example of a prescriptive folkway is the use of a napkin or saying "Excuse me" following a burp at the table.

Conformity to the norms of society is encouraged by sanctions and by the internalization of norms. **Sanctions** are the responses of others, positively or negatively, to one's actions. Positive sanctions are rewards for conformity to norms; whereas, negative sanctions are punishments for the violation of norms. Negative sanctions may range in severity from a disapproving glance to incarceration to mortal execution.

The internalization of norms is an important aspect of the socialization process in which the norms of society are adopted as one's own. As a result of this process, a person's violation of a social norm will bring on feelings of guilt and shame. Working together, sanctions and the internalization of norms provide a powerful mechanism for controlling social behavior, even in a "free" society.

Artifacts

Artifacts are material culture—the tangible part of culture which is comprised of molecules. Artifacts reflect the values of a society. Archaeologists can surmise much about the nonmaterial culture of ancient civilizations by examining relics of material culture.

Artifacts also reflect the technology of a culture. This is so whether or not the society works with metals such as iron or copper. **Technology** is the application in the physical environment of cultural knowledge. The use of machinery, written language, weapons, cooking utensils, tools, toys, and dwellings all indicate in some manner the way of life of a particular people. Artifacts are, in their own right, very much a part of culture.

Name _____   Date _____

Chapter 4   Culture

Chapter Exercise

(This assignment is to be carefully torn out and completed at the
direction of the instructor. The answers are to be legibly handwritten
directly on the sheets. Do not photocopy these pages, as such action
would constitute a blatant violation of the copyright laws of the United
States. Thoroughly read the assigned text before attempting to complete
a tear-out assignment. It is obvious when a student has tried to fill-in an
assignment without reading the background material.)

*Five elements of culture are symbols, language, values, norms, and artifacts.
Comment on the influence/impact of any two elements in your own culture.*

_____

_____

_____

_____

_____

_____

_____

_____

_____

_____

_____

_____

_____

Chapter 5

Socialization

Socialization is a lifelong process of becoming fully human. It is the process of social interaction by which individuals develop their human potential and learn the patterns of their cultures.

The Nature Versus Nurture Debate

"A baby cobra."

Many animals already have knowledge of how to survive and function when they are born. The female cobra snake of southwestern Asia, for instance, coils her body around the eggs when they are about ready to hatch. When the baby snakes break out of their shells, they slither immediately over the mother's body and into the jungle. The baby cobras already have the genetic knowledge (instincts) of how to feed themselves, find water, reproduce, and even to sun themselves on rocks.

Humans are not like that. The baby human needs to be fed and cared for by others until it develops and learns how to take care of itself. If you were to have a baby on a deserted island in the Caribbean, then sail away, leaving the newborn infant to care for itself, the baby would likely die. Even if you were to leave essential items with the baby—a refrigerator full of milk, a box of diapers, a toy box full of toys, and a set of encyclopedias, the baby would still not survive. Humans are social beings.

There has been a long-standing debate over which factor has the greatest impact on the behavior of humans, nature (genetic factors), or nurture (socialization). **Sociobiology** investigates the biological bases of the social behavior of animals and human beings. Because it often extended its analyses to the behavior of human beings, sociobiology initially aroused controversy. Those opposed to it often consider sociobiology a form of biological determinism and its proponents supporters of existing social systems.

John Watson, the parent of **behaviorism**, issued a challenge in the early part of the 20th century to those who insisted on sociobiological explanations of behavior. He emphasized the importance of social learning. He said that behavior is malleable, almost like clay in the hands of a sculptor. He intimated that he could take virtually any normal healthy baby and train it to be a construction contractor or a thief, or whatever he wanted it to become. This was regardless of the genetic makeup of the child. B.F. Skinner later elaborated on Watson's ideas.

A number of studies of identical twins, who share each other's genes, have not brought a conclusion to the nature versus nature debate. At best, they tend to indicate that both biological factors and social learning play important roles in human behavior.

Negative Effects of Lack of Socialization

© Jack Cronkhite/Shutterstock.com

Children who have little social contact fail to thrive in terms of physical, social, and emotional maturity into adulthood. This is why the socialization process is so essential for adequate development to occur.

Anna

Anna was a child born in Pennsylvania to an unwed mother. The mother's father was so enraged at Anna's illegitimacy that the mother kept Anna in a storage room in the farmhouse similar to an attic and fed her barely enough to stay alive. She never left the storage room or had anything but minimal contact with another human for 5 years. When authorities found her in 1938, she was physically wasted and unable to smile or speak. After intensive therapy, including language training, Anna did make some progress. She eventually learned to use some words and feed herself.

1. She had good food habits.
2. She dressed herself.
3. She kept herself clean.
4. She was toilet trained.

Though she died at age 10 of hemorrhagic jaundice, her progress clearly demonstrates the power of the socialization process and the importance of social learning (Davis, 1940).

Isabelle

© YAKOBCHUK VIACHESLAV/Shutterstock.com

Isabelle was another sequestered youngster 6 years of age when social workers discovered her. Her mother was a deaf mute who sat with her and hugged her, but Isabelle could not speak. The faculty members at Ohio State University at first thought she was blind, also, because she did not react well to stimulation. They taught her many basic life lessons. She also underwent extensive language training which had an immediate impact on her ability to function meaningfully. She is said to have attended school, married, and had her own normal family (Davis, 1947).

Harry and Margaret Harlow's Monkey Experiments

© Eric Isselee/Shutterstock.com

A considerable amount of research with nonhuman primates was conducted before Institutional Review Boards began to limit such research. The assumption when working with animal subjects is that some parallels with human behavior may be inferred.

The Harlows' research served to illustrate the possible developmental restriction and damage resulting from removing animals from their parents and others of their kind. Scientists at the University of Wisconsin bred rhesus monkeys from birth and supervised various experiments with the infant monkeys (Harlow, 1962). The conclusion was that among the monkeys, at least, becoming a functioning member of the community of like beings appears to be dependent upon social interaction. The experiments involved observation of the difference between socialization of monkeys with no contact with any other monkeys but only with inanimate surrogate mothers. One surrogate was covered with terry cloth (towel-like material) so that the baby monkey could cling to it. Another surrogate mother was simply made from hard cold wire. Variations of the experiment included cloth mothers that gave milk (through an attached baby bottle), cloth mothers that provided no milk, and wire mothers that gave or did not give milk.

The Harlows found that the infant monkeys clung to the cloth mothers for most of the time. If the cloth mother did not provide milk, the baby monkey would go to the wire mother only long enough to drink its fill of milk, then return to the much more comforting cloth mother.

The isolated monkeys never learned to adequately respond to the opposite sex and thus reproduce. When females were artificially inseminated and subsequently gave birth, they tended to ignore or even kill their own offspring, rather than nurture them as normal monkey mothers were prone to do. These experiments demonstrate that much monkey behavior is learned from others, and not necessarily instinctual or genetic. Interestingly, if otherwise isolated baby monkeys were placed together, rather than only with inanimate surrogate mothers, the developmental delay was drastically reduced, and their behavior was practically normal, including reproductive ability. Clearly then, socialization is largely dependent upon social learning.

The Looking Glass Self

© Suzanne Tucker/Shutterstock.com

You did not simply wake up one morning and decide to build your self-concept from scratch. We do not start from a blank slate and choose the characteristics of ourselves that we would like to have. There is no "cafeteria" full of characteristics, from which we can pick and choose to build ourselves. Charles Horton Cooley, a student of George Herbert Mead at the University of Chicago, introduced the idea of **the looking glass self**. Cooley said that the conceptions we have of ourselves are derived from the responses of others to us. It is a lot like looking into the "looking glass," or mirror of society. When different people particularly significant others) tell us that we are good-looking, or dumb, or laid back, or observant, or clumsy, and so on, these become part of the way we view ourselves.

The Elements of Personality

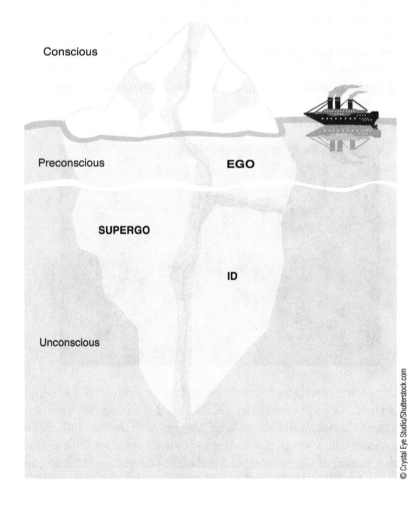

Conscious

Preconscious   EGO

SUPERGO

ID

Unconscious

The famous psychoanalyst Sigmund Freud delineated a set of elements of personality. These elements of personality are really only a construction from the mind of Freud. There are no reports from brain surgeons relating that one of these elements has been found in someone's head. Nonetheless, they are widely viewed as having some degree of relevance to the study of the socialization process.

The **id** is that part you that is a "wild and crazy person." It is the part of you that is "footloose and fancy free." It wants to soar through the heavens and experience life to the fullest extent. The id is the creative part of you. God is the Creator and you were created in His image; therefore, you have a creative spark within you. All great art, literature, and music have stemmed from someone's id

If left unchecked, however, the id, in its pursuit of limitless pleasure, may impinge on the rights of other humans. If you have something it wants, it might take it from you without permission. If it hates you, it may kill you. If it desires you, it may rape you. Clearly, there exists a need for some means of checking or controlling the id.

The **superego** is that part of you which has incorporated into itself the knowledge of good and evil, of what is right and what is wrong. It is a depository of knowledge concerning what is proper social behavior and what is improper. It is somewhat related to the concept of the conscience. The superego, if properly developed, will help a person to determine whether a particular act is appropriate or inappropriate within a given context. For instance, one should not walk around naked in public. It is perhaps just as improper, however, for one to take a shower fully dressed.

The id and superego both function at the unconscious level. The **ego** is that part of you that is your conscious mind. It includes your will and emotions. If your id and superego seem to be at enmity with each other, it is the ego (in its capacity as the will) that will make the ultimate decision of which behavior to perform.

In Freud's day, the major problem plaguing many of his clients was **repression**, or oversocialization. Many people were guilt-ridden about behavior that should have been considered normal (such as sexual relations between married partners). Their superegos were overdeveloped and their ids were underdeveloped. Today, the major problem for many people seems to be the opposite. Many people seem to be undersocialized. They exhibit little or no remorse after murdering someone or after having premarital or extramarital sex. Their ids are overdeveloped and their superegos are underdeveloped.

Stages of Cognitive Development

Swiss psychologist Jean Piaget developed a theory of cognitive development (Piaget, 1969). It involves a series of four stages though which each human progresses in the early years of the life cycle. These stages are as follow:

1. **Sensorimotor stage**, ages 0 through 2. At first, children understand their environment only through their senses and motor ability. During this stage, they begin to learn the classification of objects by acting upon them, object permanence (the realization that out-of-sight objects still exist), and how to coordinate the different parts of the body. Much of their behavior begins to be intentional and goal-directed.

2. **Preoperational stage**, ages 2 through 7. In this stage, children develop language. They understand what symbols mean, but think everyone else understands things as they do. They understand only one characteristic of a thing at a time, and begin to move from egocentric thought toward decentering.

3. **Concrete Operational stage**, ages 7 through 11. In this stage, the child's understanding expands to include concepts of time, weight, equality, distance, and so on, but is limited to concrete things they can see or manipulate.

    They learn about the conservation of quantity and the classification of objects by various criteria.

4. **Formal Operational stage**, ages 12 and older. In this stage, children can think logically about hypotheses as well as concrete facts. Critical thinking becomes a part of their repertoire, as well as a concern for values and truth. They are also beginning to be able to consider alternative futures.

Agents of Socialization

Socialization does not occur in a vacuum, nor does it "just happen" on its own. There are individuals and institutions at work constantly shaping and reshaping our patterns of behavior. These forces are referred to as "agents." A few of them are delineated as follows.

The Family

The family is the most important agent of socialization because it is the first. Children are heavily dependent upon other family members for their

very physical health and survival. The close contact inherent in the family setting means that the child will necessarily learn many patterns of behavior from them. Gender roles are learned by observing and interacting with parents and siblings. Language is passed on from one generation to the next largely through the family. Not only does the family help shape the child's personality, but it also provides the child with her position (social status) in society. Many of the values a person holds throughout her lifetime were instilled by the family.

The School

The school is an agent of socialization that has the manifest function of teaching a wide range of skills and information. There is also a latent function of the school that is commonly called the **hidden curriculum**. This refers to the teaching of values, such as success, competitiveness, and so on. The values taught in school may or may not be in harmony with those taught in the family. Some sociologists have suggested that what occurs in the hallways, on the school grounds, and in the parking lots is more important in terms of socialization than what happens in the classroom.

The Church

Only about 50% of people in the United States are socialized to any extent by a church, synagogue, or mosque. If children are involved in a church, it is usually for only a few hours per week, at most. By contrast, they are in school for

30 or more hours per week, interacting with peers for 40 or more hours per week, and the average child in the United States watches 30 hr of television per week. These other influences often communicate variant values. Religious organizations must have quality programs in order to make the most of what little time they have to influence children.

Peer Group

© CREATISTA/Shutterstock.com

Peers may be defined as people with common interests and social position and who are usually about the same age. The peer group differs from the family, school, and church in that there is little or no direct adult supervision. New behaviors, therefore, become possible. A sense of new found freedom and independence from the family is experienced. The individual is finally free to do whatever she wants. There is, however, such a thing as **peer pressure**—a tendency toward group conformity. This may sometimes involve feeling "pressured" to perform behaviors one might not actually desire to carry out. Many people have said that the first time they smoked, drank alcohol, took drugs, or had premarital sex was when they were pressured to do so within a peer group setting. Peer pressure is not necessarily negative. Certain peer groups may actually influence participants to good works.

Mass Media

The mass media comprise the agent of socialization that encompasses channels of communication directed to vast audiences. Some examples include radio, television, movies, books, popular music, newspapers, video games, magazines, computer software, and the Internet.

The mass media tend to spread culture; that is, knowledge, beliefs, customs, skills, and behavior. They change the way we experience the world. For example, a normally neutral experience such as going to bed can be changed by a mass medium (horror movies) into a frightening one. The mass media may also enhance our experiences in various ways. For instance, a boring event (parade, sporting event, or political convention) may be viewed as more exciting or interesting than it would normally be by providing close-ups, supplying comments, hype, and so on.

Concerns About Television:

Social scientists have criticized television for a number of reasons.

1. Television tends to be a passive medium rather than an interactive one.
2. Television programming does not tend to be not very reflective of reality. Most of the characters and families are depicted as wealthy or well-to-do.
3. Television advertising creates wants and needs that would not otherwise exist. Parents are often villainized through advertising. Repeated exposure to TV commercials turns children into mini salespersons who make demands on the parents for what they see advertised. Children tend to believe commercials. Fred Flintstone and Barney Rubble said a cereal was "chocolatey enough to make you smile." When children were asked why they wanted the cereal:
   a. Two-thirds responded that they wanted it because of the chocolate taste (Atkin & Gibson, 1978).
   b. Three-fifths wanted it because it would make them smile.
   c. One-half wanted the cereal because Barney and Fred like it.
4. Commercials teach children a number of attitudes:
   a. All problems are resolvable.
   b. All problems are resolvable fast.
   c. All problems are resolvable through some technology, such as a drug, detergent, toy, fast food, vehicle, computer.
5. TV's effects on sexual attitudes have also been hashed and rehashed. The fact is that there are numerous depictions of copulation in which the partners are not married. Many programs feature incest, rape, prostitution, and gay and lesbian characters and themes.

6. The effects of television violence have been discussed for decades. The more TV children watch, the more accepting they are of aggressive behavior. Children's attitudes toward violence can be changed if adults discuss the violence with them, explaining the unreality of television violence. Violence on TV has been measured in terms of:

   a. **Prevalence**—The extent to which violence occurs at all in the program.

   b. **Rate**—The frequency of violent episodes.

   c. **Role**—The number of characterizations of victimization.

7. If children watch a great deal of TV violence, they will be more prone to aggressive violence than those children who do not watch TV violence. Role models act as stimuli to produce similar behavior in the observer. The behavior is learned by being imitated, rewarded, or reinforced in a variety of ways. There are three steps necessary for this process:

   a. Exposure to the stimulus

   b. Acquisition of the message

   c. Acceptance of the message

8. Persons who often watch TV:

   a. Tend to be more suspicious and distrustful of others.

   b. Think that there is more violence in the world than reality suggests.

Name _____   Date _____

Chapter 5   Socialization

Chapter Exercise

(This assignment is to be carefully torn out and completed at the direction of the instructor. The answers are to be legibly handwritten directly on the sheets. *Do not* photocopy these pages, as such action would constitute a blatant violation of the copyright laws of the United States. Thoroughly read the assigned text before attempting to complete a tear-out assignment. It is obvious when a student has tried to fill-in an assignment without reading the background material.)

Explain Cooley's "looking glass self" concept in relation to your own experience.

_____

_____

_____

_____

_____

_____

_____

_____

_____

_____

_____

_____

_____

_____

Chapter 6

Social Groups and Organization

Statuses and Roles

Status

The term **social status** refers to a recognized social position that an individual occupies within society. A **status set** is all the social statuses a particular person holds at a given time. A given person, for example, might be a son, a pastor, an African American, an Episcopalian, a novelist, a husband, a father, a tuberculosis victim, and a dove hunter, and upper middle-class.

A **master status** is the one status most important in establishing one's social identity. If one has AIDS, for instance, that fact might shape the self-concept and the way others view the individual, regardless of all other statuses that person occupies, such as physician, U.S. Senator, or magazine editor.

Status inconsistency refers to aspects of an individual's status or statuses that might appear contradictory. For example, a woman football player may experience inquisitive remarks about how being female seems inconsistent with the playing of full-tackle football.

Ascribed status is a social status into which one is born or otherwise involuntarily placed. Race and social class when young are examples. In a **caste system,** nearly one hundred percent of all social positions are ascribed.

Achieved status, conversely, is a status that is assumed voluntarily and that reflects a significant measure of personal ability and effort. A person who was born into a lower-class family but graduated from college and is now upper middle-class would serve as an example of achieved status. Such a move would be called upward social mobility.

Role

© Sudowoodo/Shutterstock.com

A **role** is a set of norms or expected behavior patterns, obligations, and privileges attached to a particular social status. A **role set** is a number of roles attached to a single status. For example, a person occupying the status of school teacher plays the role of classroom manager, instructor, and colleague to other teachers.

Role conflict refers to the incompatibility among the roles corresponding to two or more statuses. For example, a school teacher may have her own daughter in class. She is both the student's teacher and the student's mother. The temptation might arise to either show favoritism toward the daughter or to be particularly tough on the daughter because of the role conflict.

A similar problem that can arise is called **role strain**. This refers to incompatibility among roles corresponding to a single status. For example, a physician plays the role of compassionate healer. At the same time, however, she might also be a businessperson who sues her patient for payment, whom she is treating for a stress-related illness.

Social Groups

In order to understand what a social group is, it will be helpful to first discuss what a social group is not.

1. First, a social group is not an **aggregate**. An aggregate is a number of people who happen to be in the same place at the same time. A number of people walking on a city street at a randomly chosen moment might be an example of an aggregate. They do not necessarily know each other nor interact on a regular basis.
2. A social group is also not a **category**. The term category refers to a number of people with common characteristics, but who seldom or never interact with each other. All blue-eyed nurses or all college graduates are examples of categories.

A **social group**, therefore, refers to two or more people who have a high degree of common identity and who interact on a regular basis. Examples might include such entities as a baseball team, a college class, or a nuclear family. According to sociologist Charles Horton Cooley, there are two major types of social groups (Cooley, 1909):

1. **Primary group**: This is a typically small social group in which relationships are both personal and enduring. Examples include a small family, a friendship clique, or, perhaps, college roommates.
2. **Secondary group**: This is a typically large and impersonal social group based on some special interest or activity. A college class and a large business firm might be examples of secondary groups.

Social groups have also been classified by Ferdinand Tönnies (pronounced "Turn-yes") in a somewhat similar manner in terms of Gemeinschaft and Gesellschaft (German terms for "community" and "society"). **Gemeinschaft** relates to groups that tend to be very personal, possibly rural, and informal. **Gesellschaft** groups are more urban and impersonal.

Looking at the Difference between Gemeinschaft and Gesellschaft

Gemeinschaft	Gesellschaft
Tradition oriented	Future oriented
Resistant to change	Look to rapid change
Emphasis on customs	Emphasis on codified laws
Social relationships long-lasting	Social relationships more transitory
Social relationships personal, affectionate	Social relationships more impersonal, anonymous

Gemeinschaft	Gesellschaft
Little division of labor	Complex division of labor
Interrelated roles	Segmental roles
Emphasis on ascribed roles	Emphasis on achieved roles
Agricultural and extraction industries	Manufacturing and service industries
Caste system of social stratification	Class system of social stratification
Homogeneous population	Population of diverse cultural backgrounds
Ascribed status important	Achieved status important
Economically self sufficient	Increasingly complex economic interdependence
Simple technology	Increasingly complex technology
"Folk" entertainment such as carnivals	More synthetic entertainment, i.e. spectator sports
Apt to be patriarchal	More gender equality
Informal education, illiteracy widespread	Emergence of mass education
Usually small in size	Usually large in size
Family is focal unit of society	Kinship group loses importance to economic and political relationships
Primary group emphasis	Secondary group emphasis
Family loyalty important	Society loyalty important
Society in harmony with nature	Society control of nature important
Religion is important unifying factor	Religion is separate and diverse
Little or no social disorganization	Raising of social disorganization/ anomic
High social integration	Low social integration
Cooperation is an important social process	Competition is an important social process

Group Leadership

DIFFERENCE BETWEEN
BOSS VS. LEADER

BOSS
- Drives employee
- Depends on authority
- Inspires fear
- Says, " I "
- Places blame for the breakdown
- Knows how it is done
- Uses people
- Take credit
- Commands
- Says, " Go "

LEADER
- Coaches them
- On goodwill
- Generates enthusiasm
- Says, " We "
- Fixes the breakdows
- Shows how it is done
- Develops people
- Gives credit
- Asks
- Says, " Let's go "

© Keepsmiling4u/Shutterstock.com

Social groups always have some kind of leadership. There are two ways of categorizing group leadership.

1. **Instrumental and Expressive Leadership**
   a. **Instrumental leadership** emphasizes the completion of tasks by a social group. An instrumental father may put pressure on his children for academic performance or to participate in music or athletic activities. An instrumental pastor may try to mobilize her congregation for missions, evangelism, a building program, or ministry to the poor.
   b. **Expressive leadership** emphasizes the collective well-being of the members of a social group. The expressive parent may not have a performance agenda for the family members, but will simply be interested in nurturing them and "being there" for them. The expressive pastor may not implement very many programs in the church, but will do a lot of visitation of the members, providing them with ample counseling and fellowship opportunities.

2. **Involvement of Members in Decisions**
   a. The **authoritarian leader** makes all the major decisions. This type of leader is autonomous and the members simply go along with her decisions.

   b. The **democratic leader** includes the members in the decision-making process. She may actually make the final decision, but only after receiving free, open, and welcome input from all the members. She may have actually been elected to the position of leadership by the members and is therefore responsible to them.

   c. The *laissez-faire* **leader** tends to de-emphasize her role as leader, choosing, instead, to allow the organization to drift in whatever direction the course of least resistance might take it. This is a weak form of leadership which is usually rather ineffective.

Social Organization

Group Size

© ARENA Creative/Shutterstock.com

German sociologist Georg Simmel (pronounced "Zimmel") emphasized the importance of group size (Simmel, 1950). He insisted that **as group size**

increases arithmetically, the number of relationships tends to increase arithmetically.

In a **dyad**, or social group of two persons, there is only one relationship. In a **triad** (a social group of three persons), however, there are three relationships.

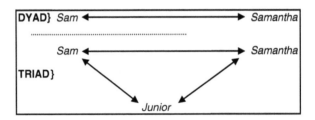

The number of group members has increased by only one, but the number of relationships has increased by two. Simmel said that it would be virtually impossible to maintain a primary group of more than 15 persons, because the number of relationships is 105! That many intimate, long-term relationships would, indeed, be wearisome to sustain.

Bureaucracy

Max Weber, as previously discussed, delineated the ideal qualities of a **bureaucracy** (Weber, 1922). These include such features as specialization, a hierarchical arrangement of leadership, rules and regulations, a high degree of technical competence, impersonality (treating everyone the same, regardless of personal relationships), formal, and written communications. Weber depicted a bureaucracy, with all its faults (mountains of "red tape" and seemingly endless chains of command), as—nonetheless—the most efficient way of getting things done when large numbers of people are involved. Governments, universities, the Church, and all other formal organizations function much better with bureaucratic structures in place than they would be able to do without them.

The Iron Law of Oligarchy

Robert Michels (pronounced "mee-kels") was a German sociologist who lived and worked in Italy. He isolated what is considered to be one of the few "laws" in sociology, the iron law of oligarchy (Michels, 1911). This law states that every group, regardless of size or democratic intentions, will sooner or later become an oligarchy. **Oligarchy** refers to "rule by a few." Those who are designated to take care of the day-to-day concerns of the group are acquainted with the needs and resources of the group and their opinions about the decisions of the group are therefore solicited by the other members. This gives these individuals an inordinate level of influence. Over time, they tend to become the leaders of the organization. Michels' assertion has not been successfully challenged to date. It seems to be a reality in every known group.

Group Conformity

"What was the decision making process that led to hiring a cat?"

Group Conformity can be defined as the tendency of individuals to adopt the standards and behaviors of the group. There are several important studies that have become classics in this area.

Solomon Asch

Solomon Asch studied group conformity within the context of visual perception (Asch, 1952). He set up several students in an experimental situation in which they were asked to tell which one of the lines on a card with three lines of various lengths matched the length of the line on another card. The other parties had been previously coached to give an incorrect answer. The "subject" was then asked to choose which of the lines matched. More than 33% conformed by answering incorrectly, even though the answer was obvious. The only possible explanation is the tendency of humans toward conformity with the group.

Stanley Milgram

Another experiment was conducted by a student of Asch's, Stanley Milgram, who became a professor at Yale University. This experiment was conducted because Milgram was interested in the question of why ordinary German citizens carried out orders from government officials involving the killing of Jews and others during the Nazi regime (Milgram, 1965).

The experiment involved a researcher (Milgram), a "teacher" (the subject in the experiment), and a "learner." The learner (actually a professional actor) was in an adjacent room separated by one-way glass so that he could not see the researcher and teacher, but they could see him. He was strapped into a chair somewhat resembling an electric chair with electronic wires attached to his head, arms, and chest. The teacher was told that the learner was supposed to have memorized certain academic material and should be able to answer questions. When an incorrect answer was given, the teacher was instructed by the researcher to administer an electric shock by pulling a lever on a panel with markings from 0 to 450 volts. The learner acted as though he was receiving an electric shock. Ordinary household current is 110 volts and is enough to kill a human being. Electric dryers use 220 volts.

Of the numerous subjects tested in the same experiment, none questioned the procedure before 300 volts. Two-thirds went all the way to 450 volts! The actor would jerk in the chair, sometimes screaming, then slump as though dead. The subjects were assured that there would be no repercussions to them for this action, since Milgram was a legitimate authority figure. He was a Yale professor with a government grant, and besides, the learner should have learned the answers to the questions as he had agreed to do.

Groupthink

"Space shuttle Challenger disaster. Space shuttle exhaust plumes entwined around a ball of gas a few seconds after the explosion caused by ruptured O-rings. Jan. 28, 1986."

Irving L. Janis is best known for his study of **groupthink**, which refers to a reduced capacity for critical thinking caused by group conformity (Janis, 1989). Groupthink is considered to have been responsible for bad decisions concerning the United States' lack of preparation for the Japanese bombing of Pearl Harbor, despite ample warnings from military personnel. The United States' involvement in the Vietnam conflict, the ill-conceived and executed Bay of Pigs Invasion of Cuba, the Iran-Contra Affair, and the Space shuttle Challenger disaster are further examples of the results of group conformity through groupthink.

Name _____   Date _____

Chapter 6   Social Groups and Organization

Chapter Exercise

(This assignment is to be carefully torn out and completed at the direction of the instructor. The answers are to be legibly handwritten directly on the sheets. *Do not* photocopy these pages, as such action would constitute a blatant violation of the copyright laws of the United States. Thoroughly read the assigned text before attempting to complete a tear-out assignment. It is obvious when a student has tried to fill-in an assignment without reading the background material.)

Describe a situation you know about (or perhaps from your own experience) in which "group conformity" or "groupthink" took place.

_____

_____

_____

_____

_____

_____

_____

_____

_____

_____

_____

_____

_____

_____

Chapter 7

Social Deviance

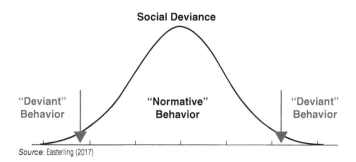

Social Deviance

"Deviant" Behavior — "Normative" Behavior — "Deviant" Behavior

Source: Easterling (2017)

The term **deviance** refers to the recognized violation of cultural norms. Norms are ideas of expected behavior. Deviance, therefore, is a residual category of behavior, since it is statistically on the fringe of what would be considered "normal" behavior.

Crime is the violation of norms that have been formally enacted into criminal law. **Juvenile delinquency** is the violation of legal standards by children or adolescents. Deviance, however, is not limited to crime. Spitting on the sidewalk may be considered deviant in some cultural settings, but it is not a crime. In other places, the same behavior may, in fact, be a crime or it may be perfectly acceptable normal behavior.

Deviance is a product of society. That is to say, it exists only in relation to cultural norms. It is the definition of others that is important. For example, if no one had ever spat on a sidewalk, there would be no cultural expectations about it, one way or the other. If you were to spit on the sidewalk in this context, you would not be censored, although some people might think that it was a particularly nasty act. If you or someone else then started habitually spitting on the sidewalk, there might be a meeting of community leaders to decide how to stop this behavior. It would then become a deviant act, since others are reacting negatively to it.

Biological Explanations of Deviance

Caesare Lombroso

Some early researchers concluded that deviance was due to biological factors. An Italian physician named **Caesare** Lombroso (1876/2006) theorized that criminals have distinctive physiological characteristics. He identified them as:

+ Low foreheads
+ Long arms
+ Beady eyes
+ Excessive hairiness

Lombroso viewed criminals as throwbacks to earlier stages of hominid evolution. He wandered through Italian prisons and found several people with the characteristics listed above. This was obviously a flawed methodology. There were many people who had these same characteristics who were not in prison.

William Sheldon's Body Type Theory

William Sheldon examined body types and tried to link these with delinquency and criminal behavior (Sheldon, Hartl, & MacDermott, 1949). He concluded that there are three basic body types with corresponding personality characteristics (somatotypes):

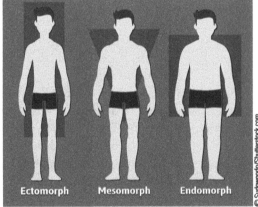

Ectomorph	Tall, thin, lean, delicate, poor muscles	Quiet, fragile, restrained, nonassertive, sensitive
Mesomorph	Muscular, athletic	Active, assertive, vigorous, combative
Endomorph	Short, fat, plump, buxom, developed visceral structure	Relaxed, sociable, tolerant, comfort-loving, peaceful

Sheldon linked mesomorphs with criminal and delinquent behavior. Why do you think he made this deduction? Could it be because he thought that the muscular and athletic person is able to bully someone and then run away quickly?

Sheldon's research has been criticized extensively. It makes use of a sample that is nonrepresentative, since many people are short and thin, or tall and fat, tall and muscular, and so on. Still, it was a step toward the attempt to understand the complexities of deviant behavior.

Glueck and Glueck

The husband and wife research team of Glueck and Glueck also found a link between the mesomorph body type and delinquency (Glueck & Glueck, 1950). Unlike Sheldon, however, they did not argue that body type caused the criminal behavior. Their research at Harvard University in the 1930s centered around variables in addition to body type, particularly the early onset of juvenile delinquency as a harbinger of a delinquent career.

Glueck and Glueck found that the most important factor was family relationships. Others included physical and mental factors such as intelligence, mental disease, and physique. Physique, or body type, is only one minor factor in deviant behavior, and certainly not causal in any sense.

The "Super Male" Fallacy

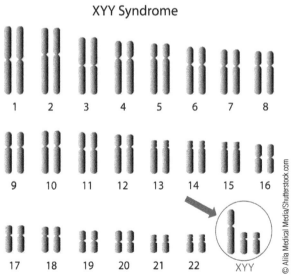

"XYY, super male syndrome genome."

More recent research has uncovered the fact that some males have an extra "Y" chromosome in their genes. In the U.S. prison population, about one in one hundred men have the **XYY chromosomes**. In the U.S. population at large, however, about one in one thousand men have the XYY chromosomes. Clearly, there is a significantly high proportion of men in prison with the XYY. Most people with XYY chromosomes are not in prison, though, and to generalize about this genetic characteristic is manifestly inaccurate and dangerous. The popular conclusion that the extra Y chromosome places the individual in extreme risk of committing deviant acts and even violent crimes is unfounded.

A Psychological Theory of Deviance: Containment Theory

Reckless and Dinitz (1968) derived a theory relating criminality to a personality type. They hypothesized that two personality traits may help prevent a person from violating social norms. These traits are:

1. A positive self-concept
2. A strong conscience

© Leah-Anne Thompson/Shutterstock.com

Subsequent studies indicated that there was, indeed, a positive relationship between these personality traits and the lack of a delinquent record. Reckless and Dinitz called this idea "**containment theory.**" They viewed delinquency as unsuccessful socialization. Their study included "Good Boys" and "Bad Boys," based on nondelinquent and delinquent behavior, respectively.

Good Boys	Strong conscience, handled frustration, and identified with cultural norms and practices
Bad Boys	Weaker conscience, little toleration for frustration, did not go along with conventional culture

(Reckless and Dinitz 1968)

The Good Boys had fewer run-ins with the law. The conclusion was they had the ability to control or "contain" their deviant impulses.

The Structural-Functional Perspective

"World Trade Center September 11, 2001."

The Functions of Deviance

Some sociological concepts may at first seem counterintuitive. Durkheim (1895) indicated that some deviance may be functional for society.

1. **Unity**—In the first place, a heinous crime or other blatant act of deviance may bring about unity among the population in their opposition and/or reaction to it. For example, when the Oklahoma City bombing took place in 1995, Oklahomans worked together in an unprecedented manner, providing relief, rescue efforts, blood drives, and so on. There was a very similar unity dynamic in operation following the terrorist attacks on the World Trade Center towers in New York City and the Pentagon in Washington, D.C. on September 11, 2001.

2. **Boundary maintenance**—A second way in which Durkheim indicated that some deviance may be beneficial is called boundary maintenance. This refers to the fact that when the members of society see the response of others to deviant acts, they then know whether those acts are considered acceptable behavior within the context of that society. In other words, when some deviance occurs and is reacted to, it lets the rest of us know the boundaries of our behavior. For example, if your classmate were chewing gum in school and was disciplined for it, you would discern that you probably should not chew gum in school yourself, thus adding another "boundary" to your repertoire of acceptable behaviors.

3. **Vested interests**—Veblen (1899) provided a third reason why some deviance may be functional, at least for certain facets of society. He maintained that there are certain groups that have vested interests in preventing the complete abolition of deviance. This idea is similar to Herbert Gans' arguments for the functions of poverty, such as those discussed in Chapter 3. There might also be a discussion of the functions of crime, based on the various vested interests that might benefit from it. For example, if there were no more crime, it might mean the laying off of all police officers, criminal justice workers, and those in the penal system. Security alarm companies and insurance companies would be hurt, because people would no longer need many of their products or services. It might even lead to a major economic catastrophe. A small amount of crime is needed, therefore, to perpetuate the bureaucratic and capitalistic systems now in place.

Merton's Social Strain Theory of Deviance

Merton (1949), in his **social strain theory**, outlined a typology of responses to the societal goal in the United States, which he identified as material success or "the American Dream." Some people respond differently from others for various reasons. They may accept the societal goal and the culturally approved means of achieving it, such as getting a job, entering a profession, and becoming an entrepreneur. Others may reject the goal, but accept the means of achieving it, or any combination. This may be because they feel that the goal is out of reach for them so they might "innovate" by engaging in criminal activity. These possibilities are summarized in the following figure.

Social Strain Theory Of Deviance		
The Conformist	Accepts the goal	Accepts the means
The Innovator	Accepts the goal	Rejects the means
The Ritualist	Rejects the goal	Accepts the means
The Retreatist	Rejects the goal	Rejects the means
The Rebel	Rejects the goal and substitutes with a new goal	Rejects the means and substitutes with a new means

Source: Merton (1949).

The social strain theory has some explanatory power for some categories of deviance, such as economically motivated crime and cults and communes. It offers no explanation, however, for "crimes of passion" or violent crimes.

Symbolic Interaction Paradigm

Labeling Theory is the assertion that deviance and conformity result from the process by which individuals are defined or labeled by others. **Primary deviance** refers to an activity that is initially defined as deviant. In secondary deviance, the label becomes part of the  person's identity and self-concept, thus affecting her behavior. **Stigma** is a powerful negative social label that radically changes a person's social identity and self-concept. It is usually attached in a **degradation ceremony**, such as the sentencing of a criminal in a formal court setting.

The reinterpretation of a person's past in terms that are consistent with a present label is called **retrospective labeling**. For example, if a priest molests a child, people will often begin to revise the past in their memories, making statements like: "Come to think of it, he always did like to be around children." It is a result of secondary labeling stemming from the attachment of a stigma.

The Medicalization of Deviance

The **medicalization of deviance** (Foucault, 1963) refers to the identification as diseases or illnesses patterns of behavior that were previously considered in moral terms. Spencer (1898) viewed society as analogous to a living organism. A problem or "disease" in one part of the organism affects the entire organism. Early sociologists built on this idea and arrived at the conclusion that deviant behavior could be thought of as "social disease" (Durkheim, 1925) and "social pathology" (Mills, 1943; Lemert, 1951).

Pathology is a medical term that indicates the interpretation and diagnosis of disease and the changes caused by disease. The early social pathologists were concerned with crime, mental illness, drug abuse, and suicide. Today this list has been expanded to include alcoholism, stress, smoking, child abuse, obsessive–compulsive tendencies, pedophilia, spouse beating, spiritual abuse, overeating, under-eating, marital difficulty, compulsive gambling, divorce adjustment, compulsive shopping, bereavement, trichotillomania, rape, Vietnam veterans, depression, postpartum depression, anxiety and panic attacks, sexual addictions, codependency, mood swings, and many other behaviors. There is a tendency to treat such "ailments" in a hospital or clinical setting.

Undoubtedly, the hospitals and clinics benefit monetarily from treatment programs, and some individuals and families are aided by the treatment. To the extent that they ameliorate suffering and facilitate economic growth, treatment programs may be regarded as functional for society. Overall and in the long-term, however, the trend toward the medicalization of deviance can be thought of as dysfunctional in several ways.

Whatever Became of Sin?

The medicalization of deviance removes responsibility from the individual. According to Parsons' (1953) **sick role** concept, sick people are not responsible for their conditions. Being sick is unpleasant and becoming sick is not a matter of moral choice. People are "stricken" by sickness through no fault of their own. Those who become sick, therefore, are not to be blamed or punished for their maladies.

Popular 1970s and '80s entertainer Flip Wilson performed a celebrated comedy routine in which he would use as his excuse for outlandish stunts, "The devil made me do it!" It rang true to his audiences because of the hesitancy of most of us to accept the blame for our own actions.

Psychiatrist Menninger (1973) wrote a book entitled *Whatever Became of Sin?* in which he decries the all-too-common cop-out "It's not my fault." He insists that as adults, each person is responsible for the deeds done in her own body. Blaming behavioral problems, particularly addictive ones, on a genetic "predisposition" or chemical imbalance or on one's parents, employer, and so on, though at times there may be some basis for such claims, implies a biological or psychological determinism that is not entirely satisfactory for most social scientists.

The Social Nature of "Dysfunctional Behaviors"

The medicalization of deviance also removes responsibility from the society which continues the perpetual production of perpetrators of deviance. Even if a particular treatment program should actually help an individual or family, it will not have changed the social system in which the problem was originally initiated, incubated, and eventually produced. Medicalized deviance may be an individual's problem in a narrow context, but it is at root a social problem. Reiman (1979) has stated that the failure to focus on the social responsibility for deviance literally acquits the existing social system (hence, it's oligarchic or plutocratic leadership) of any charge of injustice. Let us use the problem of alcoholism to illustrate this principle.

Society allows the advertising of alcoholic products. There have been wars that were fought but never declared, such as the Korean and Vietnam "conflicts." There have been wars that were declared but never fought, like the War on Poverty and the War on Drugs. How can we say that the War on Drugs has not been fought? Isn't there a Drug Czar appointed by the President and a huge Drug Enforcement Agency? Yes, but the War on Drugs does not aim at alcohol, which is the drug of choice in the United States, including the White House, Lincoln, Hayes, and Trump having been the only U.S. presidents in who were teetotalers. George W. Bush, the 43rd U.S. President, was a former heavy drinker, but stated that he quit drinking in 1986 after determining alcohol to be a problem for him.

The advertising of smoke tobacco products on television and radio was banned in the United States in 1971. There was a decrease in the number of new smokers in 1972 and the decline has continued every year since. Today, smoking (with the recent exception of cigar smoking) has virtually become socially unacceptable and legislative statutes as well as voluntary efforts are creating smoke-free environments for work, dining, study, and recreation. Lawsuits against the large tobacco companies have driven them to diversify their investment of capital to nontobacco industries or to market their tobacco products in the Third World. Macionis (1992) has said, "The American tobacco industry is not breathing as easily as it once did."

Why have we not done the same with alcohol? Tobacco related deaths number over 300,000 per year in the United States, due to a variety of diseases, including heart disease, cancer of the mouth, throat, and lungs, bronchitis, and emphysema. This is indeed reprehensible, but far more damage is done to our society by alcohol abuse, in terms of automobile accidents, broken homes and careers, child abuse, and violent criminal acts, than tobacco or any other drug—including marijuana, heroin, cocaine, and speed. Eighty percent of all fire deaths, 65% of drownings, and 70% of fatal falls are related to alcohol use (Bartholomew, 2007). In the workplace, alcoholism is responsible for absenteeism, excessive medical bills, and poor job performance, making it the most costly type of substance addiction.

The giants of the alcohol industry, such as Anheuser-Busch, Coors, and Philip-Morris (Miller Brewing), spend around $4.6 billion dollars on advertising in order to convince the public that alcohol drinking is respectable and socially desirable (Ramirez, 2014). Much of the marketing has been directed at young people, the obvious purpose being to secure a new generation of users. These corporations, in their profit-oriented activities, have been responsible for getting many Americans addicted to dangerous substances.

A simple ban on alcohol advertisements on television and radio would benefit our society far into the next century. This could result in a true War on Drugs. Formidable opposition to such a proposal could be expected from the beer and wine producers and distributors, the advertising agencies with alcohol clients, and the owners of television and radio networks and stations. Past attempts at prohibition have failed. The right to sell and consume alcoholic products is not in question; but is it really necessary to promote and advocate alcohol consumption? Similar reports could be related about numerous additional medicalized deviancies, amply illustrating the social nature of so-called dysfunctional behaviors.

Bonum Ex Nocentibus

The medicalization of deviance ignores certain economic deterministic truths of the social inequality inherent in a market-driven economic system. In the United States, 80% of the wealth (money and goods—including real estate and stock ownership) is held by the top 20% of the population, whereas the bottom 20% control no wealth at all (U.S. Bureau of the Census, 2010).

One is reminded of Smith's (1776/1937) great paradox of *bonum ex nocentibus* ("a good product from an evil source"). He claimed that "from individual self-interest and the personal pursuit of profit comes the greatest good for the greatest number of people." By this Smith meant that in the process of self-interested entrepreneurship, many jobs are generated and essential or desirable commodities are made accessible to the public through the production, distribution, and consumption of goods and services. The profits themselves are subsequently diffused throughout the economy by means of spending and further investment. The paradox stems from the nature of "self-interest" or selfishness, the heart of which is avarice—greed—the love of money, the root of all evil (St. Paul, 65 AD).

One can argue that many social problems identified as individual deviations from societal norms are actually outgrowths of the pursuit of profits, legal or illegal, ethical or unethical. Consider the drug trade, the liquor and liquor service industries, the pornography industry, the tobacco companies, the various weapons manufacturers, the credit card companies, and the casino industry. Do the captains of these enterprises really care at all about the well-being of individuals and families, or only about their own continued profits at others' expense?

The Placebos of False Consciousness

The medicalization of deviance contributes to what Marx called "**false consciousness**" (Marx, 1867) by hiding from view the "class consciousness" that would reveal the underlying root causes (radix) (Feagin & Feagin, 1990) of deviance-related social problems. The opiates of the masses (sport, television, alcohol, religion, etc.) detract the public's attention from the exploitation and alienation that lie at the heart of society's problems.

The myriads of (predominately "for profit") treatment programs produce the convincing illusion that something worthwhile is being done about society's "behavioral problems." The use of the word "treatment" is particularly deceptively comforting because it gives the impression that the problem is being "treated;" that is, alleviated, assuaged, "taken care of," and by professionals, no less. "Oh well, we have a treatment program for that, so let's worry about this other problem."

One person's efforts at recycling may not save a forest, but if one tree can be saved the endeavor will have been worthwhile. The essence of the problem, however, does not lie in the lack of recycling effort, but in the destruction of forests. If one compulsive gambler is effectively assisted by a treatment program, it will have served a constructive purpose, but it will not have prevented the creation of many more compulsive gamblers. Treatment programs, unfortunately, do not prevent the creation of millions more child abusers, pedophiles, spouse beaters, overeaters, undereaters, drug addicts, alcoholics, rapists, and suicidal individuals, ad infinitum.

Out of the Frying Pan . . .

The treatment programs resulting from the medicalization of deviance turn the individuals "treated" back into the same social milieu in which the problem was incubated in the first place (Glassner & Freedman, 1979). Clinical sociologists and sociological practitioners point out that the "treated" individual will likely once again be subjected to the same underachieving kids, nagging spouse, exploiting boss, stacks of unpaid bills, and negative media reporting as before the treatment. In the case of alcohol, she will view the same commercials and advertisements which strongly advocate the use of the substance. She may still associate with the same friends and drinking-buddies she had before treatment, and her society will still baptize the use of the substance as a proper means of the ceremonial observance of weddings, wakes, anniversaries, and other celebrations and holidays.

The individual will likely have already been labeled as deviant and entered into secondary deviance through a paradigm shift in her self-concept. The struggle to become unstigmatized after having spent several years in a deviant career can be a dreadfully perplexing experience. The few widely-heralded success stories applauded in the media do not adequately reflect the reality of repeat offenses after "treatment" and the extent of reversion to deviant status. The "success rates" of certain treatment programs (such as those dealing with pedophiles) are near zero percent.

Monetary and Social Costs of the Microlevel Focus

In addition to draining the individual's and the family's resources, the expensive, temporary, isolated treatment of individuals inflicts a severe noncost-effective depletion on societal income. Individual-oriented treatment programs absorb resources that could be used for the transformation of society toward a more just and equitable model. Such a transformation would involve minimizing racism, sexism, ageism, economic inequality, and moral/spiritual depravity.

The social costs of not implementing a deeply-rooted social overhaul will be tremendous. Entire future generations will remain chained to addictions, abuses, exploitation, and insufficient social resources to maintain a state of relative health—physical, mental, and emotional well-being. The continued focus on microlevel solutions for society-wide problems will reinforce the abiding endurance of these problems throughout perpetuity.

The Vested Interest Leviathan

The medicalization of deviance creates a vested interest (Veblen, 1919) industry of politically and economically influential professionals whose very training and careers depend upon the treatment of individuals. The treatment programs which arise to meet the "challenge" are usually associated with clinics and hospitals that are hungry for expansion of services to enhance market share and therefore profits from individuals and insurance companies. Not only are the perpetrators and victims said to require treatment, but also the families of both perpetrators and victims. This tendency is economically beneficial to the hospitals and clinics, their stockholders, therapists/physicians, their employees, their advertising agencies, the advertising media, and the pharmaceutical companies with chemical "solutions" for virtually every problem.

The medicalization of deviance has constructed a system of individualized microlevel treatment programs that can be beneficial on a limited basis for a few individuals and their families. We should not be satisfied with such a social arrangement, however, because it tends to treat only the symptoms but does not change the society of which they are but indicative emanations. Like the application of topical salve on a cancer the roots of which are in the bone marrow, the blood, or an internal organ, the process is an expensive exercise in futility.

The Social Conflict Perspective

The social conflict perspective views the creation and enforcement of social norms as being biased against the less powerful individuals and groups in society, and also as reflecting the interests of the ruling capitalistic elites. The result is that laws will be ineffective when their application threatens corporate profits or the social elite. The social conflict paradigm predicts that justice systems in capitalist societies tend not to be neutral in terms of "blind justice," but will actually serve those in positions of wealth, power, and prestige.

Conflict theorists often pose the accusation that capitalist justice systems aim to protect the wealthy from crimes by the poor and disadvantaged, as opposed to the prevention of poor perpetrators' exploitation of other poor people. The power elites prefer theories that blame lower class moral depravity for their situation rather than systemic social problems.

Differential Labeling

"Former Presidential candidate Hillary Clinton."

The social conflict perspective also focuses upon the fact that who and what are defined as deviant are linked to social power. Norms and laws tend to reflect the interests of the powerful. **Differential labeling** is the idea that the plentiful resources of the powerful allow them to resist the label of deviant. For instance, during Barack Obama's presidency beginning in 2009, five people were convicted and sentenced to prison under the Espionage Act for leaking or carelessly handling classified or sensitive information. The five were John Kiriakou, Shamai Leibowitz, Jeffrey Sterling, former State Department official Stephen Kim, and Bradley Chelsea Manning. Presidential candidate and former Secretary of State Hillary Clinton used a private server to store, receive, and send official classified e-mails. The director of the Federal Bureau of Investigation stated that she "violated laws governing the handling of classified information," yet she was not penalized in any way, though her actions were more serious than any of those of the individuals who were prosecuted.

Crime

The phrase "white-collar crime" was coined in 1939 during a presidential address given by Edwin Sutherland to the American Sociological Society. **White collar crimes**, according to Sutherland, are crimes committed by respectable people in the course of their work. They may be of any of the following varieties:

1. Personal crimes, such as those involving income tax or credit card fraud
2. Abuses of trust, such as embezzlement or bribery
3. Incidental to and in furtherance of organizational operations, such as antitrust violations, insurance fraud, deceptive advertising, or safety violations
4. Full-time business, such as stock swindles and telemarketing scams
5. Government crime, such as the HUD Scandal in the 1980s, the Watergate Hotel break-in, the Iran-Contra Scandal, and the Holocaust (Sutherland, 1949)

Computer Crime

Computer crime is a branch of white collar crime. It can be defined as any illegal act for which knowledge of computer technology is used to commit the offense. Computer crime may be categorized in a number of ways:

✦ **Internal Computer Crimes**—Financial records
✦ **Telecommunication Crimes**—Internet; E-mail
✦ **Computer Manipulation Crimes**—Embezzlement
✦ **Support of Criminal Enterprises**
✦ **Hardware and Software Theft**
✦ **Computer Sabotage**—Viruses (Easterling, 2017)

A Profile of "The Criminal"

1. **Age**—Official crime rates rise sharply during adolescence and the early 20s, declining thereafter. Ages 15–24 (15% of population) account for 50% of arrests.

2. **Sex**—Males are involved in 76% of property crime arrests and 88.6% of violent crime arrests. The arrest rate for women, however, is increasing twice as fast as that for men.

3. **Social Class**—Arrests for violent and property crimes in the United States disproportionately reflect those of low social class. Persons of lower social standing are also disproportionately the victims of violent and property crimes. Only a small proportion of lower class persons are convicted of crimes. Most crimes are committed by a few hard-core offenders. If white collar crime is included, the "common criminal" has much higher social standing.

4. **Race**—Whites are involved in 60.9% of arrests in the United States. Blacks represent 12.5% of the population and 37.1% of arrests. It is important to remember that arrests do not equal guilt; cultural prejudices prompt police officers to arrest nonwhites more readily than Whites. Blacks are disproportionately represented among the disadvantaged classes. If the definition of crime included business fraud, toxic waste dumping, embezzlement, bribery, and cheating on income tax returns, the proportion of White criminals would certainly rise (U.S. Department of Justice, 2014).

All Users of Illegal Drugs		Inmates in Prisons on Drug Convictions	
White	66.0%	White	37.5%
Black	12.6%	Black	40.5%

Source: U.S. Department of Justice (2014); U.S. Department of Human Services (2014).

Most personally threatening crime is committed by a small fraction of the population. What is this small fraction like?

The **typical offender** is a young male—15–24 years of age. Juvenile offenders are at risk to become adult offenders. Adult offenders are likely to have been juvenile offenders. Being labeled a criminal by the criminal justice system marks a person for further arrests and convictions.

In a large sample conducted in Philadelphia 35% of men had a first arrest; of these, 54% had a second arrest. Among men arrested six times, 80% had a seventh arrest. The average seriousness of the crime rose with each subsequent arrest.

Criminologists have found that chronic or habitual offenders, 5%–7% of the population, are responsible for just over 50% of all arrests. Seventy percent of all convictions by 1981 of men born in 1953 were of the 5.5% who had six or more convictions. This tells us very plainly that close scrutiny of a small proportion of the population can reap great benefits for a comparably small expense.

Easterling's review of research in this area found that chronic offenders are disproportionately recruited from the population of children and adolescents who are aggressive early in life. There are **five major predictors of chronic offending**:

1. Inconsistent, indifferent, or harsh parenting
2. Troublesome childhood behavior
3. Low tested intelligence (IQ below 90)
4. Poor economic conditions
5. Parents with criminal records

Boys who were hardest to raise between 1 and 5 years of age:

1. Started offending earlier
2. Were arrested younger
3. Committed more crimes
4. Committed more serious crimes
5. Were more than 4 times as likely to be multiple offenders as were boys who were easy to raise

Delisi (2006) at Iowa State University used a population of 500 adult career criminals, descriptive and regression analyses produced five key findings.

1. Offenders first arrested at age 14 were among the most chronic, versatile, and dangerous offenders and were justifiably the threshold in differentiating early from late starters.
2. Those arrested in middle childhood were rare, yet accumulated hundreds of career arrests.
3. Persons first arrested at ages 16 or 17 were most likely to be convicted of felonies and sentenced to prison.
4. The most violent offenders were first arrested at ages 14 or 15.
5. While early onset was undoubtedly important, 62% of offenders with extensive criminal careers were not initially arrested until adulthood.

Delisi's conclusion is that these findings added empirical specificity to the theoretical and empirical significance of experiencing an early arrest. These studies are not meant to alarm, but are helpful for criminal analysis. In fact, most children with the early precursors do not become serious offenders, but most serious offenders have shown the precursors early in life.

There are a number of types of crimes according to the FBI **Crime Index (2016)**. This typology of crimes includes:

1. **Crimes against the person**—Crimes against people that involve violence or threat of it
   a. **Murder**—the willful killing of one human being by another
   b. **Aggravated Assault**—an unlawful attack by one person on another for the purpose of inflicting severe or aggravated bodily injury
   c. **Forcible Rape**—the carnal knowledge of a female forcibly and against her will
   d. **Robbery**—taking or attempting to take anything of value from the care, custody, or control of a person or persons by force or threat of force or violence and/or putting the victim in fear
2. **Crimes against property**—Crimes that involve theft of property belonging to others
   a. **Burglary**—the unlawful entry of a structure to commit a serious crime or a theft
   b. **Larceny-Theft**—the unlawful taking, carrying, leading, or riding away of property from the possession of another
   c. **Auto Theft**—the theft or attempted theft of a motor vehicle
   d. **Arson**—any willful or malicious burning or attempt to burn the personal property of another

The Criminal Justice System

The Courts

After arrest, a suspect's guilt or innocence is determined by a **court**, an official body charged with adjudicating legal cases. In principle, our courts rely on an adversarial system involving attorneys in the presence of a judge who upholds legal procedures. In practice, about 90% of criminal cases are resolved before they come to court through **plea bargaining**, a legal negotiation in which the prosecution reduces a defendant's charge in exchange for a guilty plea. This spares the system the time and expense of court trials. It sometimes leads to what is called **Bargain Counter Justice**, which means that defendants (who are presumed innocent) are pressured to plead guilty.

Punishment has traditionally been carried out in public, presumably so that it will serve as an example to would-be offenders. Does punishment uphold social morality? In other words, does it work? Let's investigate, shall we?

Criminal Recidivism refers to subsequent offenses committed by people who were previously convicted of crimes. Sixty-three percent of people released from incarceration are rearrested within 3 years. Forty-one percent return to prison within 3 years.

Sociologist Edwin Sutherland put forth the **Theory of Differential Association**. This theory stated that placing a person in prison for a long period of time will simply strengthen the individual's criminal attitudes and skills. There is a great deal of criminal socialization that takes place in the prison system. Once released, furthermore, prison inmates receive the stigma of being ex-convicts, an obstacle to successful integration into the larger society. This makes the establishment of a new career difficult and frustrating, thus leading to the reentering of the criminal lifestyle.

Only about one-third of all crimes come to the attention of police. Of these, only one in five results in an arrest. Clearly, there is a great amount of criminal activity that escapes punishment, and the punishment itself does not effectively prevent criminal activity from taking place.

Traditionally, social scientists have offered four justifications of punishment:

1. **Retribution**—subjecting an offender to suffering comparable to that caused by the offense. This position views society as a system of moral balance. It is often expressed by the Old Testament injunction: "An eye for an eye, and a tooth for a tooth."

2. **Deterrence**—the attempt to discourage criminality through punishment. This position views people as rational and self-interested beings. There are two types of deterrence:
   a. **Specific Deterrence**—demonstrates to the offender individually that crime does not pay.
   b. **General Deterrence**—the punishment of one person serves as an example to others.

3. **Rehabilitation**—reforming the offender to preclude subsequent offenses. Rehabilitation assumes that crime results from an unfavorable social environment. It focuses on the specific problems of each offender.

4. **Social Protection**—rendering an offender incapable of further offenses. This can be accomplished either:
   a. Temporarily—through incarceration or probation
   or
   b. Permanently—through capital punishment, castration, life without parole, and so on.

Prisons are places of confinement for those convicted by or awaiting trial. Prisons accomplish social protection by keeping offenders off the streets, but they offer little constructive learning and rarely rehabilitate inmates. They are also havens for a destructive level of physical and sexual violence.

Capital Punishment

Capital Punishment is simply the penalty of death for a crime. It is permitted in 31 states in the United States. Capital punishment has been shown to have limited value as a general deterrent in the United States. In fact, those states that permit capital punishment continue to have the highest murder rates.

States in United States with Death Penalty		
Alabama	Louisiana	Pennsylvania
Arizona	Mississippi	South Carolina
Arkansas	Missouri	South Dakota
California	Montana	Tennessee
Colorado	Nebraska	Texas
Florida	Nevada	Utah
Georgia	New	Virginia
Idaho	Hampshire	Washington
Indiana	North	Wyoming
Kansas	Carolina	
Kentucky	Ohio	
	Oklahoma	
	Oregon	

Source: Death Penalty Information Center (2016).

"Nations with capital punishment in red color."

Police Deviance

A major problem within the criminal justice system of the United States is deviant behavior among police officers. The following is a typology of police deviance.

1.   **Occupational Police Deviance** involves deviant behavior committed during the course of normal work activities. It is sometimes referred to as police corruption. Examples include accepting bribes or theft during a criminal investigation.

2.   **Abuse of Authority** refers to any action by a police officer without regard to motive, intent, or malice that tends to injure, insult, trespass upon human dignity, manifest feelings of inferiority, and/or violate an inherent legal right of a member of the police constituency in the course of performing "police work."

3.   **Physical Abuse** (police brutality) occurs when a police officer uses more force than is necessary to effect a lawful arrest or search, and/or the wanton use of any degrees of physical force against another by a police officer under the guise of the officer's authority.

4.   **Psychological Abuse** occurs when a police officer verbally assails, ridicules, discriminates, or harasses individuals and/or places a person who is under the actual or constructive dominion of the officer in a situation where the individual's esteem or self-image is threatened or diminished.

5.   **Legal Abuse** refers to the violation of a person's constitutional, federally-protected, or state-protected rights by a police officer (Easterling, 1999).

A few examples of police deviance, according to actual court records, include abuse of sick leave, failure to adequately enforce traffic laws, lying and perjury, lying about drug use, failure to investigate possible crimes while off duty, commission of a crime, threatening another with physical violence, unexcused absences from work, use of excessive force against a citizen, unacceptable job performance, use of offensive language, drunkenness, excessive parking tickets, leaving duty to conduct personal business, off-duty firearms incidents, failing to complete reports, failing to obey a direct order, conduct unbecoming an officer, recommendation of an attorney, misuse of firearms, accepting gratuities, unauthorized release of police records, falsifying overtime, failure to report misconduct of a fellow officer, failure to inventory confiscated property or evidence, sleeping on duty, cheating on a promotional exam, sexual improprieties, patronizing a bar while on sick leave, and refusing to take a polygraph test.

Street Gangs

In the United States there are 800 gang cities, 10,000 street gangs, and over 500,000 members of gangs. These numbers do not include motorcycle "clubs," prison gangs, supremacist groups (skinheads, etc.), tagger crews, and "normal" adolescent peer groups that occasionally engage in illegal activity. What are **street gangs**?

1. Groups of young people/range in age from 10 to 30.
2. Cohesion is fostered by their acceptance of or commitment to delinquent or criminal involvement.
3. Principally but not exclusively male.
4. Principally but not exclusively minority in ethnicity or race normally but not necessarily territorial.
5. Highly versatile in their criminal offenses.
6. Not predominantly violent, but disproportionately violent when compared to other youth groups or individuals (Easterling, 1999).

Most gang cities emerged after 1985. Some reasons for the proliferation of street gangs in the United States include a number of factors. The spread and deepening of the urban underclass has led to persistent and pervasive poverty, increased racial segregation and density, and increased working class unemployment. These factors sow the seeds of street gang response.

Local youth depend less on what adult society has to offer, and more on each other. Reducing street gang violence cannot be reduced by police suppression, court crackdowns, legislative hardening, street-level intervention programs, community mobilization, or early prevention efforts. Why not?

Gang culture has been diffused throughout society. Movies such as *Colors, Boyz 'N the Hood, American Me, The Cross and the Switchblade,* and *West Side Story,* among many others, have served to popularize gangs and gang membership. There have been many TV news reports and documentaries on gangs. Youth-oriented videos on MTV and other channels tend to glamorize gangs through gangsta rap music. Millions of youngsters have learned how to dress, talk, act, and feel like gang members through the abundance of such media presentations.

Even police and research experts contribute to this diffusion through lectures, seminars, demonstrations, and workshops on gang behavior. The depiction of gang life has become a commodity to be marketed.

Many national and local efforts to control or curb gang activities have met little success. In fact, gang behavior often increases when crackdown efforts are initiated. Therefore, I offer four ways to strengthen gang bonds:

1. a jail sentence—yields reputation
2. arrest and release—yields invincibility

3. targeting by police—builds reputation
4. media attention—builds reputation

Maslow's hierarchy of needs

© Piateresca/Shutterstock.com

It is helpful to gain insight into what needs might be fulfilled through gang membership. Maslow's (1954) hierarchy of needs is one listing of basic human needs. Gang membership seems to be—in some cases—a means of satisfying several of those needs. A life-changing Christian conversion experience has also been proven to be a powerful way of lessening the perceived need for gang membership, as evidenced by the success of the Teen Challenge organization.

Terrorism

In general, the practice of **terrorism** has been defined by the Federal Bureau of Investigation as the unlawful use or threatened use of violence by individuals or organized groups against people or property with the intention of intimidating or coercing societies or governments, often for ideological or political reasons. **Counter measures** are organized plans and activities designed to impair the effectiveness of terrorist acts.

Significance

The 1995 Oklahoma City bombing and the September 11, 2001 attacks on the World Trade Center and the Pentagon are only two of thousands of terrorism events in world history. In all instances, the act of terror is widely regarded as unethical by the parties who are attacked. Ironically, however, it is most often guided by a particular set of ethics held by the attacking party. Timothy

"Police and army patrol the streets 1 week after Paris attacks and 4 months before the ISIS suicide bombings on Brussels airport."

McVeigh and the September 11 attackers believed that the United States was an evil entity and that their actions were justified.

The term "terrorism" dates from the **Reign of Terror** (1793–94), which was a period during the French Revolution in which 30,000 people were drowned, hanged, or beheaded. The September 11, 2001, attacks by Al Qaeda on the World Trade Center and the Pentagon prompted calls by political leaders for a world "war on terrorism." For terrorists and anti-terrorists alike, it has seemed appropriate to adopt the terminology of war. A terrorist attack is almost always followed by reprisals, which in turn yield further terrorist attacks, which in turn lead to further reprisals.

An essential element of terrorist actions is that they are **attempts at communication**. Through the direct material and human damage they cause, terrorists hope to convey certain "messages" which the target group will interpret, understand, and act upon.

The impact of a terrorist attack often extends far beyond the individuals actually harmed. There is nearly always a powerful jolt to the population's emotions. People become frightened, angry, insecure, disoriented—in short, terrorized. This effect is precisely the aim of the terrorists. The target population is emotionally coerced to react as the perpetrators wish. Often, anyone who does try to communicate with the terrorists is branded a "collaborator," and anyone who denounces atrocities committed by the opponent's own group is labeled a "traitor." The result is a closed circle that excludes inner criticism as well as attempts to truly understand the enemy's position.

Just War Theory

Unless an individual is an absolute pacifist who would never take any military action for any reason, she must ethically give some account of what can justify it. In the *Summa Theologicae*, Aquinas (1273/1948) presented the general outline of the most commonly accepted body of ethical theory that is applied to the study of terrorism and counter terrorism. His **Just war theory** gave both a justification of war and the kinds of activity that are permissible in war.

Just war theory has two key divisions—the *Jus ad bellum* and *Jus in bello*.

The *Jus ad bellum* gives the conditions under which it can be right to resort to war. It relies upon six such conditions (Aquinas, 1273/1948):

1. War must be declared and waged by legitimate authority.
2. There must be a just cause for going to war.
3. War must be waged only with a right intention.
4. It must also be a last resort.
5. That there must be reasonable prospect of success.
6. The violence used must be proportional to the wrong being resisted.

The *Jus in bello* is concerned with the permissible methods by which a legitimate war should be waged. Under the *Jus in bello*, there are basically two governing principles.

1. **The Principle of Discrimination**. This limits the kind of violence that can be used, principally by placing restrictions on what counts as legitimate targets. A major part of the Discrimination Principle concerns the immunity of noncombatants from direct attack.
2. **The Principle of Proportionality**. This principle limits the degree of response by requiring that the violent methods used do not inflict more damage than the original offence could require.

A common element in a discussion of ethics and terrorism is the observation that "one man's terrorist is another man's freedom fighter." Placing bombs on buses or in shopping centers, airports, sporting events or concerts, abducting, torturing, and killing the inhabitants of some village in order to "send a message" to the other party are actions carried out with little consideration for the individual victim's ethical status; that is, whether or not she has done anything to deserve this kind of treatment. Locke (1690/1986) said in his *Second Treatise of Civil Government* that legitimate violence should be directed against perpetrators and not those who have no part in the offence.

Supreme Emergency

"Supreme Emergency" is an argument which attempts to justify both terrorism and counter terror measures. It says that a political community defending itself against external aggression (and hence fulfilling the requirements of *Jus ad bellum*) and facing a danger that is both imminent and serious, may be justified in letting military necessity override the noncombatant immunity requirement of *Jus in bello*.

Ethical caution—a heightened degree of making certain ethical rules are not being violated—is called for when the argument of supreme emergency is used. The fact that one has no other option to achieve a goal but to use violent means does not necessarily mean that violent means is ethically justified. For instance, it might be true that a person's only chance of survival is to kill another person and have that individual's heart implanted into his body. Still, this does not imply that he would be ethically justified in killing that person.

When agents of a national group that does not yet have a state of its own commit acts of terrorism against recipients nondeserving of violent interference, not as a response to a supreme emergency, but simply to achieve national independence, they also send a message to the rest of the world that theirs will be a state that is likely to be disrespectful of the rights of individuals, possibly even of those of their own people.

Counter Measures

"Counter terrorism" could be taken to refer to a fight against terrorism conducted itself by terrorist means, but to define it properly, **counter terrorism** should mean "measures by state agencies designed to combat terrorism." This is equivalent to the ethical necessity for the police force of any city to arrest and bring to justice murderers and robbers within its jurisdiction. Not to do so would be tantamount to accepting that some people may violate innocent citizens' most basic rights and get away with it.

The ethical criticism of terrorists attacking innocent persons has an obvious relevance also for those states and agencies that employ military means to combat terrorism. To the extent that they do not want themselves to be regarded as perpetrators of unjustified acts of terrorism, they must refrain from indiscriminately killing, maiming, or incarcerating people who are unrelated to the terrorist activities they are trying to end.

The Principle of Double Effect

Keeping in mind the Just war theory, the **principle of double effect** states that an unintended but foreseen ethically bad effect of an action can be justified if the action itself as well as its intended effect are ethically permissible. Had it not been for the indiscriminant acts of the terrorists there would have been no ethical need for an anti-terrorist operation in the first place, and hence the terrorists are ethically responsible for there being a situation in which further innocent people may be killed as an unintended effect of the anti-terrorist operation.

There is a risk that anti-terrorist agencies will count all innocent victims of their operations as unintended casualties in a justified war against terrorism. This suggests that the principle of double effect should be modified by the anti-terrorist agencies in a way that extends the agent's responsibility for the recipients.

One such modification for the **minimization of unintended casualties** has been proposed by Walzer (2000), who has argued that soldiers in action should not only not intend to kill noncombatants, but also intend to protect them from being killed, even if that means risking the lives of the soldiers themselves. In practice, this would mean operations on the ground and face-to-face encounters with the terrorist enemy rather than the use of bombs and rockets that may be safe from terrorist fire, but which cannot discriminate between terrorists and nonterrorists as they drop their bombs from high altitudes. It also means that operations against terrorist bases must be preceded by careful collecting and studying of intelligence in order to make it possible to distinguish those targets that are legitimate from those that are not.

Alternatives to Violence

What sorts of responses to terrorism can be ethically legitimate? Just war theory rules out the use of terrorism to combat terrorism.

The use of violence to capture or even kill terrorists can be legitimate if it accords with the conditions of the just war theory and other principles that govern the ethics of resort to war. One of the most crucial conditions is that of **Last Resort**. This doctrine is based on the idea of the ethical superiority of peace over war. The resort to war must be reluctant and realistic alternatives to violence must be considered.

A necessary element among alternatives to violence is the attempt to understand terrorist grievances. Attending to the grievances of the terrorists may be a precondition for defeating the terrorist campaign and ignoring them may contribute to increasing the terrorist threat. The slogan "no negotiating with terrorists" may be an impediment to progress.

Discussion between the parties can be helpful, but the chances of success are not assured. The risk is nevertheless worthwhile. Sometimes talking is the only alternative to violence and the readiness to talk with a person amounts to recognizing that person as a human being. This tends to defuse the well-known strategy of dehumanizing the adversary and can lead to real progress.

Financial and other sanctions have been placed by many countries on organizations that directly or indirectly support terrorists. Such measures usually include restrictions on or withdrawal of trade rights, diplomatic ties, and membership in international organizations or forums. Sanctions have been successful in gaining cooperation from Liberia and Libya, but were not effective in the cases of Iraq and North Korea.

Military Tribunals

Few aspects of the war on terrorism have provoked as much criticism as President Bush's military order of November 13, 2001 dealing with the detention, treatment, and trial of certain noncitizens in the war against terrorism. Hundreds of Al Qaeda and Taliban suspects have been imprisoned at Guantanamo, a U.S. Naval base on the southern tip of the Island of Cuba. They are being held for trial by military tribunals (military courts).

Some attorneys arguing for the suspected terrorists have attempted to have the trials moved to civilian courts. In truth, President Bush's military order does have legal precedent and meets four justifying ethical principles:

1. Each suspect is presumed to be innocent until proven guilty beyond a reasonable doubt.
2. Competent legal advice is available to each suspect.
3. The death penalty requires a unanimous vote.
4. There is a formal appeals process (Easterling, 2017).

Profiling

Searching or screening for terrorist suspects by means of **descriptive profiles** has been used for decades by Israel and a few other countries. After September 11, 2001, the United States began the profiling of flight passengers.

Profiling does not normally raise deep ethical issues for most people, but some concern was expressed regarding the **Patriot Act** that was passed in the wake of the September 11 attacks. The fear was that the new law had little to do with catching terrorists but a lot to do with increasing the strength of the government to infiltrate and spy on organizations and individuals.

Certain rules, if followed, tend to legitimize a profiled search.

1. There must be a clear and present danger for the security of the country or a group of citizens.
2. Profiled searches must be carried out by a proper legitimate authority.
3. General privacy protection guidelines must be followed (Easterling, 2017).

The Oklahoma City Bombing

On the morning of Wednesday, April 19, 1995, the world was shocked by the news of a terrorist bombing in downtown Oklahoma City, Oklahoma. It was the worst bombing in recent U.S. history, second only to the bombing of Pearl Harbor, Hawaii, in 1941.

One hundred sixty-eight people were killed and more than 500 others were injured by a 4,800 pound bomb made of fertilizer and left in a rental truck parked in front of the Alfred P. Murrah Federal Building. Over 800 people were in the building at the time. The explosion occurred at exactly 9:02 a.m. Many of the victims were doing business in the Social Security office on the first floor.

A day-care center called "America's Kids," located on the

© MWaits/Shutterstock.com

"Oklahoma city National memorial."

second floor of the nine-story building, was buried beneath tons of concrete and steel. Twenty children were killed. A 37-year-old nurse died of head injuries due to falling debris while attending to victims.

The building was built in 1977 under the Carter administration and housed offices of the Bureau of Alcohol, Tobacco, and Firearms, the Federal Bureau of Investigation, and many other federal agencies. It featured an all-glass front, which made it more vulnerable to a bomb than a building of solid steel and concrete might have been. Federal law enforcement officials speculated that this may have been one reason why the terrorists chose the Alfred P. Murrah Federal Building for the attack.

The Explosion

The detonation was felt more than 30 miles away and was detected by seismographs as far away as Denver, Colorado. The blast created a crater in the street in front of the building 8 ft deep and 30 ft in diameter. The bomb consisted of ammonium nitrate and diesel fuel, along with nonelectronic fuse devices and various chemicals to heighten its devastating effects.

In addition to the Murrah Building, much of the downtown area of Oklahoma city was destroyed, including the Young Men's Christian Association (YMCA), First United Methodist Church, St. Joseph's Cathedral, the Journal-Record Building, the Oklahoma Water Resources Board, and the C. R. Anthony Corporate Headquarters. Thousands of people were required to leave their apartments due to structural damage. Other parts of the world had been ravaged by terrorism and the violence of war. This event was considered to be different and particularly tragic because it was in the normally secure and quiet "heartland" of the Midwestern United States, and was therefore completely unanticipated.

Rescue efforts

Sixty-four ambulances responded to the alarm. President Clinton declared a national emergency. The Federal Emergency Management Agency (FEMA), the Oklahoma City Fire and Police Departments, and 116 municipal, state, and county agencies assisted in the bombing aftermath. Also involved were the police and fire departments from Tulsa, Oklahoma, as well as 11 search and rescue squads from cities across the country.

There were many heroic acts performed after the bombing. The people of Oklahoma were admired by the world for the way they pitched in to help others. Many comments were made about the lack of looting and profiteering that often accompany a disaster of this magnitude. About 50 specially trained dogs were used in the attempt to locate victims. The debris was carefully sifted for any incriminating evidence that might be found.

The suspects

The perpetrators of the bombing were identified as Timothy McVeigh and Terry Nichols, who were later convicted of the crime in federal court. McVeigh was arrested near Perry, Oklahoma, 60 miles north of Oklahoma City, by Oklahoma Highway Patrolman Charles Hanger within 90 min of the detonation of the bomb. He was arrested on five misdemeanor traffic and weapons charges. It was only later determined that he was the chief suspect in the case. McVeigh was transported by military helicopter to Tinker Air Force Base near Oklahoma City, where he was arraigned on federal charges. Traces of the explosive substances used in the bombing were found on his clothing and in his car. Nichols was arrested in Herington, Kansas, where quantities of bomb-making materials were discovered in his storage building. The yellow Ryder truck used in the bombing was rented in Junction City, Kansas, a short distance from both Ft. Riley and McVeigh's and Nichols' residence in Herington.

McVeigh, age 27, and Nichols, age 40, both joined the U.S. Army on the same day in 1988, and served together in C Company of the 16th Infantry Battalion at Ft. Riley, Kansas. McVeigh served in the Gulf War and received the Purple Heart. Nichols was discharged from the Army at his own request, due to "personal hardship." The two men spent a considerable amount of time in Kingman, Arizona, as well as in Michigan, where Nichols was raised (McVeigh was originally from near Niagara Falls, New York). Neighbors said the two, along with Terry's brother James, frequently tested small bombs on James' farm near Decker, Michigan.

Both men were linked with an anti-government group called the Michigan Militia, a 12,000-member right-wing organization which has engaged in extensive military training and once planned an invasion of a U.S. military installation. U.S. Representative Steve Stockman, of Texas, received a fax from the office of Michigan Militia advocate Mark Koernke. The message was an update only moments after the bombing occurred. Congressman Stockman had sent a letter to U.S. Attorney General Janet Reno a month earlier warning against an alleged "impending raid" against anti-government groups by federal agents.

Significance of April 19

The date of the Oklahoma City disaster seems to hold some importance for certain anti-government racist and militia groups with which the suspects have been identified. The bombing occurred on the anniversary of the tragic burning of the Branch Davidian compound near Waco, Texas, in 1993. Cult leader David Koresh, who claimed to be Jesus Christ, ordered the buildings burned after refusing to turn himself in to federal authorities for weapons and child molestation violations. Many militia groups blamed the government for the ensuing fire, in which 82 people—including Koresh—died. The North Texas Militia erected an engraved memorial at the Waco site on the day of the bombing.

April 19 is also the anniversary of the beginning of the Bureau of Alcohol, Tobacco, and Firearms' and the Federal Bureau of Investigation's 1992 siege of white separatist Randy Weaver at Ruby Ridge, Idaho. His wife and son were killed by federal agents in subsequent gun battles. On the same day of the Oklahoma City bombing, white separatist Richard Wayne Snell was executed by Arkansas authorities for murdering a Jewish man and an African American man. Militia groups further point out that the Revolutionary War began on April 19, 1775, in Lexington, Massachusetts.

The Aftermath

On April 23, the entire nation participated via television in a memorial service for the victims. President Clinton, Reverend Billy Graham, and Reverend Carlton Pearson officiated in this solemn yet inspiring service. The site of the Alfred P. Murrah Building has been converted into a memorial park.

The U.S. Congress apportioned a total of 39 million dollars to help businesses and churches damaged in the Oklahoma City bombing. About 90 businesses applied for government assistance in rebuilding and reestablishing their operations.

In the aftermath of the bombing incident, the U.S. Senate passed an anti-terrorism bill by a vote of 91 to 8. Among other items, the bill provided for the following:

1. Create a new federal crime of "international terrorism committed within the United States" punishable by death.
2. Expand federal wiretapping and surveillance powers.
3. Allow the Justice Department to investigate crimes based on the political beliefs and associations of suspects.

Timothy McViegh was executed by lethal injection on June 11, 2001, at the Federal Correctional Complex in Terre Haute, Indiana. Terry Nichols was sentenced to 161 consecutive life terms without the possibility of parole, setting a Guinness World Record and is incarcerated at ADX Florence, a super maximum security prison near Florence, Colorado. He shares a cell block that is commonly referred to as "Bombers Row" with Ramzi Yousef (New York City World Trade center bombing in 1993) and Ted Kaczynski (the "Unabomber"). Michael Fortier testified against McVeigh and served more than 10 years of a 12-year sentence for failing to inform authorities about the plot. He was released in 2006, but has changed his identity under a witness protection program.

Name _____   Date _____

Chapter 7   Social Deviance

Chapter Exercise

(This assignment is to be carefully torn out and completed at the direction of the instructor. The answers are to be legibly handwritten directly on the sheets. Do not photocopy these pages, as such action would constitute a blatant violation of the copyright laws of the United States. Thoroughly read the assigned text before attempting to complete a tear-out assignment. It is obvious when a student has tried to fill-in an assignment without reading the background material.)

"Recidivism" (repeat offenses)refers to people who spent time in prison, were properly released, then repeated their crimes and were incarcerated once again. Try to think of reasons why the recidivism rate is between 67% and 75% in the United States.

_____

_____

_____

_____

_____

_____

_____

_____

_____

_____

_____

_____

Chapter 8

Social Gerontology

© Monkey Business Images/Shutterstock.com

For what reason should one study aging, the elderly, and the process of getting older? Understanding the elderly and the process of aging will help one gain understanding of society. It is logical to expect that if you do not die prematurely, you will be old someday. While this fact may not be at the forefront of most people's minds when they are still relatively young, the actual truth is that one of most people's major goals in life is to become old. Isn't that why folks fasten their seat belts, try to eat healthy diets, and exercise regularly? Through the study of the elderly and aging, we are really studying our own futures and the stages of life that may be common within the context of whatever cultural milieu may be surrounding us.

Gerontology means the study of aging and the elderly. The term comes from the Greek words "geron," meaning "old person," and "logos," meaning reason. The biological and primarily medical study of aging is referred to as **geriatrics**. Gerontology treats old age as a distinct social category. People who study aging are called **gerontologists**.

The Four Facets of Aging

There are **four facets of aging** that are commonly described by gerontologists. It is worthwhile to emphasize that chronological age is very distinct from biological, psychological, or social age. It is not uncommon to see a 65-year-old who may act and/or appear younger than someone who is 50 years of age. If the culture of a given society has a tendency toward favorable, respectful, and positive perspectives on aging and the elderly, there will be less prejudice toward the elderly as well as less self-loathing among those growing older. If the phenomenon of aging is viewed less positively, the opposite will be true.

1. **Chronological aging**—related to the number of years since the calendar date of a person's birth.
2. **Biological aging**—related to the physical changes that tend to reduce one's level of activity or energy as she progresses through middle-age to the later years. Hardening of the arteries, worn joints, or breathing problems are often typical.
3. **Psychological aging**—related to cognitive and behavioral changes, including personality and mental functioning that occur as persons grow older.
4. **Social aging**—relates to changes in a person's statuses, roles, or relationships among the members of her kinship structure, her friends, and in work or volunteer organizations. This facet of aging is relevant to the disengagement theory of aging, discussed later in this chapter.

Trends

There has been a trend in the United States and all other industrialized nations toward an increasingly older average age. In the United States, gerontologists refer to this phenomenon as **the graying of the United States**. For instance, in the year 1900, the average age in the

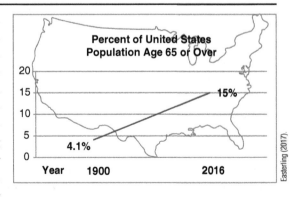

United States was 22.9 years and only 4.1% of the population was aged 65 or

older. By 2016, the average person in the United States was age 37.8 and 15% of the population was aged 65 or over (a 300% increase).

Several explanations have been advanced concerning this trend. The first explanation is related to the so-called **Baby Boom** that occurred immediately after World War II. Millions of American servicemen and women returned home to their sweethearts and established families. A great number of babies (approximately 36,000,000) were born between the years 1945 and 1965, followed by a sharp drop in the birth rate. Of course, those "baby boomers" have been growing steadily older each year, driving up the average age of the country.

An additional factor in the graying of the United States is an **increasing life expectancy**, due primarily to advances in medical technology. A man born in 1900, for example, could expect to live only to age 48, whereas a man born in 1999 had a life expectancy of 72.8 years. The life expectancy numbers for women are similar: 51 in 1900 and 82.2 in 1999. Greater life expectancies naturally contribute to a higher average age for the general population.

A third reason for the aging of the population in the United States is an increase in **family planning and abortion**. The average family in the country has only 1.8 children, down from 2.3 children in the early 1980's. Since 1982, the majority of families have no children at all. Each year since the 1973, Supreme Court decision in Roe v. Wade legalized abortion, 1.5 million abortions have been performed in the United States each year. This means that there are 1.5 million fewer children each year than there would have been without Roe v. Wade. Abortion has severely impacted colleges, because each year there are fewer college-age persons. In 1991 (the first year children born in 1973 would begin attending college), there were 1.5 million fewer potential college students. In 1992, there were 3 million fewer potential students, in 1993, there were 4.5 million fewer potential students, and in 1994, and every year since, there have been 6 million fewer potential students. These factors further contribute to the trend of an increasingly older population.

Gerontologists are keenly interested in the impact a graying population will have on future generations. They point out that there will be tremendous demands on Social Security and the health-care system as more elderly people need these services.

Another prediction is that **agism**, the belief that older people are somehow innately inferior to younger people, will slowly give way to increasing social status and respect for the elderly as they exercise more political clout due to their growing numbers. **Stereotypes** of the elderly portray them in nursing homes, helpless, confused, resistant to change, nonsexual, and unhappy. In reality, only

5% of persons aged 65 or older are institutionalized in the United States. Most of the elderly do not have false teeth, use a cane, and are not disabled.

There will be increasing respect for the elderly as more and more advertising features their needs and older actors make commercials as well as feature films and television programs. The number of Americans aged 65 and older is projected to more than double from 46 million today to over 98 million by 2060, and the 65-and-older age group's share of the total population will rise to nearly 24% from 15%.

"The older population is becoming more racially and ethnically diverse. Between 2014 and 2060 the share of the older population that is non-Hispanic white is projected to drop by 24 percentage points, from 78.3% to 54.6%. The changing racial/ethnic composition of the population under age 18, relative to those aged 65 and older, has created a **diversity gap** between generations. Older adults are working longer. By 2014, 23% of men and about 15% of women ages 65 and older were in the labor force, and these levels are projected to rise further by 2022, to 27 % for men and 20% for women. Many parts of the country—especially counties in the rural Midwest—are **aging in place** because disproportionate shares of young people have moved elsewhere." (Mather, 2016)

Positive Developments

1. Over the past 50 years, the proportion of those 65 years of age or older with bachelor's degrees has increased from 5% to 25%.
2. As a result of mortality reduction measures, Americans are living to 79 years of age, on average. This figure was 68 years in 1950.
3. Between 1990 and 2013, the gender gap in life expectancy decreased from seven years to only five years (76 years for men versus 81 years for women).
4. Older Americans are immensely better off financially today than in 1966, when 30 % were below the poverty rate. The figure was 10% in 2016. (Adapted from Mather, 2016)

Challenges

1. There is a greater obesity rate among senior citizens than in past generations, with approximately 40% in that category.
2. Though the economic condition of the elderly has improved overall, greater proportions of Hispanic (18%) and African American (19%) older persons have incomes below the poverty level.
3. The number of divorced elderly has dramatically increased from earlier generations. Since 1980, the number of divorced older women has increased from 3% to 13% and for older men, the increase has been from 4% to 11%.

4. The older a person becomes, the greater the likelihood of living alone; for instance, the percentage of women living alone at ages 65–74 is 27. The figure is 42% for the ages of 75–84, and 56% at age 85 or older.

5. There are expected to be one million more Americans needing nursing home care by 2030 (2.3 million) than there were in 2010 (1.3 million). This is largely due to the fact that the "Baby Boomers" (born between 1945 and 1965) are growing older.

6. It is predicted that the number of Americans with Alzheimer's will triple to around 14 million by the year 2050.

7. There will be a 50% increase in expenditures for Social Security and Medicare by 2050. (Adapted from Mather, 2016)

Age stratification refers to the unequal distribution of wealth, power, and privileges among people of different ages. In the United States, persons of middle age seem to be in control of most of the institutions of society. As the "baby boomers" age, however, the United States may move toward becoming a **gerontocracy**, a state in which the elderly have the most wealth, power, and privileges. China and Russia are examples of gerontocracies.

Theories of Gerontology

There are a number of theories concerning aging and the retirement process. These theories are

1. **Disengagement Theory.** This theory is based upon structural-functional theory. It insists that the elderly tend to begin to disengage from positions of social responsibility before disability or death occurs. A society can accomplish in this way the orderly transfer of statuses and roles from on older generation to a younger one.

2. **Continuity Theory.** This theory is also based upon structural-functional theory. It states that stable personality traits and routines tend to persist over the years (e.g., John has retired yet still runs 5 miles every morning).

3. **Activity Theory.** This theory is based on the symbolic-interaction paradigm. It posits that a high level of activity affords people a greater degree of personal satisfaction in old age.

An anonymous author wrote the following piece. Please do not read it as an offensive statement or as judgmental, but as an anachronistic insight that can help younger people understand the great amount of change that older Americans have experienced in their lifetimes.

For All Those Born Prior to 1945

Consider the changes we have witnessed: We were born before television, before penicillin, before polio shots, frozen foods, Xerox, plastic, contact lenses, Frisbees and "the pill."

We were before radar, credit cards, split atoms, laser beams, and ballpoint pens; before panty hose, clothes dryers, electric blankets, air conditioners, drip dry clothes—and before humans walked on the moon.

We got married first and then lived together. How quaint can you be?

In our time, closets were for clothes, not for "coming out of." Bunnies were small rabbits and rabbits were not Volkswagens. Designer jeans were scheming girls named Jean or Jeanne and having a meaningful relationship meant getting along well with our cousins.

We thought fast food was what you ate during Lent, and outer space was the back of the Riviera Theater.

We were before house husbands, gay rights, computer dating, dual careers, commuter marriages, and computer marriages.

We were before day care centers, group therapy, and nursing homes. We never heard of FM radio, CD Rom, electric typewriters, artificial hearts, word processors, yogurt, or guys wearing earrings. For us, time sharing meant togetherness—not computers or condominiums; a "chip" meant a piece of wood, hardware meant hardware, and software wasn't even a word!

In 1940, "made in Japan" meant junk and the term "making out" referred to how you did on your exam. Pizza Hut, Burger King, and instant coffee were unheard of.

We hit the scene when there were five and dime stores where you bought things for nickels and dimes. Sanders' or Wilson's sold ice cream cones for a nickel. For one nickel you could ride a street car, make a phone call, buy a Pepsi Cola, or enough stamps to mail one letter and two post cards. You could buy a new Chevy Coupe for $600.00, but who could afford one? It was a pity, too, because gas was eleven cents per gallon.

In our day, cigarette smoking was fashionable, grass was walked on and mowed, coke was a cold drink, crack was in the sidewalk, and pot was something you cooked stew or chili in. Rock music was Grandma's lullaby and AIDS were helpers in the principal's office.

We were certainly not before the difference between the sexes was discovered, but we were surely before the sex change; we made do with what we had. We were the last generation that was so dumb as to think you needed a husband to have a baby!

No wonder we are so confused and there is such a generation gap today. But we survived! What better reason to "party down?"

Life Extension

According to a popular myth, Juan Ponce De Leon, the Governor of Puerto Rico was searching for the "The Fountain of Youth," a spring that supposedly restores the youth of anyone who drinks or bathes in its waters, while he was exploring the area known today as Florida. The story goes that Ponce de León was informed by Native Americans that the Fountain of Youth was in a mythical land called "Bimini." Similar accounts of such a fountain have been related around the globe for millennia.

The Stanford Center for Longevity and Time conducted a survey of 2,330 American adults and found that 77% wanted to live to be 100. Another third of those surveyed wanted to live past 90. The study also found, however, that most people are not living in a manner conducive to a long and healthy life (Sifferlin 2016).

Many religions offer the possibility of eternal or everlasting life, which seems to have a calming or even healing effect for their adherents. This sort of afterlife is usually envisioned as distinct from physical life. Whatever the inward desire that most people may have to keep on living in the physical realm, most do not treat the desire seriously enough to take determined measures to accomplish it. There have been a few steps efforts in this regard and the likelihood of success is becoming slightly greater as life extension concepts proliferate and the number of such attempts increase over time. **Life extension** is the belief and subsequent efforts to achieve ongoing perpetual life for humans.

Transhumanism

© Chaoss/Shutterstock.com

The opening sentence of Alan Harrington's (1969) book, *The Immortalist* (, is this: "Death is an imposition on the human race, and no longer acceptable." He goes on to make an argument for the dedication of science and technology to the effort aimed at eliminating death for humans. He advocates the use of medicine, surgery (such as brain or head transplants), and other means, to achieve this end. He advocates the cryogenic freezing of humans until the scientific ability to prolong life has progressed.

Transhumanism is a cultural and intellectual movement that believes the human condition can and should be improved through the use of advanced technologies. Transhumanists are intrigued by technologies that can augment physical and intellectual capabilities beyond what humans' natural capability (hence, the term "transhuman)." The movie *Limitless* is about a chemical variation on this theme. Life extension is the core element of transhumanism. Transhumanists believe that eternal life may eventually be possible through

1. Genetic engineering
2. Nanotechnology
3. Cloning
4. Transcranial direct current stimulation
5. Mind uploading (to a computer)
6. Other emerging technologies

Transcranial direct current stimulation (tDCS) speeds up reaction times and learning speed by running a weak electric current through the brain. It has repeatedly been utilized by the United States to train military snipers.

The Singularity

Kurzweil (2012) discusses **the technological singularity** which is the phenomenon of artificial intelligences (AIs) surpassing human beings as the smartest and most capable life forms on the Earth. This, according to Kurzweil, will take place around 2045. Technological development will be taken over by machines that can think, act, and communicate so quickly that normal humans cannot even comprehend what is going on. The machines enter into a "runaway reaction" of self-improvement cycles, with each new generation of AIs appearing faster and faster. Kurzweil posits that from this point forward, technological advancement will be explosive, under the control of the machines, and thus cannot be accurately predicted.

The "Singularity" is an extremely disruptive, world-altering event that will forever change the course of human history. Kurzweil insists that the extermination of humanity by violent machines is unlikely (though not impossible) because sharp distinctions between man and machine will no longer exist thanks to the existence of cybernetically enhanced humans (transhumanism) and uploaded humans (their minds uploaded into computers).

Name _____   Date _____

Chapter 8   Social Gerontology

Chapter Exercise

(This assignment is to be carefully torn out and completed at the direction of the instructor. The answers are to be legibly handwritten directly on the sheets. *Do not* photocopy these pages, as such action would constitute a blatant violation of the copyright laws of the United States. Thoroughly read the assigned text before attempting to complete a tear-out assignment. It is obvious when a student has tried to fill-in an assignment without reading the background material.)

Express your observation of how an older relative or someone you know well has experienced the aging process.

_____

_____

_____

_____

_____

_____

_____

_____

_____

_____

_____

_____

_____

_____

Chapter 9

Race and Ethnicity

Race, Ethnicity, and Minority Groups

The term **race** refers to a category of people with common biological traits passed on from one generation to the next. It is usually thought of in terms of such things as facial features, skin color, body type, hair texture, etc.

In the Nineteenth Century, scientists concluded that there are three races:

1. **Negroid** —generally corresponding to black Africans
2. **Caucasoid** —generally corresponding to white Europeans
3. **Mongoloid** —generally corresponding to the Asian peoples

Today, there are probably no pure races. This is due to thousands of years of interbreeding among the races. It is ridiculous to talk about percentages of race in a single human being. If a person claims to be one-eighth of a given race, which one-eighth of her body is of that race? Is it her left leg? Her spleen, esophagus, and her right ear? Can you see how silly this is? Suppose you were to line up everyone in the world according to skin color, in order from darkest to lightest, then you observed them as you rode by the line in an automobile at 55 miles per hour. You would never be able to tell when one skin color ended and the next began, it would be so gradual. It is easy to see why race—especially skin color—is not a very good way of differentiating among peoples.

Perhaps a better way of distinguishing among categories of people is ethnicity. **Ethnicity** refers to a cultural heritage shared by a category of people. Ethnicity is based upon such cultural factors as religion, language, food preparation, music, modes of dress, customs of mate selection, marriage and family patterns, national origin, etc. Though sometimes linked to race, ethnicity is significantly different in that it can be changed if people choose to adopt a new way of life.

A third term often used to distinguish groups of people is through the concept of the minority group. A **minority group** is a category of people defined by physical or cultural characteristics who are subject to some social disadvantage. Women are a minority group in the United States because they meet the rigorous test of this definition. They have defining physical characteristics and earn about seventy percent of what men earn in the same occupation. What about other groups with which you are familiar? Blacks, Hispanics, homosexuals?

Even though the concept of race is largely debunked by social scientists today, they are still obligated to address it because of the **Thomas Theorem**. The Thomas Theorem was framed by sociologist W. I. Thomas, a student of George Herbert Mead at the University of Chicago. Thomas said that even though a given phenomenon may not be real, if it is *thought* to be real, it can be real in its consequences. Even though race is a poor and scientifically meaningless concept, since so many people think it is a valid reality, it can be real in its consequences, such as prejudice and discrimination.

Prejudice and Discrimination

Prejudice (prejudgment) is an unfounded generalization about a category of people. A **stereotype** is a description of a category of people that persists even in the face of evidence to the contrary. **Racism** is an extreme form of prejudice which involves the belief that one "racial" category is superior to or inferior to another. There are a number of theories about the origin and operation of prejudice.

1. **The Scapegoat Theory**—One person or category of people is
    unfairly blamed for the problems of another. This is based on a
    part of the Day of Atonement proceedings in the Hebrew Book
    of Leviticus (16:21–22), where the high priest imputed all the sins
    of the people into a goat which was then led into the wilderness.

    > The high priest (Aaron at the time) "shall lay both his hands
    > upon the head of the live goat, and confess over him all the iniqui-
    > ties of the children of Israel, and all their transgressions in all their
    > sins, putting them upon the head of the goat, and shall send him
    > away by the hand of a fit man into the wilderness: And the goat
    > shall bear upon him all their iniquities unto a land not inhabited:
    > and he shall let go the goat in the wilderness."

2. **The Authoritarian Personality**—from Theodore Adorno—a
    personality trait (authoritarianism) explains prejudice. Two factors
    contribute to an authoritarian personality: (a) a low level of
    education plus (b) harsh and demanding parents. Adorno theorized
    that the frustration and aggression intended for the parents are
    aimed at powerless groups, as in the Scapegoat Theory. In the case
    of Nazi Germany, this frustration and aggression were directed
    toward the Jewish people.

3. **The Culture Theory of Prejudice**—from Emory Bogardus— Prejudice is learned through the socialization process and passed on from generation to generation.

4. **Social Conflict Theory**—largely from Karl Marx—Prejudice arises as justification for economic oppression. Prejudice serves the interests of the capitalist class by manipulating racial or ethnically diverse working class groups to blame each other for their low status, rather than their "true oppressors," the capitalist class. The strategy is to "divide and conquer," thus keeping the lower classes under subjection. For example, poor whites blamed blacks or recent immigrants for taking their jobs in northern U.S. factories, rather than realizing that the factory owners were exploiting all of the laborers.

5. **Ethnic Competition**—from Fredrik Barth—the mutually opposed efforts of rival ethnic or racial groups to secure the same objectives. In other words, contention among individuals and groups tends to be shaped by perceived competition for available resources. This form of prejudice is often limited to specific geographic areas.

6. **Ethnic Conflict**—a form of rivalry in which groups try to injure one another in some way. Examples:
   a. Whites and Native Americans—warfare
   b. Whites and Asians—immigration restrictions
   c. Whites and Blacks—lynchings, race riots

7. **Ethnic Stratification**—a form of rivalry in which powerful ethnic groups limit the access of subordinate groups to societal resources, including wealth, power, privilege, jobs, education, and politics.

8. **Ethnic Change**—an application of the Hegelian dialectic to ethnic groups. Ethnic or minority groups, as well as their relations with one another and the larger society, are continuously in a state of change. Conflict can either change or preserve a system of ethnic stratification. All history is a process of struggle, oppression, and more struggle.

Discrimination means treating various categories of people differently. Discrimination is good when making food choices or when choosing a mate (Christians are not to be unequally yoked together with unbelievers). In terms of educational and employment opportunities, however, discrimination is one of the great maladies of the world. Simply stated, prejudice is an attitude, whereas discrimination is an action.

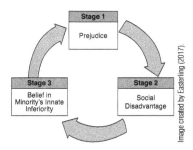

THE CYCLE OF PREJUDICE AND DISCRIMINATION

Stage 1—*Prejudice begins, often as an expression of ethnocentrism or an attempt to justify economic exploitation.*

Stage 2—*As a result of prejudice, a minority is socially disadvantaged, occupying a low position in the system of social stratification.*

Stage 3—*This social disadvantage is then interpreted not as the result of earlier prejudice and discrimination, but as evidence that the minority is innately inferior, unleashing renewed prejudice and discrimination, by which the cycle repeats itself.* (Myrdal, 1944).

Black Lives Matter movement originated among the African American community in response to killings of blacks by police, but also addresses broader issues. The purpose is reportedly to draw attention to injustices to blacks and to insist that their lives are important. Twelve percent of blacks killed by police are unarmed, compared with only 6% of whites. Upon hearing the phrase "Black Lives Matter!" someone might counter with "No! ALL lives matter!" Though this may be a good statement with good intentions, it would be similar to the following scenario.

Imagine a number of people advocating for research to find a cure for colon can-
cer. Perhaps they had the disease or had family members directly affected by this
disease and were focused on finding a viable treatment or even a cure. Someone
hearing them promote the "Cure for Colon Cancer" program might respond
with "No! Cures for ALL Diseases!" This would draw attention away from
the purpose of the original group, thus undermining their worthwhile cause.
Such a scenario demonstrates why it is so very important to try to understand
what others are saying and why they are saying it before trying to get them to
understand your position.

(Easterling, 2017).

Alternative Social Arrangements

Assimilation is the process by which members of minority groups gradually modify their ways of life to conform to patterns of the dominant culture.
Integration means incorporation as equals into society. To integrate is to
form into a whole, to unite. **Miscegenation** refers to the biological process of
interbreeding (sometimes called **amalgamation**).

Pluralism refers to a state in which all racial and ethnic groups are socially
distinct but have roughly equal social standing. Switzerland is commonly
described as a pluralistic society because it is comprised of three culturally distinct
ethnic groups with roughly equal political and social standing:

1. The French-speaking Swiss
2. The Italian-speaking Swiss
3. The German-speaking Swiss

Segregation is the physical and social separation of categories of people.
An extreme form of segregation is the **caste system**—a system of social
stratification based almost entirely upon ascribed status.

Genocide refers to the violent (attempted) extermination of one category
of people by another (sometimes called **annihilation** or **ethnic cleansing**).
This has been attempted against Jews, Armenians, Native Americans, and
many other groups throughout history.

Endogamy is marriage *within* one's social group or category. **Exogamy**,
on the other hand, is marriage *outside* one's social group or category. For
example, a Baptist might marry a Buddhist or an upper class matron might
marry a working class carpenter's helper.

Affirmative Action

Affirmative action refers to a public or private program designed to equalize hiring and admission opportunities for historically disadvantaged groups by taking into consideration those very characteristics which have been used to deny them equal treatment. Affirmative action does not mean reverse discrimination and does not give preferential treatment to people of color and women.

Affirmative action began in response to blatant and persistent institutionalized discrimination in the United States. A brief historical outline of some of the major historical events follows:

1943—Fair Employment Practices Commission; could only ask employers for voluntary compliance to stop discriminating

1948—President Truman issued an executive order ending segregation in the Armed Forces

1954—Supreme Court decision Brown v. Board of Education, Topeka. Banned public school segregation

1964—Civil Rights Act

a. Banned discrimination based on race, color, creed, national origin, and sex

b. Established the Equal Employment Opportunity Commission

c. Banned different standards for white and black voting rules

d. Banned discrimination in public accommodations

e. Banned discrimination in federally supported programs and institutions; e.g., hospitals, colleges, and road construction

1967—The Philadelphia Plan—Minority hiring quotas

1971—Commission on Civil Rights defined Affirmative Action as the Elimination of:

a. Word-of-mouth recruitment among all-white or all-male work force

b. Recruitment exclusively in schools or colleges that are all one sex or predominantly nonminority

c. Discrimination against married women or forced retirement of pregnant women

d. Advertising in male and female help wanted columns if sex is not a legitimate occupational qualification

e. Job qualifications or tests that are not substantially related to the job

1978—U.S. Supreme Court case, Regents of the Univ of California v. Bakke, "Reverse Discrimination" against majority students is not allowed. Racial quotas in college admission decisions violate the Equal Protection Clause

2003—Grutter v. Bollinger case involving the University of Michigan, U.S. Supreme Court decision to allow colleges and universities to use race as one component in their admissions policies

Martin Luther King, Jr.

Dr. Martin Luther King, Jr. was a Christian minister who led the Civil Rights Movement in the United States in the 1950s and 1960s. He was born January 15, 1929, in Atlanta, Georgia. His father and his grandfather were Baptist preachers.

King entered Morehouse College at age 16. He received his B.A. degree in sociology in 1948. He then entered Crozer Theological Seminary, where he was elected president of the student body and received his Bachelor of Divinity degree in 1951. He had the highest academic average in his class.

Martin Luther King entered Boston University in 1951. While there, he met and married Coretta Scott. They eventually had four children. He received his PhD in philosophy in 1955, and though it was later determined that portions of his dissertation had been plagiarized, the violation was not so egregious as to warrant revocation of the degree.

Dr. King became a Baptist pastor in Montgomery, Alabama, where he led the successful Montgomery bus boycott. He founded and led the Southern Christian Leadership Conference, a Civil Rights organization.

In 1959, Dr. King traveled to Africa and to India, where he met with Prime Minister Nehru. He intentionally learned about the successful nonviolent civil disobedience tactics of Gandhi. His insistence on nonviolence is often credited for averting a major race war in the United States. For this, every American should be eternally grateful.

By this time, the Civil Rights leader was well-known nationally and internationally. He was jailed in Birmingham, Alabama, and other places. He led a massive March on Washington in 1963, where he gave his famous "I Have a Dream" speech. This march, along with other factors, is thought to have led to the passage of the Civil Rights Act of 1964 and the Voting Rights Act of 1965.

Dr. Martin Luther King, Jr., was assassinated April 4, 1968, in Memphis, Tennessee, by a white separatist, James Earl Ray. His life and legacy are largely responsible for much of the progress in United States race relations since the 1960s.

School Busing

In general, the term **school busing** has meant the provision of rides to school for children, primarily in rural areas. Specifically, it refers to the use of buses to transport children to public schools outside their neighborhoods in order to achieve racially balanced student body compositions.

Busing was introduced early in the 1970's, but quickly became controversial. Compulsory busing was vigorously fought by parents who insisted on their right to enroll their children in schools within their residential neighborhoods. Proponents of the policy, however, said that school busing was a necessary element in the struggle to end school segregation.

Integration is the complete social and legal equality of all the categories of people in a society. In an integrated society, there is no systematic racial discrimination in voting, employment, education, etc. The term segregation refers to the physical or social separation of categories of people. In a segregated society, people of various races rarely encounter one another as equals.

De jure segregation is the requirement of segregation by law. The Jim Crow Laws were a long series of laws passed in Southern states from after the Civil War until the early 1950's, ensuring the division of society into distinct racial categories. **De facto segregation** is the informal practice of the separation of the races without the enforcement of formally written laws.

A significant aspect of de jure segregation was the requirement of separate schools for African Americans and whites. An important U.S. Supreme Court case involved Linda Brown, a 7-year-old girl in Topeka, Kansas, who, on the basis of the color of her skin, was denied the right to enroll in the local school only four blocks from her home. She was required to attend a school for African Americans 2 miles away. Her parents sued, and the landmark case of **Brown v. Board of Education, Topeka, Kansas**, resulted in the May 17, 1954 ruling that segregation necessarily meant an inferior education for African Americans. The Supreme Court declared separate schools for whites and African Americans to be unconstitutional.

The Brown decision overturned the existing doctrine known as the principle of **separate but equal**. That doctrine resulted from an 1896 Supreme Court decision in the case of **Plessy v. Ferguson**, which held that racial segregation could continue only if equal facilities were provided for African Americans and whites. In reality, the facilities provided for African Americans, including schools, tended to be consistently inferior.

The attempt to utilize school busing as a tool in achieving integration was not mandated by Brown v. Board of Education, Topeka, but arose indirectly from its antisegregation order. Subsequent court decisions did directly address busing, however. The 1968 Virginia court decision in Green v. New Kent County School Board ordered the school officials to do "whatever was necessary" to end educational discrimination. Such an order is called affirmative action.

The 1971 North Carolina case **Swann v. Charlotte-Mecklinburg Board of Education** concluded with the ruling that the courts could require busing as a remedy to segregation if the school officials refused to implement desegregation measures. School busing was ordered by courts across the country during the 1970s. White students were bused to previously African American schools in Cleveland, Ohio, Los Angeles, California, and Boston, Massachusetts, among many other places. In some instances, African American students were bused from the inner cities to previously white schools in suburban areas, most notably in Indianapolis, Indiana, and Wilmington, Delaware.

Effectiveness/Fairness Issues

The idea of school busing was an unpopular one from the very beginning. It met with opposition from prejudiced whites who desired a segregated society. Also opposed, however, were both whites and African Americans whose children were likely to be bused. They considered the practice to be patently unfair. This is paradoxical because busing was originally implemented with the purpose in mind of bringing a measure of overdue fairness into the educational arena. These parents complained that busing placed an undue hardship on the children, who were themselves innocent and undeserving of being forced to endure long bus rides away from the familiar surroundings of their own communities.

Many African American parents strongly opposed the busing of their children out of their neighborhoods because the distance to the new school made it difficult for them to be involved in their children's educational process. It is very inconvenient to drive all the way across a large city for PTA meetings and parent-teacher conferences, much less the numerous plays, athletic events, concerts, etc., in which many students are involved.

African Americans further objected to quotas such as those prescribed by James Redmond, Superintendent of Schools in Chicago (no elementary school should be comprised of over 15% African American students; no high school should be comprised of over 25% African American students). This policy was designed to halt so-called **white flight**, the movement of white families from the cities to the suburbs in order to avoid extensive association with minorities. African Americans argued that such quotas meant that African American students would remain in the numerical minority even in their own neighborhood schools. Another perspective, from the "Black Power" movement, insisted that only African American teachers and parents possess the compassion and motivation to communicate effectively with African American students, and this could be best achieved in their own schools.

Despite the negative reaction from much of the public, advocates of busing claimed that positive academic and social effects would result from the practice. They held that racially heterogeneous classrooms would yield great benefits in reduced prejudice and discrimination in the future. Even though there might be some temporary discomfort and inconvenience involved in its implementation, the advantages of busing would eventually far outweigh its disadvantages.

In 1966, the U.S. Office of Education issued a report on the equality of educational opportunity. This study, known popularly as the Coleman Report because it was directed by the highly respected sociologist Robert Coleman, observed the effects of desegregation on academic performance. The major finding was that the greatest determinant of scholastic achievement is the educational level of one's fellow students. Disadvantaged children were found to perform better when their classmates were from more privileged backgrounds. The study also noted, however, that the disadvantaged students might suffer lowered self-esteem. Overall, the Coleman Report encouraged the practice of school busing.

Later Developments

Around 1980, both the U.S. Congress and the courts began a philosophical change with regard to school busing. The consensus emerged that before busing could be required of a school system, it must be proven that the segregation in the system was "intentional." This is rather difficult to prove, because it would ultimately require the reading of the minds of the school officials.

Presidents Reagan and Bush appointed federal judges who opposed the use of busing to achieve school desegregation. California voters passed a referendum banning the required busing of students to achieve the goals of integration. This referendum was held to be constitutional by the U.S. Supreme Court in 1981. At that time, the complicated forced busing program implemented in Los Angeles in 1978 was ended.

The Supreme Court indicated in 1986 that busing in a city could end when officials decide that segregation no longer characterized the community's schools. In 1991, compulsory busing was dealt its death blow by the Supreme Court's ruling that Oklahoma City could end school busing even though integration had not been achieved. This ruling was stated to be on the basis that everything had been done that could be done to eliminate the effects of decades of discrimination.

The demise of school busing has signaled the end of most efforts in the direction of integration in the United States. The Supreme Court ruled against certain forms of affirmative action in 1995. The country seems to be headed in the direction of cultural pluralism, in which various racial and ethnic groups remain socially distinct, but have roughly equal social and political standing. It is unlikely that school busing will be reattempted in the foreseeable future.

Name _____   Date _____

Chapter 9   Race and Ethnicity

Chapter Exercise

(This assignment is to be carefully torn out and completed at the direction of the instructor. The answers are to be legibly handwritten directly on the sheets. Do not *Do not* photocopy these pages, as such action would constitute a blatant violation of the copyright laws of the United States. Thoroughly read the assigned text before attempting to complete a tear-out assignment. It is obvious when a student has tried to fill-in an assignment without reading the background material.)

Share an event in which you observed or even personally experienced prejudice or discrimination.

_____

_____

_____

_____

_____

_____

_____

_____

_____

_____

_____

_____

_____

_____

Chapter 10

Sex and Gender

© Lisa S./Shutterstock.com

Sex and Gender Terminology

The term **sex** refers to the division of humanity into biological categories of male and female. Female and male chromosomes are patterned in the following manner:

$$XX = \text{Female}; XY = \text{Male}$$

The **primary sex characteristics**, the genitalia, are distinguished at birth. The **secondary sex characteristics** emerge at puberty and they are not directly linked to reproduction.

The **hermaphrodite** is a person born with combination of male and female organs. A **transsexual** is a person who feels that he/she is one sex when biologically he/she is the other.

The term **sexual orientation** refers to the manner in which people experience sexual arousal and achieve sexual pleasure. **Heterosexuality** is attraction to the opposite sex. *Homosexuality* refers to attraction to the same sex. **Bisexuality** is a term used for nonmutually exclusive sexual attraction.

Asexuality is a term that could be used to describe a eunuch or other nonsexual person. A **eunuch** is generally a castrated male.

Gender is expected behaviors or traits attached by culture to each sex. Males tend to be socialized masculine. **Masculinity** has traditionally been characterized by assertiveness, physical strength, competitiveness, and insensitivity. These may in fact be stereotypes, but they have been fairly consistently been believed to be natural traits for males. Females tend to be socialized **feminine**, incorporating such traditional stereotypical traits as submissiveness, dependence, tenderness, intuitiveness, etc.

A third gender is known as androgyny. **Androgyny** refers to socializing a child with the best characteristics of both masculinity and femininity. The first chapter of Genesis says that God made both the male and female in His image. This would indicate that God is neither fully masculine nor feminine. He is not a human, in fact, but a spirit. Jesus was clearly a man, and a ruggedly masculine one at that. Still, on occasion, He was able to demonstrate "feminine" compassion. In Luke 13:34, He expresses His desire to gather the inhabitants of Jerusalem together as a hen gathers her chicks under her wings. The Holy Spirit, furthermore, is known as "the comforter," a traditionally feminine role.

Sexism and Patriarchy

© Marcin Sylwia Ciesielski/Shutterstock.com

The term **sexism** refers to the belief that one sex is innately superior or inferior to the other. It is often considered to be similar to racism in its damaging impact.

Sexism is the basis of **patriarchy**, a form of social organization in which males dominate females. Patriarchy appears to be universal, that is, it seems to be the pattern in every known society of the past or present. There are families, businesses, and occupations that are obviously **matriarchal** (dominated by women), such as nursing and kindergarten teaching. Matriarchy, however, is not anywhere extended to an entire society. In several of the Iroquois tribes, the women decided which male would be the leader of the group and they had the power of impeachment; nonetheless, it was the men who made all other major decisions in the life of the tribe.

One result of sexism and patriarchy is unequal pay for women and men in the same occupations. Women in the United States earn about 75%–80% as much as men in identical occupational positions. Women are more likely than men to live in poverty. Other aspects of sexism and patriarchy include sexual harassment, woman battering, rape, and other forms of violence against women. Twenty-five to fifty percent of wives in the United States are physically assaulted by their husbands. A woman is more likely to be injured by a male family member or close friend than in an automobile accident.

The Women's Liberation Movement

The **women's liberation movement** is a social movement for the social equality of the sexes and against patriarchy and sexism. The movement was very active in the 1800s and early 1900s and received new vitality in the social action environment of the 1960s.

Early goals of the women's liberation movement included the abolition of slavery, **women's suffrage** (the right to vote), and the prohibition of alcoholic beverages. The first two have been accomplished, and the third seems to be a hopeless cause. Women also campaigned for equality of educational opportunity; today, there are more women than men attending colleges in the United States.

More recently, the goals of the movement have centered on such issues as reproductive choice, improving the status of women, and the sharing of both breadwinning and household tasks. Further goals include equal pay for equal worth and challenging gender-based inequality in every major social institution: the family, religion, military, politics, economy, education, health care, journalism, entertainment, and law.

The United Nations has sponsored large gatherings of women in Egypt and China, which opened women's rights issues for international debate. The U.S. Senate nomination hearings for Supreme Court Justice Clarence Thomas drew national attention to the problem of sexual harassment. Thomas was approved, despite the accusations of University of Oklahoma law professor Anita Hill. The murder trial and subsequent acquittal of the former Buffalo Bills football player O. J. Simpson, in likewise, brought the issue of violence against women into the public focus.

Beginnings of the Movement

Saint Paul is reported to have written in 55 AD, "In Christ there is neither Jew nor Greek, neither male nor female." It was not until 1696, however, that Mary Astell, in "An Essay in Defense of the Female Sex," declared that "souls are equal." She insisted that women's minds should be developed as well as those of men. A woman identifying herself as Sophia wrote in a 1739 book, *Woman Not Inferior to Man*, that the differences between the sexes are only due to education, custom, and circumstances. She proposed that no woman should be denied access to education or entry into any profession, including the military.

The political philosopher David Hume opposed confining women to the domestic sphere. John Stuart Mill held similar views. Mary Wollstonecraft, the mother of Mary Shelley, the author of *Frankenstein*, wrote the most influential early feminist publication in 1792, entitled *Vindication of the Rights of Women*.

She called in this work for the complete equality of men and women, particularly in the area of education.

In the United States, the first sizeable gathering of feminists was organized by Elizabeth Cady Stanton. It was known as the Women's Rights Convention and was held at Seneca Falls, New York, in 1848. Two years later, another women's rights activist, Lucy Stone, organized a similar convention with the support of Julia Ward Howe. These groups combined in 1863 to form the Women's National Loyal League under the leadership of Susan B. Anthony. This organization proposed a women's suffrage constitutional amendment in 1878, which Congress rejected.

In 1890, the National American Women's Suffrage Association was formed. Before the year's end, Wyoming became the first state to give women the right to vote (in state and local elections). Carrie Chapman Catt was elected as the president of the organization in 1900. She led the movement with large marches and demonstrations throughout the country. Finally, in 1920, the 19th Amendment became the law, giving all women age 21 or over the **right to vote** in the United States. Women in England received the right to vote in 1918, if they were aged 30 or older. In 1928, the voting age for women was lowered to 21.

The Canadian experience with regard to women's suffrage was similar. It was granted in 1916 in Manitoba, Saskatchewan, and Alberta. The other provinces were slower to give women the right to vote, with Quebec holding out until 1940.

Recent Developments

The French feminist Simone de Beauvoir published a book in 1953, *The Second Sex*, which became a catalyst for a second wave of feminist activism in the 1960s. Influential on the movement in the United States was *The Feminist Mystique*, written by Betty Friedan and published in 1963. The decade of the 1960s was a period of widespread progress in many areas of civil rights, which placed the country in a favorable mood for considering the demands of women.

The **National Organization for Women** (NOW) was founded by Betty Friedan in 1966. It continues to be the most outspoken and influential organization involved in the crusade for women's rights. Another powerful group was begun in 1971, the National Women's Political Caucus. Leaders of this association for addressing women's issues in the government realm have included Shirley Chisholm, Bella Abzug, and Gloria Steinem, the politically active publisher of Ms. Magazine.

These groups and others led the attempt in the early 1970s to amend the Constitution of the United States with a simple statement called the **Equal Rights Amendment**. The wording was as follows: "Equality of rights under the law shall not be denied or abridged by the United States or by any State on account of sex." It was approved by the House of Representatives in 1971 and by the U.S. Senate in 1972, but failed the necessary ratification by the states.

Types of Feminism

It is generally recognized that there are three major types of feminists today (Easterling, 2017).

1. The first classification, sometimes referred to as **Liberal Feminism** (also called "Equity Feminism"), includes the mainstream organizations and advocates the availability of maternity leave and child care for working women. Liberal feminists further seek equality in the workplace, education, and in the political realm. They have persistently urged Congress to consider renewing the passage of the Equal Rights Amendment. Though there is a marginal group called "Feminists for Life," most liberal feminists favor legalized abortion.

2. Another category of feminist is that of the **Socialist Feminists**. This group tends to link the social disadvantages of women largely to the capitalist economic system. Though capitalism is the most productive type of economic arrangement, these women believe that it tends to benefit certain categories of people much more than others. The socialist feminists view social reform, the goal of the liberal feminists, as inadequate. They advocate a complete socialist revolution (by violent means, if necessary) as the only way to ensure equality for all men and women.

3. The category known as **Radical Feminism** tends to seek a gender-free society or even a matriarchal society. They argue that men have run the world long enough and have not eliminated wars, poverty, etc., so perhaps it is time to give women a chance. Some groups advocate escaping from male domination through lesbianism. Others promote goddess worship as a rejection of traditional religions,

which they often view as patriarchal. One radical feminist group calls itself the Society for Cutting Up Men (SCUM). Another has named them as the Women's International Terrorist Conspiracy from Hell (WITCH).

Women and Christianity

Women stayed with Jesus through the crucifixion, whereas the men went fishing. They were the first at the tomb after the resurrection and were also the first to proclaim the resurrection of Jesus Christ. The first preacher to the Jews was a woman (Anna–Luke 2:37–38).

A number of women, including Mary, the mother of Jesus, partici-pated in the first prayer meeting (Acts 1:14). They were present and they were participants in the great Pentecostal outpouring of the second chap-ter of Acts.

The first European convert to Christianity was a businesswoman, Lydia. The highly honored "virtuous woman" of Proverbs 31 was in the real estate business.

The following passage from Numbers 27:1–8 indicates God's attitude toward women:

Then came the daughters of Zelophehad, the son of Hepher, the son of Gilead, the son of Machir, the son of Manasseh, of the families of Manasseh the son of Joseph: and these are the names of his daughters; Mahlah, Noah, and Hoglah, and Milcah, and Tirzah.

And they stood before Moses, and before Eleazar the priest, and before the princes and all the congregation, by the door of the tabernacle of the congregation, saying,

Our father died in the wilderness, and he was not in the company of them that gathered themselves together against the Lord in the company of Korah; but died in his own sin, and had no sons.

Why should the name of our father be done away from among his family, because he hath no son? Give unto us, therefore, a possession among the brethren of our father.

And Moses brought their cause before the Lord.

And the Lord spake unto Moses, saying,

The daughters of Zelophehad speak right: thou shalt surely give them a posses-sion of an inheritance among their father's brethren; and thou shalt cause the inheritance of their father to pass unto them.

Homosexuality and Marriage

© Syda Productions/Shutterstock.com

In many areas of the world, there has been an increasing amount of political and religious advocacy for homosexual practices, same-sex marriage, and alternate sexual identities. There are a great many perspectives from which one might draw in order to arrive at a position on this phenomenon. The most stable foundation on which to build a position is Holy Scripture, which is a dependable guide (2 Timothy 3:16–17). Since the Bible speaks to the nature of human beings and their sexuality, it is important to understand and articulate what it teaches on these issues that can at times be controversial and divisive.

Some theologians have proposed revisionist interpretations of relevant biblical texts that are not necessarily based upon the best exegesis and translation. This was predicted a long time ago by Saint Paul in 2 Timothy 4:3, "For the time will come when people will not put up with sound doctrine. Instead, to suit their own desires, they will gather around them a great number of teachers to say what their itching ears want to hear."

Historically, homosexuality has been defined as an emotional, psychological, or physiological problem. In recent years, mental health organizations have been heavily lobbied to remove homosexuality from the list of classified diagnostic pathologies. It was removed from the American Psychiatric Association's *Diagnostic and Statistical Manual of Mental Disorders* (DSM) in 1987. It is regarded by many people as nothing more than a morally neutral personal preference or a naturally occurring aspect of human biological diversity.

In Scripture, male and female genders (cultural roles) are clearly defined. The consistent ideal for sexual experience in the Bible is purity for those outside a monogamous heterosexual marriage and faithfulness for those inside such a marriage.

From the traditional Christian perspective, homosexual behavior is sin because it deviates from scriptural teachings. When God called the Hebrews to be His people, He delivered them through a series of miracles from slavery in Egypt. He entered into a covenant relationship with them and provided means by which they should live life as His established pure, sacred, and blameless people, conditional upon whether or not they would obey His commandments and follow His principles. The Torah (the teachings of the first five books of the Bible) included specific prohibitions of homosexual practice, such as in Leviticus 18:22: "You shall not lie with a male as with a woman; it is an abomination." This is repeated in Leviticus 20:13.

The New Testament also prohibits such behavior. In the time of Saint Paul, the city of Corinth was particularly known for sexual promiscuity. It was an international crossroads of commerce and prostitution. In Romans 1:25–32, Paul is speaking about male homosexuality and lesbianism:

24 Wherefore God also gave them up to uncleanness through the lusts of their own hearts, to dishonour their own bodies between themselves:

25 Who changed the truth of God into a lie, and worshipped and served the creature more than the Creator, who is blessed for ever. Amen.

26 For this cause God gave them up unto vile affections: for even their women did change the natural use into that which is against nature:

27 And likewise also the men, leaving the natural use of the woman, burned in their lust one toward another; men with men working that which is unseemly, and receiving in themselves that recompence of their error which was meet.

28 And even as they did not like to retain God in their knowledge, God gave them over to a reprobate mind, to do those things which are not convenient;

29 Being filled with all unrighteousness, fornication, wickedness, covetousness, maliciousness; full of envy, murder, debate, deceit, malignity; whisperers,

30 Backbiters, haters of God, despiteful, proud, boasters, inventors of evil things, disobedient to parents,

31 Without understanding, covenant breakers, without natural affection, implacable, unmerciful:

32 Who knowing the judgment of God, that they which commit such things are worthy of death, not only do the same, but have pleasure in them that do them.

It is obviously the behavior itself, not whether "marriage" is involved, that is sinful. The only alternative to heterosexual marriage, according to Scripture, is celibacy for the kingdom of Heaven's sake (I Corinthians 7:7–9).

Name _____   Date _____

Chapter 10   Sex and Gender

Chapter Exercise

(This assignment is to be carefully torn out and completed at the direction of the instructor. The answers are to be legibly handwritten directly on the sheets. *Do not* photocopy these pages; as such action would constitute a blatant violation of the copyright laws of the United States. Thoroughly read the assigned text before attempting to complete a tear-out assignment. It is obvious when a student has tried to fill-in an assignment without reading the background material.)

Based on your readings, try to explain your opinions regarding the difference between sex and gender and why those simple concepts can become controversial.

_____

_____

_____

_____

_____

_____

_____

_____

_____

_____

_____

_____

_____

Chapter 11

Marriage and Family

© Monkey Business Images/Shutterstock.com

Family

The family is the basic institution in all societies. It generally arises from a social structure of kinship and marriage. **Kinship** refers to social relationships based on blood marriage or adoption. A **family**, then, is a social group of two or more people who are related by blood, marriage, or adoption, and who live together.

The **family of orientation** is the family in which the individual receives her early childhood socialization. The **family of procreation** comes into existence when the individual marries and has children of her own.

A **nuclear family** includes one or two parents, plus children, who live together. An **extended family** includes one or two parents, plus children, plus other kin, who live together. This is the sociological/ Census Bureau definition, although in popular usage, the extended family is often synonymous with the kinship system.

Strictly speaking, **marriage** is a socially approved relationship involving both economic cooperation and sexual activity. There are a number of types of marriage:

A TYPOLOGY OF MARRIAGE

Monogamy—marriage between two persons
Serial monogamy—a series of monogamous marriages
Polygamy—marriage among three or more persons

1. **Polygyny**—marriage among one male and two or more females
2. **Polyandry**—marriage among one female and two or more males

Endogamy—marriage within one's social group or category
Exogamy—marriage outside one's social group or category

The Structural-Functional Perspective of the Family

The structural-functional paradigm emphasizes the **functions of the family**. The essential functions of the family include (Easterling, 2017):

1. **Material security**—includes food, clothing, shelter, and protection from the outside world
2. **Emotional security**—love, acceptance, and relationship
3. **Socialization of children**—training them in the ways of their culture, including language and gender roles
4. **Regulation of sexual activity**—to prevent disease, maladjustment, and social disorganization
5. **Social placement**—passing on the family's social status and social class to subsequent generations

In the traditional family, the members worked together, as a team, to establish an economic undergirding. They worked the farm, milked the cows, harvested the crops, or worked in the family business, of whatever type. Each family member was an important part of the income-producing process. Children were valued for their contributions to the family's workload. Can you see why couples tried to have numerous children?

In contemporary society in most industrialized areas of the world, the family is no longer thought of as an economic unit and children are considered financial liabilities. Could this be one reason for increased incidences of abortion, child abuse, and child neglect?

In the traditional family, the entire family unit banded together for protection from enemies or invaders. It was also considered the responsibility of the total group to take care of the young, the elderly, the weak, and the infirm. In the contemporary world, however, society provides a large measure of protection and security for most people.

DUTIES OF PARENTS TOWARD CHILDREN

1. Provide food, clothing, shelter
2. Provide good example (role model)
3. Teach them right and wrong

   a.   Honesty, Obedience, Truthfulness, Purity
   b.   To respect the rights and property of others
   c.   10 Commandments
   d.   Golden Rule

4. Provide an honorable and principled home

   a.   Display the fruit of the Spirit

      i.   Love
      ii.   Joy
      iii.   Peace
      iv.   Patience
      v.   Kindness
      vi.   Goodness
      vii.   Faithfulness
      viii. Gentleness
      ix.   Self-control

   b.   Church attendance

5. Teach them about Jesus Christ

   a.   Family Bible study
   b.   Sunday School, Confirmation Class, etc.

6. Teach them to pray
7. Prepare them for college
8. Prepare them for marriage

9. Teach them the beauty and sacredness of sex
   a. Only appropriate within marriage
   b. Correct information, but sensitive to age and development of the child
10. Give them wholesome recreation
11. Keep them from evil companions

The Social Conflict Perspective on Marriage

Proponents of the social conflict perspective tend to take on a negative view of the family. They point out that the family tends to perpetuate the dominance of men over women. The family leads to conflict, they say, such as spouse battering and the physical or sexual abuse of children.

From the social conflict perspective, the family—through inheritance practices—perpetuates inequality of wealth and income by passing on family-owned property, even though the inheritors may have actually accomplished or risked little or nothing to deserve it. Karl Marx advocated the abolition of private property and viewed it as possibly the greatest evil in society.

These theorists further blame the institution of the family for the harmful effects of divorce, which is devastating for all involved parties. The abolition of the family is one of the necessary steps for a socialist society, according to Marx's Manifesto of the Communist Party. An FBI agent named Skousen (2014) outlined a number of strategies socialists thought would help bring about their goals:

1. Use technical decisions of the courts to weaken basic American institutions by claiming that their activities violate civil rights.
2. Gain control of key positions in radio, TV, and motion pictures.
3. Continue discrediting American culture by degrading all forms of artistic expression.
4. Eliminate all laws governing obscenity by calling them "censorship" and a violation of free speech and free press.
5. Break down cultural standards of morality by promoting pornography and obscenity in books, magazines, motion pictures, radio, and TV.
6. Present homosexuality, degeneracy, and promiscuity as "normal, natural, and healthy."
7. Discredit the family as an institution. Encourage promiscuity and easy divorce.

8. Emphasize the need to raise children away from the negative influence of parents. Attribute prejudices, mental blocks, and retarding of children to the suppressive influence of parents.

The Symbolic Interaction Perspective

There is no particular position concerning the family that is taken by most symbolic interactionists. Instead, there are a number of microlevel discussions involving marriage and relationships.

Social exchange theory is based upon the utilitarian philosophy of Jeremy Bentham and John Stuart Mill. It is can be likened to an economic cost/benefit model applied to social relationships. Peter Blau and others have popularized this theory.

Simply stated, **social exchange theory** posits that humans make decisions based upon some undefined internal weighing of the costs and benefits to the individual. Social exchange theory may seem crass and cold when thinking about relationships, but it can be helpful when analyzing marital problems or when considering potential mates. For example, Harry may have married Wilma because she is a good cook. She undoubtedly has a few faults (such as a tendency to nag), but Harry is willing to overlook them because the benefit of her cooking is greater than the cost of her faults. Similarly, Sarah may have wanted to marry Duane because of his family's wealth, but she decided not to marry him because of his alcoholism.

Easterling has stated that the leading cause of divorce is **unmet expectations**. Engaged couples should always seek premarital counseling, so that their expectations of marriage will be similar. If they do not heed this advice, they will be disappointed when marriage is not what they thought it was going to be like.

Marriage

There are fundamentally two kinds of love. Both kinds of love are necessary for a completely fulfilling marriage.

A TYPOLOGY OF LOVE

Romantic Love

Idealism
High emotionality
Strong sexual attractio**n**
Great need to be with the other

> *Companionate Love*
> Realism
> Trust
> Respect
> Commitment
> Friendship

Couples should stay in love and out of debt. Financial problems are seldom the actual cause of divorce. If financial problems were the principal cause of divorce, as many people claim, why do so many financially well-off couples divorce? Remember that the major cause of divorce is unmet expectations. The fact remains, however, that financial difficulties can most assuredly exacerbate already existing problems.

Politeness means to do the nicest thing in the nicest way and it is a better way to live. Couples who initiate the practice of saying "please" and "thank you" in the daily routines of their families will experience less friction and greater marital satisfaction. Greater marital satisfaction also occurs when both parties share in the housework.

The Three-Legged Stool of Commitment

A stool with only one leg is not stable. It makes sitting difficult. A stool with two legs is not much better. A **three-legged stool**, however, remains stable on practically any terrain.

What has this to do with marriage? Simply this: marriage must be a commitment on three levels. The couple should, of course, be **(1) committed to each other by name**. On days in which they may be in particular disagreement, this commitment may be temporarily jeopardized. A broader, more stable commitment is called for. Thus, the couple should be **(2) committed to their relationship**—to their marriage. Even if you are temporarily upset with your spouse, you can still be committed to your marriage. Thirdly, they should be **(3) committed to the institution of marriage**, itself, as a sacrament and a holy estate, entered into at the wedding before both God and human witnesses.

Marriage is a solemn covenant, and should not be entered into unadvisedly. A covenant cannot be broken without dire consequences because it involves vows by which the parties promised to uphold each other at least until death.

DIVORCE

Divorce is a way of dissolving a legal marriage, which permits the partners to remarry if they choose. It differs from an **annulment**, which declares a marriage invalid because of some defect in the contract. Divorce involves the recognition that a marriage has irreparably failed and that at least one of the partners has no desire to continue the marital relationship.

Unsuccessful marriages may be dealt with in other ways. For example, instead of divorcing, the partners may choose to remain together for religious or family reasons, or they may decide to live apart without breaking their legal ties.

The marriage and divorce institutions of the West are derived from ancient Hebrew and Roman sources. In Jewish law, a wife did not have the right to divorce her husband, but she did have the right to remarry if her husband divorced her. This is recorded in Deuteronomy 24:1: "When a man takes a wife and marries her, if then she finds no favor in his eyes because he has found some indecency in her ... he writes her a bill of divorce and puts it in her hand and sends her out of his house ... and if she goes and becomes another man's wife ..."

In the Roman Empire, marriage was not a legal formality; a man and a woman simply began to live together in a permanent household. The only legal requirements were that the parties be citizens above the age of puberty and that they have the consent of their families. Both the husband and the wife possessed property separately. Either could put an end to the marriage; the law required only a clear indication of the intent to divorce, such as a formal letter.

In the eyes of the Christian church, marriage was indissoluble. Canon law, as it developed during the Middle Ages, became the law of the Christian countries of Europe with respect to marriage and divorce; under it, divorce was not allowed. Separation was permitted in the case of adultery or extreme cruelty; it was also permissible if one of the partners had left the church. Canon law concerning divorce could be summarized by the phrase from the marriage ceremony: "What therefore God hath joined together, let not man put asunder" (Matthew 19:6).

When Martin Luther and other Protestants broke away from the Roman church in the 16th century, they adopted a different view of marriage. Luther called it "an external worldly thing, subject to secular jurisdiction, just like dress and food, home and field." The Protestants, therefore, permitted divorce on specific grounds, such as adultery, cruelty, or desertion. In England, a different tradition prevailed. Legal divorce was instituted after HENRY VIII broke away from the Roman Catholic Church, but it was obtained through Parliament rather than through the courts. Every divorce required a separate act of the House of Lords. Divorce was therefore expensive and accessible only to the rich and powerful. This system of legislative divorce continued in England until 1857, when Parliament established the Court for Divorce and Matrimonial Causes.

The early American settlers brought with them three different views of divorce:

1. The Roman Catholic view that marriage was a sacrament and that there could be no divorce
2. The English view that divorce was a legislative matter
3. The Protestant view that marriage and divorce were secular matters to be handled by the civil authorities

The United States has a divorce rate that is among the highest in the world, and in recent decades it has held fairly steady. Only Eastern European countries have higher divorce rates.

RATIO OF DIVORCES TO MARRIAGES, U.S.

Year	Ratio
1960	33%
1970	44%
1980	53%
1990	51%
2000	50%
2010	53%

There was a slight decline in the U.S. divorce rate from 1980 to 2000. Social scientists believe that some reasons for this decline of the divorce rate include

1. The fear of contracting HIV
2. Longer courtships
3. More people living together outside of marriage
4. Later average age at time of marriage (27 for women and 29 for men)

The divorce rate has risen since 2010. This could be due to a virtual major news media blackout regarding the dangers of the ongoing full-scale world-wide HIV epidemic. People are possibly not as hesitant to jump from partner to partner as they were when HIV was more prominently discussed in the news. Why the media are hesitant to report the truth is a mystery, though there have been some medical advances and more people are undergoing treatment, but the misery and death aspects of the disease make it as undesirable as ever.

NUMBER OF PEOPLE LIVING WITH HIV GLOBALLY

2000	28.9 Million
2005	31.8 Million
2010	33.3 Million
2011	33.9 Million
2012	34.5 Million
2013	35.2 Million
2014	35.9 Million
2015	36.7 Million

Americans who get divorced are likely to remarry. In 2013, 64% of the U.S. divorced men had remarried, compared with 52% of the divorced women. Eighty years earlier, two out of three divorced persons did not remarry.

Divorce can be a devastating experience. While the divorce is in progress, and for some time afterward, both parties may feel personally rejected, cheated in the economic arrangements, misrepresented legally, bitter about the coparental arrangements, lonely because they have lost friends, and afraid of living alone.

In the United States, the mother traditionally has been granted custody of the children unless she is found unfit by the courts. The father is usually awarded the right to visit the children regularly. Prolonged and bitter struggles for legal custody have often scarred parents, children, and grandparents.

Just a decade or two ago, many counselors tended to advise couples that divorce is better for the children than living in a home in which there is strife. Lately, however, the tide has turned since counselors are recognizing the devastating effects of divorce on all concerned. If divorce can be at all avoided, even when the adults do not get along well, at least the children have both parents available. The married parties should try every possible means of reconciling with each other. The benefits of an intact home for the children far outweigh any selfish personal reasons for the divorce, such as wanting to marry a third party.

Of course, spouse-battering or physical or sexual abuse of the children must not be tolerated and divorce is the proper recourse. Children must not be made to remain in an abusive situation.

The Family Budget

A budget is a plan for spending and saving. Stewardship is trustworthiness with the family finances. The parents are committing a disservice to the children if they spend recklessly and make poor financial decisions.

A well-balanced budget can help the family do the following:

1. Prevent impulse spending
2. Decide what they can or cannot afford
3. Know where their money goes
4. Increase savings
5. Protect against the financial consequences of
   a. Unemployment
   b. Accidents
   c. Sickness
   d. Aging
   e. Death

STEPS IN ORGANIZING A FAMILY BUDGET

1. The first step in organizing a budget is to estimate the family's income.
2. Next, the family should estimate their expenses.
3. Finally, they should compare their total expected income with their total planned expenses.

It is important to become an informed consumer. (Recognize quality and avoid waste). Accurate record-keeping is essential. A monthly expense record can be easily maintained using computer software or a personal budget kit available at most office supply stores.

The budget should be constantly evaluated. It can be changed to meet the family's changing needs and income. It is imperative that the budget have some built-in flexibility. The parents should listen to the other family members' comments and be prepared to compromise. They should encourage each other to stick to the plan and exercise will power.

The most important aspect of the family budget is the **tithe** (Malachi 3:10; Matthew 23:23). The word tithe literally means one-tenth. A person can live much better on 90% of her income than on 100% if the other 10% is the tithe, going into the local church. Furthermore, God has promised to rebuke the devourer for the sake of the tither (Malachi 3:11). In addition, one should give **offerings** over and above the tithe (Luke 6:38). This will cause blessings to come in abundance to the family. It is more blessed to give than to receive, because blessings come to those who give.

Identifying Codependency in Family Relationships

Codependency refers to the fallacy of trying to control interior feelings by controlling people, things, and events on the outside. In a broad sense, it is an addiction to people, behaviors, or things. There are basically **three types of codependency**:

1. **Interpersonal codependency**—the individual has become deeply enmeshed with another human being to the extent of severely

© Cartoon Resource/Shutterstock.com

"Co-dependency is a possibility."

restricting her own personal identity. It can be thought of as an "addiction" to a person.

2. **Chemical codependency**—the individual tries to fill the great emotional vacuum inside herself by ingesting alcohol or drugs.
3. **Material codependency**—"addiction" to money, food, sexuality, work, etc.

The study of codependency began in the late 1970s in Minnesota's therapy community to describe the impact alcoholism had on those married to alcoholics. In the 1980s, clinicians and counselors began to identify, both among spouses and children of alcoholics, patterns of behavior and family roles that were conditioned by the alcoholic's addictive behavior. These behaviors and roles were labeled as codependent. Therefore, "codependency" was originally a term used to explain symptoms of people who had become dysfunctional as a result of being in a relationship with an alcoholic person.

In the forefront of the movement to popularize the concept of codependency was the organization known as Alcoholics Anonymous. The founders of the organization discovered a number of factors about alcoholics that led to what is now called codependency. Many of these factors still apply to alcoholics and their families and are outlined as follows:

1. They were embittered toward God
2. They were rebellious
3. They were childishly dependent upon people close to them
4. The family was often as dependent upon the alcoholism as the alcoholic was on the alcohol itself
   a. They "enabled" the alcoholic to maintain the habit (buying, serving, or providing funds to purchase the substance)
   b. They denied the facts to outsiders
   c. They ignored or circumvented the problem
   d. It had become their comfortable way of life

The concept of codependency has expanded to include other chemical addictions, as well as behavioral and material addictions (cocaine, marijuana, heroin, eating disorders, sexual addictions, workaholism, gambling, etc.).

The "thread" of codependency can extend through the children and grandchildren and so on until the cycle is finally broken. Each alcoholic impacts at least four other people, such as spouse, children, siblings, and coworkers. The dependency or dysfunction may change with each succeeding generation. For example, the son of an alcoholic might become an alcoholic or a workaholic, and the granddaughter an alcoholic or a compulsive eater.

Potential problems resulting from codependency might include

1. Divorce or relationship difficulties
2. Substance abuse
3. Compulsive behaviors
4. Explosive anger
5. Clinical or near-clinical depression

There are a number of reasons why each individual should examine her life for codependency. This is not necessarily a negative exercise—all families have some imperfections. The first reason for self-examination is to make life more manageable. Examining one's own life will help the individual to avoid serious mistakes. It will be beneficial for the codependent spouse or other significant person, as well as for one's children and grandchildren.

Codependency has been described as the myth that one can make herself happy by trying to control people and events outside herself. A sense of control, or the lack of control, then, is at the center of the codependent person's life.

Traits of a Codependent Person

1. The codependent is driven by one or more compulsions. Examples: checking the lights and stove several times before leaving the house; always thinking about food, sex, money, or fitness. Not all compulsions are judged bad by society (keeping an immaculate house, making straight A's).
2. The codependent is bound and often tormented by the way things were in the dysfunctional family of orientation. Examples: Mom making you take off your shoes in the house to keep the floors clean or dad flying into a rage if your grades were not up to his standard.
3. The codependent's self-esteem is very low. Ask yourself the following questions as you think about your own level of self-esteem:
    a. Do you defend yourself against unfair criticism? ("No" indicates low self-esteem.)
    b. Do you criticize yourself before others have a chance to do so?
    c. Would you want someone like yourself as a best friend?
    d. Do you constantly aim self-critical thoughts at yourself?
    e. Rate your self-esteem on a scale of 1 to 10 (with 10 representing high self-esteem).
4. The codependent is certain that her happiness hinges on others. Ask yourself these questions:
    a. Do you find yourself thinking, "If certain people would treat me better, then I could be happy?"
    b. Do you react to harsh treatment by thinking, "I deserve it?"
5. A codependent tends to feel inordinately responsible for others. If a best friend's marriage breaks up, the codependent thinks, "I should have been able to help them solve their problems." There is a deep sense of responsibility for the decisions and feelings of other people. "Did I help my children enough with their homework—will they fail in school?" Ask yourself, "Do I think it is my fault when my friends or family members are hurting? What could I do to stop their pain?"
6. The codependent's relationship with a spouse or significant other person is marred by a damaging, unstable lack of balance between dependence and independence. The codependent is usually at one extreme or the other. Examples of dependence: saying or thinking "I can't live without you;" constantly borrowing money from

parents or friends. Examples of independence: "I can make it on my own in this life with any help from you or anybody else;" keeping one's feelings entirely to oneself.

7. The codependent is a master of denial and repression. It is very difficult for the codependent person to admit negative things about their parents. This may be repression of some of the problems that lie at the root of the codependency. An indication of denial is the tendency to make excuses for the parents. "He wasn't really all that bad at heart." "She really didn't mean to do and say the things she did." "They did the best they could, under the circumstances."

8. The codependent worries about things she can't change and may well try to change them. Codependents refuse to accept the truth that we cannot change other people. "If only I had trained the children better, my husband wouldn't have exploded at them like that." "If only I could make George love me, he wouldn't run around with other women." Think of three people in your family or friendship circle you would most like to change. Have actually tried to change any of these people? Have your efforts have been successful?

9. A codependent's life is punctuated by extremes. Example: Bill is a highly respected Elder in his church. His pastor sees him as deeply spiritual and full of wisdom. At work he is well-liked and performs admirably in a quiet and efficient manner. At home, though, he constantly goes into fits of rages and terrorizes his family with verbal abuse. If his office and church friends were to view a videotape of his behavior at home, they would be aghast with shock. Think about this question: "If people at your work and or school, your friends at church, and your family were asked to describe you, would they all describe the same person?" "How would each of these categories of people describe you?"

10. A codependent is constantly looking for the something that is missing or lacking in life. There is a feeling of discontent or restlessness regardless of the person's circumstances. Examples: "If only I were married, I know I'd be happy." "If I had a new car, boy oh boy, would I be satisfied with my life." Even after the person is married and has a new car, the discontent persists.

Source: Adapted from Hemfelt, Minirth, and Meier (1989).

What to Do About Codependency

Always focusing on other people and their needs and wants rather than your own tends to be the problematic element for codependent individuals. Beginning to focus on your own wants and needs is not a selfish position. It means that you are allowing the others to self-determine their own behavior without being controlled. It shows respect for their autonomy. The following are some suggestions (Lancer, 2015):

1. Don't obsess or worry about the other person. Imagine putting the person in God's hands.
2. Don't judge others, just as you don't want to be judged.
3. Don't have expectations of others; instead, meet expectations of yourself.
4. You didn't cause someone else's behavior. Others are responsible for their behavior, and you're only responsible for yours.
5. Write about your feelings in a journal. Read it to someone close to you or to a therapist.
6. Pursue your own interests and have fun.
7. Remember you cannot change or "fix" someone else. She/he is responsible for her/his own life, not you.
8. Write positive things about yourself in your journal every day. Look for things you did well or like about yourself and write them down.
9. Ask yourself how you would treat the other person if he or she wasn't your partner, child, or parent.
10. Go to a Twelve Step meeting for codependents, such as Codependents Anonymous. There are other Twelve Step groups for relatives of other addicts, such as for relatives of gamblers and sex addicts.
11. Get counseling from someone familiar with codependency. It's preferable that they are licensed in your state. They may be marriage and family counselors, social workers, addiction specialists, psychologists, or psychiatrists.
12. Pay attention to how you talk to and treat yourself. Much of low self-esteem is self-inflicted. Train yourself to speak gently and encouragingly, rather than telling yourself what you should or shouldn't be doing or what's wrong with you.

13. Start looking for the positive in your life and what you do. Make a list of things for which you are grateful for each day.

14. Stand-up for yourself if someone criticizes, undermines, or tries to control you.

15. Let go of control and the need to manage other people. Remember the saying, "Live and let live."

16. Express yourself honestly with everyone. Say what you think and what you feel. Ask for what you need.

Name _____   Date _____

Chapter 11   Marriage and Family

Chapter Exercise

(This assignment is to be carefully torn out and completed at the direction of the instructor. The answers are to be legibly handwritten directly on the sheets. Do not photocopy these pages, as such action would constitute a blatant violation of the copyright laws of the United States. Thoroughly read the assigned text before attempting to complete a tear-out assignment. It is obvious when a student has tried to fill-in an assignment without reading the background material.)

Many people do not seem to hold marriage in high regard. Explain why you feel that marriage is still important today.

_____

_____

_____

_____

_____

_____

_____

_____

_____

_____

_____

_____

_____

_____

Chapter 12

The Economy and Social Stratification

© Sakarin Sawasdinaka/Shutterstock.com

The **economy** is the social institution, which organizes the production, distribution, and consumption of goods and services. **Goods** is a term referring to things made of molecules, and the term **services** refers to human activity. In order for objects and human activity to qualify as goods and services, however, they must meet at least one of the following criteria:

1. Facilitates survival
2. Makes life easier
3. Make life more enjoyable

In a classical sense, there are thought to be four categories or sectors that may compose an economy. Others have been suggested, but do not have sufficient explanatory import to be included here (Easterling, 2017).

1. **Primary sector**—generates or extracts raw materials from the environment. This could include all agrarian or agricultural activity, as well as fishing, mining, herding, poultry, the petroleum industry, etc., in terms of growing or extracting the raw materials.
2. **Secondary sector**—transforms raw materials into manufactured goods. Examples of the secondary sector include not only manufacturing, but also the construction, shipbuilding, automobile, aerospace, engineering and textile industries, as well as utility companies, etc.
3. **Tertiary sector**—generates services rather than goods. This sector includes retail and wholesale businesses, transportation and distribution, entertainment (movies, television, radio, music, theater, etc.), restaurants, clerical services, media, tourism, insurance, banking, healthcare, legal firms, etc.
4. **Quaternary sector**—consists of intellectual activities. This sector includes government, culture, museums, aquariums, libraries, research, education, and information technology.

Economic Systems

There are two major types of economic systems. Both satisfy the definition of economy as discussed above, but each does it rather differently.

Capitalism is an economic system in which the natural resources and means of production are privately owned. Adam Smith wrote about a number of facets of capitalism in *The Wealth of Nations* in 1776.

He wrote that the **individual pursuit of profit** results in the greatest good for the greatest number of people. For example, an individual wants to make a large amount of profit, so she starts a business. Suppose this business is a factory. She will invest her own money and raise other capital through the sale of stock. She thus benefits the stockholders as well as herself if the factory turns a profit. She will have to pay engineers and architects to design the factory and a construction company to build it. These entities will pay their employees and make profits for their owners. The materials for the construction of the factory and the equipment in the factory must be purchased. The suppliers of these and all other needs of the factory will profit and pay their employees. The factory workers and employees must be paid, as well as sales personnel. The merchants who sell the manufactured items in their stores will profit and pay their employees. Consumers will benefit from the finished product. It is, in these ways, that the greatest good comes from the selfish pursuit of personal profit.

Adam Smith was also a proponent of the **laissez-faire** (literally, "hands off") system of government nonintervention in business. He indicated that the **"invisible hand" of consumer sovereignty** would regulate the market, in terms of inferior products and overpricing. Consumers would simply cease buying the inferior and/or overpriced items and purchase a competitor's offerings. The market, then, through the **law of supply and demand**, turns private vice into public good. Smith only barely addressed the issue of dishonest producers (price fixing, false advertising, planned obsolescence, etc.) by insisting that "social sympathy" prevents the violation of other's rights.

Socialism is an economic system in which natural resources, as well as the means of production, are collectively owned. Socialists oppose **private property**, which is private ownership of the means of production, such as factories, real estate, etc. Private property is not to be confused with personal property, such as an individual's wardrobe, stereo, etc. Socialists take this position on the grounds that the idea of personal property gives control to individuals who are no more deserving than others within society.

Socialism is a very expensive form of economic system, since it does not reward risk taking and hard work and does not incentivize the building of a practical infrastructure of roads, airports, electronic communications, railroads, food distribution, etc. Marx postulated that socialism can only be practical after an extended period of capitalism, during which a utilitarian infrastructure would have been constructed upon which to build a socialist society. Marx would possibly have "turned over in his grave" to see the Russian revolution, the Cuban, the Chinese, the Nicaraguan, the Chilean, etc., because those were all agrarian societies. Truckloads of Russian wheat rotted in the fields because they could not get to market on the mud-strewn trails, and they did not have the sufficient infrastructure.

Socialism is the most expensive economic system and requires an extensive and advanced infrastructure. It could never be successful in anything less than a well-developed capitalist-built environment. The world has yet to see any **dictatorship of the proletariat**—the self-appointed leaders in socialism—voluntarily stepping down from power, as Marx insisted that they would eventually do. Though it is an enamoring and attractive idealistic goal for many people, the practical aspects of implementing and sustaining socialism for extended periods are unrealistic, including its communistic eschatology. It is a utopian dream. The word **utopia** comes from Greek: οὐ ("not") and τόπος ("place") and literally means "not a place."

The motivation to work in a socialist economy is primarily **altruism**—working to improve the common welfare, as opposed to the pursuit of personal profit. Sociologists Davis and Moore (1945) proposed an idea concerning the motivation to work, widely known as the **Davis–Moore Hypothesis**. They said that since occupations vary in societal importance, differential rewards are necessary in order to motivate people to aspire to important positions. Davis and Moore used the example of a physician, who has to recoup the expenses of medical school and setting up a medical practice, after long years of strenuous training. The physician should be lucratively rewarded in order to induce capable individuals to pursue this important career track. This argument tends to break down somewhat when considering the extremely high rewards society grants to entertainers and sports stars, but some argue that those positions also provide some value to those who pay to enjoy their talents.

Socialists also insist that the **"guiding hand" of government** is necessary to ensure the meeting of the needs of the entire population. These needs include such things as food, shelter, health, transportation, etc.

Much of the world seems to be moving in the general direction of **democratic socialism**. Under democratic socialism, free elections and a capitalistic market economy coexist with governmental efforts to minimize inequality.

Liberalism

"United States Senators Bernie Sanders and Hillary Clinton"

Bernie Sanders, a U.S. Senator from Vermont, labels himself a socialist, but in the contemporary world, many socialists prefer to avoid that label and identify with the term "liberal," instead. **Liberalism** has generally been considered a political philosophy founded upon ideas of liberty and equality, but also open to new ideas and willing to discard traditional values. Today's liberals tend not to agree with Thoreau's (1849) statement, "that government is best which governs least."

Liberals use moralistic platitudes and catchy phrases such as "social justice" to appeal to those who believe that the ultimate goals of liberals are genuinely benign and beneficial for the poor. Like the Prince in Machiavelli's (1513/1985) scheme, however, the principle to which they adhere is the continual accumulation and centralization of power. Liberals often talk about freedom, especially sexual freedom, but not so much of individual freedoms like economic self-reliance, which demand moral responsibility.

Liberals tend to promote **abortion** (the killing of preborn infants) as a necessary policy to guarantee sexual freedom. Could the elimination of guilt and its effect on the moral conscience also be reasons for advocacy of abortion? Liberals tend to disagree with religions or religious persons who believe or teach that there are moral consequences for sin.

Individualism is the view that a person has intrinsic value apart from others, is responsible for her own decisions and success in life, and should be free to pursue her own best interests without undue restrictions from the state. The U.S. Constitution specifically supports individualism, which is evident in the Bill of Rights. The fundamental power struggle of liberals, though, may be framed in terms of **collectivism** as in opposition to individualism. Rand (1944) has stated, "collectivism means the subjugation of the individual to a group .... Collectivism holds that man must be chained to collective action and collective thought for the sake of what is called 'the common good.'"

In order to advance their agendas, liberals at times endeavor to create an atmosphere of crisis and fear that is used to justify their concentration of power in government. For example, the United States' involvements in World War I (Wilson), World War II (Roosevelt), the Korean Conflict (Truman), and the Vietnamese Conflict (Kennedy) were entered into by liberal administrations.

Western nations and civilization have produced an unprecedented level of liberty and prosperity for people. Christianity is the foundation of the culture upon which Western civilization was built. The first universities in the United States were founded as Christian institutions, including Harvard, Yale, and Princeton. A genuinely Christian populace will reject collectivism and support individualism. A genuine Christian people will live moral lives and support governmental policy that encourages individual and personal moral responsibility.

A morally disintegrating population will look to its government for support and sustenance, thus leaning toward a liberal stance. Why is this? Perhaps the reason lies in the reality that in order to be able to impose socialism upon a people, the ability of the people to govern themselves according to moral law must be undermined.

In Chapter 3, we alluded to Marx's 10 measures to implement a socialist state as outlined in *The Communist Manifesto*. The 10th item is "Public and free education of all children." This sounds like a wonderful thing, but it literally means that *all* children *must* have the public education designed by the socialists. There are to be no private, charter, magnet, home-school, or other alternative choices. They oppose school voucher programs, even in inner cities where minority parents seek school choice for the betterment of their children. Recently, in the city of Baltimore, Maryland, there were six high schools in which not even one student tested as "proficient" in math (Papst, 2017). Liberals tend to seek to eliminate any institutions that can weaken the state's power to socialize children. This sort of control extends to public schools, child abuse agencies, health and welfare departments, social service agencies, and all organizations that concern children.

We noted in Chapter 11 that social conflict theorists tend to adopt a negative view of the family. Socialist strategies include discrediting the family as an institution, encouraging promiscuity and easy divorce, and emphasizing the need to raise children away from the negative influence of parents. Many of the media products of Hollywood seem to endanger the innocence of children as early as possible. Some liberals seek to sexualize children, eliminate age of consent laws, and promote the normalization of pedophilia, all in the pursuit of sexual freedom. The liberal nonprofit law firm known as the American Civil Liberties Union (ACLU) defended the North American Man Boy Love Association (NAMBLA) in a 1997 case. NAMBLA advocates for changes in society's views about consensual sex between adults and minors, regardless of how young the children may be. The strategy is to attribute prejudices, mental blocks, and developmental delay of children to the suppressive influence of parents. Strong families are one of the greatest threats to the goals of liberalism. The disintegration of the American family in recent decades has possibly at least partially occurred as a direct result of such policies.

Liberals, in general, oppose the private ownership of firearms, which is often held to be the single greatest symbol of individual power. The first president of the United States, Washington (1790), said, "Firearms stand next in importance to the constitution itself. They are the American people's liberty teeth and keystone under independence. From the hour the Pilgrims landed to the present day, events, occurrences and tendencies prove that to ensure peace, security and happiness, the rifle and pistol are equally indispensable. The very atmosphere of firearms anywhere restrains evil interference. They deserve a place of honor with all that's good."

Social Stratification

Social stratification is the hierarchical arrangement of categories of people in a society. Stratification is **universal**; that is, it exists in every society. Even if all families in a society are at approximately the same level in terms of income and prestige, there will still be some form of stratification based on sex and age. Men may have more social power than women. Adults will probably have more social power than children.

Social stratification is **variable**. The system of social stratification in Bangladesh is different from the system of social stratification in New Guinea.

Another characteristic of stratification is that it tends to persist from one generation to the next. In the United States, sociologists have determined that approximately 65% of men at age 35 occupy roughly the same social positions their fathers occupied when they were at the same age. This means that about 35% of men in the United States have achieved social mobility. An example of **upward mobility** might be a person who was born into a lower class family, but through education and diligence has embarked upon a successful professional career. Such persons are often called **Young Upwardly mobile Professional Persons** (YUPPies). **Downward mobility** could be demonstrated by an individual who had high social status, like a judge, but due to corruption or alcoholism, lost his/her position and is now homeless.

Any particular system of social stratification tends to be supported by patterns of belief. Religions often endorse the *status quo* as the will of the gods. Certain people are thought to have been destined to occupy the higher positions and others to occupy lower positions. There are two major types of system of social stratification:

1. **Caste System**—based almost entirely on ascribed status. Examples:
   a. South Africa until 1994 (**Apartheid**—separation of the races).
   b. India (officially illegal, but widely practiced, particularly in rural areas. Linked to occupation and reincarnation.)
   c. **The Estate System** of Europe during the Middle Ages
      iv. First Estate—Landowner
      v. Second Estate—The priesthood
      vi. Third Estate—The knighthood
      vii. The commoners who work the land
2. **Class System**—somewhat greater potential for social mobility. Examples: Great Britain and the United States (Easterling, 2017).

United States Social Class	Typical Characteristics
Upper class (1%)	Chief executives, celebrities, or inherited wealth; income of $500,000 or more.
Upper middle class (15%)	Well-educated professionals; wide variation of incomes ranging from $82,000 to $499,000.
Lower middle class (34%)	Skilled crafts or experienced preprofessionals; income from $41,000 to $81,000. Often some college credits.
Working class (35%)	Clerical, pink- and blue-collar workers with often low job security; common household incomes range from $28,299 to $40,999. High school education.
Lower class (15%)	Below the Federal Poverty Level for a family of four ($28,290). Low-paying jobs or reliance on government assistance. Some high school education.

Understanding social stratification requires a differentiation between income and wealth. **Income** refers to all the wages, salaries, tips, commissions, receipts from rents and investments, dividends and such that a person receives during the course of a year or other standard period of time. **Wealth** refers to all the money and goods an individual or family owns or controls. Wealth can include real estate, cash, stocks and bonds, inventories, equipment, etc.

In terms of income, the highest one-fifth of the population of the United States receives 49.8% of all the income (Bureau of the Census, 2010). This has been slightly decreasing in recent years, so the statement that the rich are getting richer is not strictly accurate. The bottom one-fifth only receives 3.4% of all the income. This illustrates a great deal of income inequality. Wealth inequality is even greater. In terms of wealth, the highest one-fifth of the population of the United States own 85% of all wealth. The bottom one-fifth own 40% of all the wealth. That is, they have negative wealth—their liabilities are greater than their assets. The top 5% own 50% of all the wealth.

If wealth were in the form of bricks, some Americans would have a pile as high as the Burj Khalifa building in Dubai. The average would be about three feet high, and the poorest would have no bricks at all, only a hole in the ground.

Peterson-Wilthorn (2016) presented the Forbes Magazine 400 wealthiest Americans. The top 20 are listed in the following.

Bill Gates, richest person in the United States.

Rank	Name	Worth ($ Billions)	Source
1	Gates, William H. III	81	Microsoft Corporation
2	Bezos, Jeff	67	Amazon
3	Buffett, Warren Edward	65.5	Berkshire Hathaway
4	Zuckerberg, Mark	55.5	Facebook
5	Ellison, Larry	49.3	Oracle
6	Bloomberg, Michael	45	Bloomberg, LP
7	Koch, Charles	42	Diversified
8	Koch, David	42	Diversified
9	Page, Larry	38.5	Google
10	Brin, Sergey	37.5	Google
11	Walton, Jim	35.6	Wal-Mart
12	Walton, S. Robson	35.5	Wal-Mart
13	Walton, Alice L.	35.4	Wal-Mart
14	Adelson, Sheldon	31.8	Casinos
15	Balmer, Steve	27.5	Microsoft Corporation
16	Mars, Jacqueline	27	Candy
17	Mars, John	27	Candy
18	Knight, Phil	25.5	Nike
19	Soros, George	24.9	Hedge funds
20	Dell, Michael	20	Dell Computers

Information

In general, the term "information" has meant the communication of knowledge or intelligence obtained from investigation, study, or instruction. Information makes one aware of something, such as facts, data, occurrences, or news. It may be oriented to the past, present, or future.

The Information Explosion

Since the 1960s, society has been said to be in the "information age." This refers to the phenomenon of the transformation of the retrieval, storage, and dissemination of information into a major sector of the world's economy. It further refers to the explosion of information becoming available on a daily basis.

The total sum of humankind's knowledge doubled from 1750 to 1900. It doubled again from 1900 to 1950, again from 1950 to 1960, and again from 1960 to 1965. It has been estimated that the total sum of humankind's knowledge has doubled at least once every 5 years since then. It has been further projected that by the year 2020, knowledge will double every 73 days.

Access to Information

Sir Francis Bacon has said, "Knowledge is power." The opportunity for people to participate in economic, political, and cultural life depends upon their ability to access and use information. The fourth U.S. President James Madison said it this way: "Popular government without popular information, or the means of acquiring it, is but a prologue to a farce or tragedy, or perhaps both. Knowledge will forever govern ignorance, and a people who mean to be their own governors must arm themselves with the power which knowledge gives."

Many people fail to obtain the information they need or desire because they do not understand where to search for it, or they do not know whether the information exists, or it is difficult to locate. An important factor in helping people gain access to information is the public or private library. Libraries are no longer simply storage places for books, but places where information can be accessed. If a particular library does not have the information requested, it can usually be found through an "interlibrary loan" or other form of connection with other libraries. Library card catalogs are now available to computers at work, home, or school. This is accomplished by means of telephone connections using a piece of technology called a "modem."

Many efforts to provide information services tend to focus on upper and upper-middle income populations. Few of these activities reach the working and lower classes. New information policies and/or new information institutions may be required to achieve information democracy in the United States.

Classified Information

The United States is fundamentally considered to be an **open society**. This refers to the openness of its borders to citizens who wish to travel abroad and to visitors and immigrants from other countries. It secondarily refers to the widespread availability of information about the affairs of government and all other institutions of society. This is particularly true when the U.S. system is compared with other political systems around the world.

Since World War II, however, there has been a shift in the direction of secrecy. This began with the atom bomb, which was developed in the United States behind tight security precautions. The atom bomb was regarded as a success after its use on the Japanese cities of Hiroshima and Nagasaki because it hastened the end of World War II. Since it was built in secrecy, the experience lent favor among the American public for keeping certain types of information from public access. This idea eventually became an essential focal point of the Cold War era.

Executive privilege is the legal underpinning on which secrecy in the United States government rests. The doctrine of **executive privilege** provides that the president can justify the withholding of information when, in the president's view, the public distribution of the information would jeopardize national security or seriously hamper the ability of the government to fulfill its normal functions. The courts have ruled that executive privilege belongs only to the president and not to any other government official.

There are over 100 statutes enacted by Congress that allow or require government agencies to withhold information from the public. Such protected material includes personnel records of government employees, information on citizens' income tax returns, and the trade secrets of businesses, in the form of patents and copyrights.

There is a classification system in the U.S. government whereby information is given a security stamp and withheld from public disclosure. Officials are to place a secrecy stamp on documents that they consider to be potentially embarrassing to the United States or damaging to national security. In practice, over-caution and self-interest may cause agencies to classify as secret a substantially greater proportion of documents than is truly warranted.

Freedom of Information Act

The **Freedom of Information Act** is a law that requires executive agencies to furnish citizens and other interested parties outside of government with nonclassified information they request from the executive branch. The request may be made by "any person" anywhere in the world. The law provides for penalties to be exacted upon officials who wrongfully withhold requested information.

In 1966, the Freedom of Information Act was first passed in a rather loosely worded form that had relatively little impact. It was strengthened by amendments passed by Congress in 1974 and 1976. These amendments gave teeth to the act, requiring federal officials to provide the information requested or the reason for refusing to do so within 10 working days.

In the **Watergate scandal**, several Republicans working for the reelection of President Richard Milhous Nixon, broke into the hotel headquarters of the Democratic National Committee and stole some important documents. President Nixon subsequently resigned from office, but not until after withholding important evidence, including taped telephone conversations, for several months.

These events provided dramatic proof to the general public that official secrecy can be used to conceal criminal misconduct. Several reform organizations, like Common Cause, began to lobby against entrenched secrecy in American government, and the 1974 and 1976 amendments to the Freedom of Information Act were pushed through Congress.

The law applies to most agencies of the executive branch of the U.S. government, such as the Departments of Energy, Commerce, and the Interior, regulatory agencies, the Federal Trade Commission, the U.S. Postal Service, and the Treasury Department. Private businesses and organizations must also comply if they have entered into a contractual arrangement with the federal government. The legislative and judicial branches of the government are exempt from the law, as are the president's immediate staff.

Documents which are sought for business and commercial purposes are charged a monetary fee by the agencies for the costs involved in searching for and copying the information. This fee may be waived at the discretion of the agency, if the information is judged to benefit the public in some manner. About 60% of requests come from businesses and corporation attorneys. The remaining requests are raised by journalists, consumer groups, and academic institutions.

The Freedom of Information Act has enabled journalists to access information concerning alleged atrocities by United States armed forces in Vietnam and elsewhere, illegal political campaign contributions, details of the Kennedy assassination, etc. However, the legislation includes loopholes. There are nine categories of exceptions, such as "executive privilege," considerations of national security, the unfair revelation of trade secrets, and information that would constitute the invasion of privacy for individuals. The Freedom of Information Act is therefore not as powerful as it appears on the surface.

Information Management Systems

Since not all available information is needed immediately, systems for managing its storage and retrieval have become indispensable. A substantial amount of information can be stored and retrieved by the human brain. The continuing explosion of information becoming available, however, dictates the need for storage and retrieval of information in quantities beyond the capacity of any human brain.

Information management systems have a number of functions, including the collection and organization of information, storage, and retrieval. The conventional method of information management has utilized placing the information on paper, storing it in libraries or other information centers, and retrieving it by hand. In recent decades, however, electronic and mechanical devices have revolutionized the manner in which information is stored and retrieved. Billions of items can be stored and retrieved in powerful systems and made available to users almost immediately.

Management information systems may be cataloged into three major categories (Easterling, 2017):

1. **Systems for direct answers to queries** are generally of limited utility in that they are confined to specific subject areas and for special purposes. The user asks a question, usually by typing on a computer keyboard or using a touch-tone telephone, and the system answers the question by accessing a data base or bibliographic index. The questions have been anticipated by the system designers and some questions may be too general or outside the scope of the system.

2. **Bibliographic reference systems** usually deal with text documents. The documents are indexed according to key words and phrases, titles, subtitles, and abstracts. The user simply makes a query regarding one of the indexed items and is shown basic data concerning all the occurrences of the item in the system. An important key to the efficiency of the system is the indexing, much of which is performed by individual specialists. Electronic indexing technology is now available, but the performance of such technology is highly dependent upon varying levels of sophistication.

3. **Data base systems** store and retrieve basic information on customers, employees, inventories, students, sports data, or any other type of detailed information. A data base can be searched

and manipulated for a variety of purposes. The Internal Revenue Service (IRS), for instance, keeps a massive data base, which includes the names and addresses of taxpayers, along with their tax records and a great deal of other pertinent information. These files are accessible to the IRS at any time and are easily managed to provide information such as the names of all taxpayers within a certain income range or those who are of a particular age.

Information management utilizes computers that store the files and print or display the desired information. Files may be stored in cloud environments, on magnetic disks, cards, or tape strips, microfilm, or CD-ROM disks.

Cloud storage is not what it may seem to many users. Though the user may not have to maintain the storage details, ultimately, the data are on one or several servers somewhere. The cloud is made up of many distributed resources, but still acts as one. There is no secure cloud that is safely locked away, so it is a rich resource for both hackers and national security agencies. Because the cloud holds data from many different users and organizations, hackers see it as a very valuable target. Still, the low cost for external hosting and the swift retrieval and redundancy characteristics make cloud storage attractive for many enterprises. Good encryption practices can help to provide better security.

A very dependable means of storing information is the magnetic disk. Magnetic impulses representing zeroes and ones are ingeniously used to record data on the disk. These two numbers can be combined in a number of ways to represent letters and other numbers, punctuation marks, and a host of graphic images. The information can later be erased when it is no longer of value. A great advantage of magnetic disks is that they provide random access. This means that a specific item can be found instantly without searching through the entire file. Magnetic cards and tape strips give random access to stored data, but they do not tend to be as dependable as magnetic disks. Stacks of magnetic disks afford access to even more information than does a single disk.

An outdated but inexpensive and easily accessible information storage device is microfilm. Microfilm is utilized to record pictures and written text in reduced size. Ninety-eight pages of 8.5 by 11-in. text can be stored on a single 4 by 6-in. sheet of microfilm. Though microfilm provides fairly swift access to information, it cannot be erased and is not compatible with computer applications. It is primarily used to archive data.

The CD-ROM disk is similar to the compact disks used for musical recordings. Information is cataloged as tiny holes representing zeroes and ones which are "burned" into the disk by a laser beam. The data are subsequently read by translating the light from a laser beam that is reflected off the disk inside the computer or CD-ROM drive. A disadvantage of the CD-ROM disk is that it provides read-only memory rather than random access. This means that its information cannot be erased or changed.

Sources of Information

As the quantity of information has "exploded," so has the number of sources of information. A few of these are magazines (trade, professional, general, and specialized), books, newspapers, radio reports, television and cable programs, syndicated studies, newsletters, schools of all kinds, libraries (including the Library of Congress), the Internet, special mailings, the U.S. Government Printing Office, state and local governments, religious organizations, political action committees, experts, consultants, speakers, audio and video tapes, seminars, encyclopedias, dictionaries, atlases, almanacs, academic journals, and the human brain. Among the more significant of these sources are the Library of Congress and the Internet.

The **Library of Congress** was established by and for the U.S. Congress in 1800. Since then, it has extended its services to other government agencies, other libraries, scholars, and to the general public. It contains more than 100 million volumes in 470 languages. The catalog of the Library of Congress is accessible to users of the Internet.

The Internet was initiated during the 1960s as an undertaking of the **Department of Defense's Advanced Research Projects Agency** (DARPA). Electronic message dialog interchange expanded briskly, and the network was periodically renovated with greater speed and capacity. Management of the network shifted from the Advanced Research Projects Agency to the National Science Foundation as the number of civilian users burgeoned. The new network, to which a multiplicity of territorial and special purpose networks were attached, became known as National Science Foundation Network (NSFNET). The total system is known as the **Internet**.

On 4 April 2017, Sir Tim Berners-Lee was awarded the ACM A.M. Turing Award for inventing the World Wide Web in 1989, the first web browser, and the fundamental protocols and algorithms allowing the web to scale.

Participation in the Internet continued to surge, and the urgent necessity of a significant refurbishing of the network and expanded public service objectives were acknowledged by the U.S. Congress. Congress undertook a proactive initiative in the passage of the **High Performance Computing Act** in 1991. This act designated the spending of more than 1 billion dollars over a 5-year duration to immensely boost the speed and capacity of the network. The act also provided for connections to unite public libraries and K-12 schools with the rest of the Internet.

Commercial on-line services offer home-based consumers access to the Internet as well as a host of other information services. Computer-mediated communication, such as electronic mail (e-mail) and electronic bulletin boards, affects the daily lives of their users. America Online and Compuserve were among the better known early providers, although several cable television companies and local telephone companies also offer Internet access to their existing customers. These service companies furnish their subscribers with discussion forums, news, weather, and sports information, stock market reports, and assistance in many other areas. This phenomenon has been called the "Information Superhighway."

There are sources of information for virtually every possible area in which a person might express an interest. Sports information, for example, is readily available on radio and television. The major broadcast networks provide coverage of the Olympic Games. Sports picture cards carry photographs of professional baseball, football, basketball, and hockey players, as well as summarized statistics about individual and team performance records. In addition, every professional team and most universities have a Sports Information Director, whose job is to provide complete information about the team as well as personal information concerning the players, the coaches, and their personalities. Most teams have a "web page" on the Internet containing a great deal of information. Other major sources of sports information include daily newspapers and specialized sports magazines and books.

Information Specialists

There are a number of occupations involved in the collection, storage, retrieval, and dissemination of information. The most obvious of these are librarians, educators, and information scientists. In addition, some persons specialize in law, medicine, sports, or other specialized areas of information. Klanwatch, for example, is an organization in Montgomery, Alabama, which keeps the public informed about the activities of survivalists, militias, skinheads, and the Ku Klux Klan. Greenpeace and Worldwatch are environmentally oriented groups which gather and publish information that enhances society's awareness of environmental, pollution, and population problems.

Career opportunities exist with the **U.S. Census Bureau**, which has the task of gathering and making available demographic and economic information about the population of the United States. **Intelligence agents**, usually employees of the Federal Bureau of Investigation, the Central Intelligence Agency, or one of the branches of the armed forces, travel around the world gathering information about crime, terrorism, or matters of importance to national defense or American business interests. **Journalists** collect and edit material of current interest for presentation through news media. **War correspondents** are journalists who risk their lives to report the results of battles, the condition of troops, and other matters of interest to the general public in a time of war.

Educators teach a wide range of skills and information. One of their most important tasks is to teach students the techniques of obtaining access to desired information.

A **librarian** is a specialist in the care or management of a library, which is a place where books, manuscripts, music, video tapes, or other literary and artistic materials are kept for use but not for sale. Membership in the American Library Association and attainment of a college degree from an institution accredited by the American Library Association are common signs of librarianship but are not required for employment in the occupation.

An **information scientist** is a person who works in the area of information retrieval systems, particularly bibliographic and computerized systems. This individual may also be trained as a librarian, but tends to be specialized, whereas librarians tend to be generalists. There is a separate professional organization for information scientists, the American Society for Information Science.

New Technologies

© Rawpixel.com/Shutterstock.com

Computer video conferencing is making the idea of the "global village" a reality by permitting the interchange of messages among users. A third grade class in Oklahoma can see and communicate directly with a third grade class in Asia, Africa, or Australia. The free and direct exchange of information in such a setting is the wave of the future for families, businesses, and many other categories of users.

Marriage market intermediaries provide formats for bulletin board or video-based dating services on computer networks that enable singles to search for potential marriage partners. They are matched according to preprogrammed criteria and are given opportunities to electronically interact with likely candidates.

Parallel searching and fast text-scanning methods are continuing to speed the information search process. Automatic information storage and retrieval systems equipped with "intelligent" programming aid in medical diagnosis as well as in problems of chemical structure.

Some futurists, in speculating about the technological revolution, have predicted that the old fashioned book, printed on paper and bound with heavier stock, will soon become obsolete. There are several features of the book, however, which indicate that it may continue to have importance for some time. For one thing, book sales tend to fluctuate but are reported to be increasing to all-time highs, despite the proliferation of computers and other high-tech devices, including e-readers, such as Kindle and Nook. The book evolved over many centuries and is a very efficient object. A book may be read at home, in a library, or at the beach. It may be stored on a shelf horizontally or vertically, in a box or trunk, or easily carried. A book can be shipped to a friend or a customer, and makes a treasured gift. It is not particularly fragile and can be repaired and rebound after heavy use or recycled if no longer wanted.

Name _____   Date _____

Chapter 12   The Economy and Social Stratification

Chapter Exercise

(This assignment is to be carefully torn out and completed at the direction of the instructor. The answers are to be legibly handwritten directly on the sheets. *Do not* photocopy these pages, as such action would constitute a blatant violation of the copyright laws of the United States. Thoroughly read the assigned text before attempting to complete a tear-out assignment. It is obvious when a student has tried to fill-in an assignment without reading the background material.)

Do you believe that it is the role of society to provide healthcare, food, and other resources for every citizen? If so, how can these things be paid for in the real world? If not, how would you treat those who may be unable (through disabilities or other tragic circumstances) to care for themselves?

_____

_____

_____

_____

_____

_____

_____

_____

_____

_____

_____

_____

Chapter 13

The Sociology of Health and Medicine

"The health plan will cover you and up to three dwarves."

Health in the United States and Elsewhere

In low-income countries, there is a relatively short life expectancy. Many people pass away before adolescence. These outcomes may be due to poor sanitation, malnutrition, unsafe water, and low numbers of medically trained personnel.

In the United States and higher income countries, death rates from infectious diseases have decreased dramatically. The good news is that most people die of chronic disease in old age. How is that good news? Because the leading causes of death occur at later ages, so this means that people are living longer. **Chronic illnesses** are long-term and the symptoms tend to get worse over time. Chronic conditions are more characteristic of older people. **Acute illnesses** can be severe and have sudden-onset, but are usually short-term and the condition tends to improve over time. Younger people often have acute conditions, but recovery is possible.

The 10 leading causes of death in the United States. (CDC, 2010)

1. Heart disease
2. Cancer
3. Chronic lower respiratory diseases
4. Stroke
5. Unintentional injuries
6. Alzheimer's disease
7. Diabetes
8. Nephritis, nephrotic syndrome, and nephrosis
9. Influenza and pneumonia
10. Suicide

Health in the United States is generally good by world standards. In the United States, more is spent on health care per person than any other nation. Death is now relatively rare among young people. Women tend to be healthier than men across the lifespan. Boys and men are socialized to be aggressive and individualistic. They have higher rates of accidents, violence, and suicide. Those who self-describe as "healthy" tend to have higher income. This could be related to the ability to afford better nutrition, better health care, and live in safer and less stressful surroundings.

One measure used to compare the relative health of various populations is the rate of infant mortality. The **infant mortality rate** (IMR) is the number of deaths of infants under one year old per 1,000 live births. The infant mortality rate of the world is 42.09 (CIA, 2014). The infant mortality rate for Afghanistan is 112.8, but for the United States, it is only 5.8, and for Canada, it is 4.6.

Health-Care Systems

Health care systems are the arrangements within given societies for the provision of health care. **Health care** may be defined as activity directed toward the improvement of human health. **Health** itself has been defined by the United Nations' World Health Organization as not only the absence of disease, but also "a state of physical, mental, and social well-being."

Throughout most of history, health care was considered a responsibility of the family. In more complex societies, however, separate institutions have developed solely for the purpose of providing health care. These institutions revolve around certain occupations, such as physician, nurse, and hospital. Important issues include access to health care, the quality of care, and the rising costs of health care.

Socialized Medicine

Socialized medicine refers to a medical care system in which the government owns and operates most medical facilities and employs most physicians. In Sweden, the government provides comprehensive medical care paid for by very high taxes.

Dual System

A **dual system** is a health-care system in which a national service offers care to everyone, but wealthier citizens often choose to utilize private health-care facilities. This is the case in the United Kingdom.

Single-Payer System

A **single-payer system** is a health-care system in which the government functions somewhat like an insurance company. Some physicians work outside the government-funded system and set their own fees, but costs are regulated by the government. This is the situation in Canada. In 1978, Saskatchewan began a program of publicly-funded health care for all citizens of the province. Services were cost-free to the patients and included nursing home and other long-term care. Since then, all the Canadian provinces have enacted their own free-to-the-public health-care systems. Every Canadian now has, therefore, government-funded access to hospitalization and physician services.

The Canadian federal government pays one third and each province pays two third of the costs of health care in Canada. In the strictest sense, the Canadian system is not a case of socialized medicine, since physicians operate privately, rather than as government employees, as in Great Britain. Furthermore, they are allowed to work entirely outside the government-funded system, charging whatever fees they desire to patients willing to utilize their services privately.

Canada is one of the few countries that has held the cost of all health care to a constant proportion of the Gross National Product. Per capita health-care costs in Canada are only half those in the United States, even though most hospitals are privately owned and most physicians are in independent private practice. Only 1.5% is spent on administrative costs, making the Canadian system possibly the most efficient in the world.

The major emphasis in Canada is upon general practitioners (family practice) rather than specialists. There are twice as many general practitioners per capita in Canada than in the United States. The extreme northern areas of Canada are served by nurses who are very well trained. They are quick to refer serious problems to regular physicians. In addition to providing competent care, this "nurse-practitioner" system is an effective means of extending the reach of the formally trained physicians.

Direct-Fee System

A **direct-fee system** is a system in which patients pay directly for the services of physicians and hospitals. The United States is an example of a direct-fee system. The Affordable Care Act of 2010 implemented elements of socialized medicine. The system is essentially a private, profit-making industry in which patients pay directly for services provided by physicians and hospitals, with various insurance plans making up the difference.

Several sociological studies have shown that poor Americans have less access to health care than do other Americans. The result is that wealthier Americans enjoy better physical, mental, and emotional health than do those without abundant financial resources or insurance. This pattern remains evident throughout the life cycle. Nevertheless, health care is available to all Americans through indigent care and several other social mechanisms.

The **Social Security Act of 1965** proposed amendments that put into effect a program of hospital insurance for persons aged 65 and older and a supplementary medical insurance program to aid the elderly in paying health-care bills. **Medicare** pays a portion of medical costs for people aged 65 or over (15% of the total population). First was **Medicare Part A**. Part A is hospital insurance for the elderly, financed by Social Security payroll taxes. This provision pays approximately 80% of many major hospital expenses for the aged.

Second was **Medicare Part B**. Part B is supplementary medical insurance for the aged to help pay for 80% of physician care. Prescription drugs are not covered. The elderly beneficiary pays premiums for Medicare Part B.

The third part of the 1965 Act was called **Medicaid**, designed to pay for health care for the elderly poor and other low-income people. Medicaid is jointly financed by each of the 50 states and matching federal revenues. There are differences in the ways in which various states administer Medicaid because it is administered by each of the states to their own welfare recipient groups. This generally includes those with incomes below the "poverty level." In 2017, the official poverty level for a family of four was $28,290 annual income. Medicaid pays benefits for 20% of the total population.

Health maintenance organizations (HMOs) are organizations that provide comprehensive medical care to subscribers for a fixed fee. The costs and benefits vary.

In the United States, most Americans have traditionally opposed government intervention into the economy and into matters presumed to be personal, such as health. There is strong resistance to the idea that society is responsible for meeting basic human needs in health, income, housing, or welfare. Despite this situation, the U.S. Congress passed the **Affordable Care Act** (ACA, also known popularly as "Obamacare") in 2010. The bill itself was 2,700 pages and with all the accompanying regulations, it was a massive document of approximately 20,000 pages. Speaker of the House of Representatives Nancy

Pelosi made the astounding statement to the Representatives before the vote, "We have to pass the bill so that you can find out what's in it." The ACA made significant changes to the U.S. health-care system. Those elements that are most often publicized are the following:

1. All families must pay an insurance tax (this is why the U.S. Supreme Court has characterized the ACA as a "tax").
2. Customers cannot be dropped due to illness or preexisting conditions.
3. Caps on lifetime expenses cannot be set.
4. Parents have to use family health-care plan until child is 26.
5. Coverage refusal due to preexisting conditions cannot be made (this element of the ACA began in 2014).
6. Insurance coverage will be required for everyone with penalties for noncompliance.

By 1960, the United States had become the world's leading country with regard to research in the biomedical sciences and by 1970, the **National Institutes of Health** had the world's largest and most diversified concentration of biomedical investigators. Among all the nations of the world, the United States is definitely the leader in this area. It has many more research centers with established standards of excellence and more research dollars with which to work.

The dollar cost of medical care in the United States has increased faster than inflation. The health-care system accounts for more than one tenth of the Gross National Product, which is approximately $17 trillion. As of 2017, there were six states where physician-assisted suicide is legalized and 12 others with legislative proposals for it. Insurance companies would greatly prefer the issuance of death-inducing pills rather than to pay for sometimes costly life-saving measures.

Malpractice insurance is a type of liability insurance purchased by health-care practitioners to protect against lawsuits for accusations of misdiagnosis, mistreatment, or other errors. It is a major factor in medical costs in the United States, because Americans are more likely to file lawsuits than are residents of many other countries.

Hospitals in the United States also spend billions of dollars on advertising and offer many **amenities**— creature comforts to effect convenience and pleasure. Such amenities add to spiraling health-care costs. For example, some childbirth hospital wards offer (for an extra fee, of course) recessed lighting, soft colors and comfortable birthing beds, full-sized tubs, refrigerators stocked with juice and bottled water, flat-screen TV and WiFi, deluxe food service for two (with vegan and veggie meals), complimentary hotel-style robes, hair stylists, manicures and pedicures, personal parking and a **doula** (a personal assistant to help the mother and family before and during childbirth, and/or postpartum).

Social Epidemiology

Social epidemiology is the study of the distribution of disease or relative health in a society's population. An **epidemic** is a spreading of disease—usually fairly quickly—within a specific geographic area. The **Bubonic Plague**, also known as the "Black Death," stretched from 1340 to 1750 AD, and killed around 50% of the European population. About 650 cases are still reported each year, primarily in Africa, but few cases have recently occurred in Colorado and New Mexico.

Sir Percival Pott investigated an outbreak of cancer of the scrotum among young chimney sweeps in 1775. In animal experiments, he discovered that soot was a carcinogen (cancer-causing agent). The solution was frequent washing, changing clothing, and requiring a higher age before a child could become an apprentice in the trade.

Similarly, **John Snow** discovered that a cholera epidemic in London was related to water contaminated by sewage. In 1854, he prevailed on authorities to shut down a particular water pump at Broad Street and the epidemic withered away.

Louis Pasteur did not invent the **germ theory of disease**, but his work verified its explanatory power in terms of the causes of some diseases. The theory states

© Belish/Shutterstock.com

Louis Pasteur is responsible for Pasteurization, a process that kills microbes in food and drink, such as milk, juice, canned food.

that many diseases are caused by microorganisms (popularly called "germs"). Germs are too tiny to be seen with the naked eye. The theory goes that germs enter into humans, animals, or plants and their growth and reproduction can cause or transmit disease. **Pathogenic** (disease-causing) microorganisms may be viruses, bacteria, fungi, or the like, and the diseases they cause are called infectious diseases.

The germ theory is essentially universally accepted, but there are criticisms. Germs are literally everywhere, and therefore cannot be determined to be the "cause" of disease unless there is also an explanation for those who did *not* contract disease in their presence. Germs should therefore be considered as only one necessary component of many diseases. Sociologists tend to emphasize the importance other factors in addition to the presence of pathogenic microorganisms. For instance, social inequality affects people's health. Some of those intervening variables might include

1. Socioeconomic status
2. Nutrition
3. Heredity
4. Environmental factors
5. Individual immunity traits
6. Cultural practices
7. Public health efforts
8. Lifestyle patterns

Acquired immune deficiency syndrome (AIDS) is a condition caused by infection with the **Human immunodeficiency virus** (HIV). HIV/AIDS is considered a **pandemic**—an outbreak of sickness that continues to spread over a large territory. Often, the person infected with this virus has no symptoms or possibly cold or flu-like symptoms that are not alarming. As the infection progresses, though, it begins to interfere more with the person's immune system. This exposes the individual to enhanced risk of serious infections such as tuberculosis. The later symptoms are called AIDS and very often lead to death if untreated.

HIV is spread primarily by unprotected homosexual or heterosexual sex (including anal and oral sex), contaminated blood transfusions, hypodermic drug, or other needles, and from mother to child during pregnancy, delivery, or breastfeeding. In much of the world, it is related to homosexual activity, but in Africa, it is largely heterosexually transmitted. There is no known cure or vaccine other than supernatural intervention by God. Antiretroviral treatment can slow the course of the disease and some people receiving such treatment seem to enjoy a fairly long life expectancy. Without treatment, an average AIDS victim lives about 11 years. AIDS has been responsible at least

40 million deaths around the world. HIV/AIDS is considered a pandemic—a disease outbreak which is present over a large area and is actively spreading.

Ebola is a hemorrhagic fever caused by specific viruses. Victims tend to begin to bleed both internally and externally, and there is a high incidence of death, with approximately 50% of victims dying of the disease within 16 days. The virus spreads by direct contact with body fluids, such as blood. There have been over 15,000 confirmed deaths in all countries, primarily Ghana and Sierra Leone.

The **Zika virus** is spread by particular mosquitoes (daytime-active Aedes mosquitoes). Its name comes from the Zika Forest of Uganda, where the virus was first isolated in 1947. Zika virus is related to the dengue, yellow fever, Japanese encephalitis, and West Nile viruses. As of 2017, it cannot be prevented by medications or vaccines. The most fearful characteristic is that Zika can spread from a pregnant woman to her baby. This can result in microcephaly, in which the infant's head is very small and often the brain does not develop properly. It can also result in other birth defects. Many nations have issued warnings, cautioning pregnant women against travel to countries with high Zika incidence and even advising women not to become pregnant until further research can be conducted.

Medical Technology

Society shapes health in major ways. There is a great deal of contrast in patterns of health in low-income and higher income countries. Ethnicity, class, gender, and age are linked to health.

Cultural standards of health change over time.

A society's technology affects people's health. **Technology** is the application of knowledge to solve practical problems in the physical world. **Medical technology** is the application of knowledge in the form of tools, medicine, and practices to solve problems related to health and disease. Since the fifteenth century, there have been three major breakthroughs in dealing with diseases:

1. Sanitation (sewers, septic systems, and the availability of clean water)
2. Anesthetics for surgical procedures
3. Inoculations

More recently, there are three major developments happening all at once:

1. The Human Genome Project and its usage
2. Organ transplants without the body's rejection of the new material
3. Successful cancer research

Name _____   Date _____

The Sociology of Health and Medicine

Chapter Exercise

(This assignment is to be carefully torn out and completed at the direction of the instructor. The answers are to be legibly handwritten directly on the sheets. *Do not* photocopy these pages, as such action would constitute a blatant violation of the copyright laws of the United States of America. Thoroughly read the assigned text before attempting to complete a tear-out assignment. It is obvious when a student has tried to fill-in an assignment without reading the background material.)

Answer the following based upon your readings. In your own opinion, what would be the ideal health-care system for your country?

_____

_____

_____

_____

_____

_____

_____

_____

_____

_____

_____

_____

_____

_____

_____

Chapter 14

The Sociology of Religion

Religion

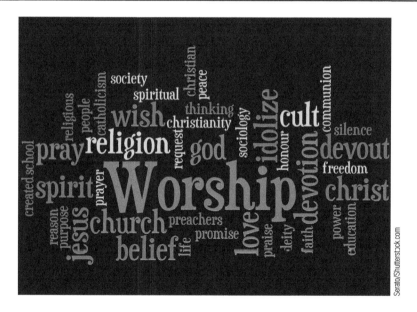

Serato/Shutterstock.com

Religion has been defined by Durkheim as a system of beliefs and practices built upon the recognition of the sacred. The **profane** includes all the ordinary elements of everyday life. The **sacred**, on the other hand, which is defined as extraordinary, inspiring a sense of awe, reverence, or even fear. A totem is an object, usually an element of the natural world, that is imbued with sacred qualities.

According to structural functionalism, the major **functions of religion** include the following:

1. Social cohesion—the members of the religious group tend to be unified around their beliefs.

2. Social control—most religions tend to support the laws of the land.
3. Meaning and purpose—religion helps explain the meaning of life, death, and existence, itself.

These functions are especially important during particular circumstances, such as the following:

1. When discrepancies exist between the society's ideal practices and its actual practices, such as a widespread breakdown of morality. This is where the society needs the church to fulfill a prophetic function.
2. In the face of personal suffering or death.
3. During group crises of leadership failure, war, conquest, or natural disasters.

Marx referred to religion as "the opiate of the masses." An opiate is a derivative of opium, a narcotic, which gives the individual a false sense of euphoria. His use of this famous phrase means that Marx thought that religion causes people to think primarily about the joys of life after death rather than about how to improve society.

Contrary to Marx' derogatory attitude toward it and unfounded statements about it, religion has actually been a major factor in positive social change in many situations. The **abolitionist movement** was a largely Christian effort to end slavery. The **Civil Rights movement** was an essentially Christian crusade, as well. It was a cluster of strategies and groups in the United States during the 1950s and 1960s with the overarching goal of bringing to an end racial segregation and discrimination against African Americans. The idea of **liberation theology**, though misused by socialists and communists, is based upon the obedience of Moses to go to Pharaoh and demand that he let God's people go free.

German sociologist Ernst Troeltsch popularized the idea of the **church/sect continuum**. By continuum is meant that a given organization may not be completely within any one category, such as the denomination or the sect. The **denomination** (what Troeltsch called "the church") tends to be well integrated into the larger society. Its clergies are generally formally trained and work full time in the ministry. A **sect** does not tend to be well integrated into the larger society, has informal worship styles, and part-time or lay ministers. An **ecclesia** is always formally allied with the state, e.g., the Church of England. A **cult** has little or nothing in common with other religious organizations in the society. Examples include Scientology, the Unification Church, the World Mission Society Church of God, and "Heaven's Gate."

Variation in Religious Beliefs

There are thousands of religious organizations around the world. The six largest are outlined below.

Christianity

Christianity is the world's largest religion with approximately 2.2 billion adherents in 2015. It began as a Middle Eastern sect with its roots in Judaism. Christianity is **monotheistic** (belief in one true God), not **polytheistic** (belief in many gods).

Some people think that Christianity is polytheistic because of the Trinity. The **Trinity** refers to the fact that God has three expressions, the Father, the Son, and the Holy Ghost.

Christianity is based on belief in the divinity of Jesus, which he died on a cross for the sins of humankind, and rose from the dead. It became an ecclesia in the fourth century AD. A major division occurred in the eleventh century between the Roman Catholic and the Orthodox Churches. Another division occurred during the **Protestant Reformation**, which was a revolt against perceived excesses and abuses of the Catholic Church. A time line of the Reformation follows:

✦ 1517—Albert of Brandenburg, archbishop of Mainz, sponsored a sale of indulgences to pay for, among other things, construction of Saint Peter's Basilica in Rome. In response, Martin Luther, an Augustinian monk, posted his 95 theses on the door of the castle chapel in Wittenburg, Germany, where Luther was a university professor. The theses invited debate over the legitimacy of the sale of **indulgences** (an ancient practice, later discontinued, involving the forgiveness of sins in exchange for a payment of money to the Catholic Church). Copies of the theses spread rapidly over Europe. The papacy took steps against Luther as a heretic, but the University of Wittenburg faculty supported Luther.

✦ 1520—Luther published his three famous treatises: "An Open Letter to the Christian Nobility of the German National Concerning the Reform of the Christian Estate," "The Babylonian Captivity of the Church," and "On the Freedom of a Christian." He won powerful support.

✦ 1521—Luther was **excommunicated**. This means that he was banished from the Catholic Church and could no longer receive the sacraments through the Church. He refused to recant unless proven wrong by the Bible or by "clear reason."

✦ 1530—Many German princes and cities signed the Augsburg Confession as an expression of the evangelical faith.

✦ 1555—The Peace of Augsburg provided that each German prince could determine the religious affiliation of the territory he ruled. The Protestant Reformation swept over Northern and Eastern Europe.

Christianity is perhaps best characterized by the **Gospel** (good news) message. The Gospel actually begins with a bit of bad news, the fact that everyone has sinned. The Bible says, "For all have sinned, and come short of the glory of God" (Romans 3:23). All the best church members have sinned at some time in their lives. If you are honest, you will admit that you have sinned, right?

In fact, the Bible says that if anyone says that she has not sinned, she is a liar (I John 1:10).

"There is none righteous, no not one" (Romans 3: 10). "All we like sheep have gone astray; we have turned every one unto his own way" (Isaiah 53:6). Many people are "lost" like stray sheep. To be "lost" means you don't know the way. Have you strayed from God's way and tried to live life your own way?

"The wages of sin is death; but the gift of God is eternal life through Jesus Christ our Lord" (Romans 6:23). The wages, or result, of sin is death. This means **spiritual death**, or separation from God. That may not sound very bad, but realize this: spiritual death leads to **Hell**, which is an everlasting Lake of Fire. Revelation 20:15 says, "And whosoever was not found written in the Book of Life was cast into the Lake of Fire."

That may sound scary, but do not worry. I have good news for you. Even though you have sinned, you do not have to go to Hell. The free gift of God is eternal life through Jesus Christ our Lord. Eternal life means living in **Heaven** (the abode of God) forever and also having a life of love, joy, peace, and abundance while you are still here in this life. Does it sound too good to be true? Many people have missed it because it is so easy.

Jesus said, "Behold, I stand at the door and knock: if anyone hear My voice and open the door, I will come into him, and sup with him, and he with Me." (Revelation 3:20). Jesus is knocking at the door of your heart. If you will simply open the door of your heart by asking him to come in, He will. He will come into your heart and life to dwell in you and make you a new creature. You will be on the road to Heaven. You will have eternal life.

You are strongly advised to turn away from your sin today and pray this prayer:

> *Father-God, I have sinned. I am sorry for my sins. Please forgive me. I open my heart by faith right now and ask Jesus Christ to come into my heart and live in me. Thank You for saving and forgiving me. I promise that I will live my life for You as You teach me Your ways. In Jesus' name, amen.*

If you refused this offer of the free gift of eternal life through Christ Jesus, the Lord, please read on. An **extraterrestrial being** (ET) from another planet has visited me. "It" asked permission to live in me.

"It" is not parasitic, but prefers to live in human beings. "It" sees through my eyes and hears through my ears. The ET thinks independently of my thoughts, although "It" can read my thoughts.

This ET communicates with dolphins and whales and other beings. I actually have found references to "It" in ancient Earth writings.

The planet from which this ET has come is known as Planet Heaven. The Being's name is Jesus Christ.

The ET has given me a "spirit guide." This spirit guide acts as a sort of spiritual gyroscope that keeps me honed in on the correct pathway of life leading to my next evolutionary leap, which will be two-fold:

1. A body which can walk through walls and will never grow hungry or cold, known as "The Glorified Body."
2. A mind which understands the most far-reaching and intricate workings of the universe, known as "The Mind of Christ."

The spirit guide is known as "The Holy Ghost." The ET is coming to Planet Earth in the near future to take me and all who believe on Him on a Star Trek to Planet Heaven. The liftoff will be known as "The Rapture of the Church." "Then the Lord Himself shall descend from Heaven with a shout, with the voice of the Archangel, and with the trumpet of God: and the dead in Christ shall rise first: Then we which remain shall be caught up together with them in the clouds, to meet the Lord in the air: and so shall we ever be with the Lord (I Thessalonians 4: 16-17)."

Lewis (1946) quoted the words of G. K. Chesterton, who said, "Hell is a monument to human freedom." There are literally thousands of "How To" books available these days. This section deals with the subject of how to avoid Heaven. It will tell you how to get into the Lake of Fire and burn forever.

You definitely have a choice. Here is a word of encouragement: you can go to Hell. Yes, can do it! You have probably heard quoted the words of Edison (1932), "Genius is only one percent inspiration and 99 percent perspiration." But that is not the way it is with going to Hell. It is really very simple and requires little or no effort at all. Adolf Hitler worked very hard to get there, but he did not have to.

There are a few barriers to overcome. If you are serious about going to a place of eternal torment where you will suffer in utter loneliness, you must at any cost avoid exposure to the Gospel of Jesus Christ. When you hear a preacher on the radio, turn her off. Never watch Christian programming on TV. Never attend a Bible-believing Church or Sunday school. Never read the Bible, God's Holy Word. Any of these may cause you to change your mind about wanting to be tortured and fried throughout eternity. The only way to get to heaven is by receiving Jesus Christ as your Savior and Lord. An ancient book, which even Satan herself believes, says, "The wages of sin is death but the gift of God is eternal life through Jesus Christ our Lord." Therefore, the only way you can ever get to Hell, where there is much weeping and wailing and gnashing of teeth because of intense pain and suffering, is by refusing God's free gift of eternal life through Jesus Christ.

If you never want to see any of your family or friends again and you want to be in outer darkness and in the presence of evil demons, refuse to invite Jesus Christ into your life. He said, "Behold, I stand at the door and knock; if anyone hears my voice and opens the door of his heart, I will come into him, and have fellowship with him, and he with Me (Revelation 3:20)."

I have plainly and clearly told you how to go to Hell, where the fire is not quenched and the worm dieth not. Here is my advice, however, believe on the Lord Jesus Christ and be saved today. I would not wait another five seconds. Get on the road to Heaven.

Pray this prayer:

"Father-God, I know that I am a sinner and cannot save myself. By faith, I gratefully receive Your gift of salvation. I invite the Lord Jesus Christ to come into my heart and life. Thank You for Your death on the cross for my sins. In Jesus' name, amen."

One of the more common neuroses today is that of the Christian who is sooooo worried about being "in God's perfect will." This person prays earnestly for God to "reveal" to her her purpose in life—her ministry, her spiritual gifts, where she should be, what her major and minor should be, ad infinitum. Of course, this is admirable, but for many, it becomes a hand-wringing, nail-biting source of anxiety and consternation.

Chill out. Suppose for just a moment that you are in the unenviable, tragic, and shameful circumstance of not being where you should be right now. You dirty dog! How dare you heap shame and dishonor upon the name of Christ and His holy Church. You should be stoned. We should be wagging our fingers at you, humiliating you for your utter failure as a child of God, as a Christian, and yes!—even as a pretender at being a decent human being! You are a fake, a failure, and a contributing factor in the pathetic demise of Christendom and civilization as it has been known here-to-fore.

Now let us further suppose the dire results of your wrong placement on this planet. Suppose you are tithing from the wrong paycheck. Receiving divine revelation from the wrong translation of the Bible. Testifying of the saving grace of Jesus Christ to the wrong people! Getting the wrong people healed, delivered, set free, and baptized in the Holy Ghost through the power of Christ. Praying through with the prayer of faith in long hours of sweet fellowship with God in intercessory prayer in the wrong prayer closet! Fellowshipping in precious Koinonia with the wrong saints! Lifting up the weary hands of the wrong discouraged pastor. Bringing reconciliation into the wrong broken families. Assisting the wrong widows and orphans, homeless, lonely, destitute, and hungry. Tearing down the wrong walls of bondage. Wrestling against the wrong spiritual wickedness in high places. Casting out the wrong demons. Overcoming the wrong temptations. Receiving the wrong blessings of god on your life and ministry. Walking in divine favor with God and the wrong people. Equally yoked together with the wrong believer in a Godly marriage relationship characterized by romance, trust, respect, friendship, and commitment. Training up the WRONG CHILDREN in the way they should go and in the nurture and admonition of the Lord.

If you find yourself in such a despicable and miserable position, don't worry too much; don't you suppose that God will forgive you? It is more important to be who and what God wants you—and all Christians—to be than where He wants you to be. In Acts chapter 8, verse 40, Philip was who God wanted him to be, doing what God wanted him to do, so God transported him from the Ethiopian eunuch to Azotus.

What does Scripture say? "The steps of a neurotic person who is worried about being in the right place at the right time are ordered of the Lord?" No, "the steps of a good person are ordered of the Lord." "He leadeth me in the paths of neurosis, confusion, and quandary about being in the right place at the right time for His Name's sake?" No, "He leadeth me in the paths of righteousness for His Name's sake."

Be a Christian—pray, give, forgive, witness, study your Bible, be sweet, loving, gentle, kind, and competent—wherever you are. "There is therefore now no condemnation to those who are in Christ Jesus (Romans 8:1)." That, after all, is where you should be: in Christ Jesus, seated with Christ in the Heavenliness.

Islam

Crystal mosque with moon and star in
Kuala Terengganu, Malaysia.

Islam is the second largest religion in the world. It has 1.6 billion adherents. By some accounts, it is the fastest growing religion. It is the dominant religion in the Middle East, in North Africa, and in Indonesia.

Islam is based on the life of Muhammad during the seventh century AD. The religion itself is called **Islam**. The correct term for an adherent is **Muslim**, and the word **Moslem** should be used only as an adjective.

The sacred book of Islam is the **Koran**. It contains many references to the Old Testament. The basic precept is that all people should submit to the will of **Allah**, the one true god, according to Islam.

There are two major divisions of Islam. The **Shi'ite** (pronounced "she-ite") branch claims that its priesthood is composed of the direct descendants of Muhammad and Fatima. Shi'ite Islam is the ecclesia of Iran. The **Sunni** (pronounced "sue knee") branch is much larger. Both types of Islam tend to be very patriarchal toward women and emphasize an obligation to defend the faith against unbelievers.

Hinduism

Hinduism is the third largest religion in the world, with about 1 billion adherents. It is said to be the oldest of the major religions and is the primary religion in India. **Hinduism** includes the worship of many gods and the belief that after one dies, he/she will return to life in a different form. Most Hindus live in India. Hinduism is strongly linked to Indian culture, which has hindered its diffusion to other parts of the world. It is not linked to the life of any individual, such as Jesus or Muhammad.

The beliefs and practices of Hinduism are highly variable. There are, however, several shared concepts:

1. **Dharma**: responsibility within a moral universe
2. **Karma**: belief in the progress of each person's soul
3. **Reincarnation**: a type of rebirth which recurs each time the individual dies
4. **Nirvana**: a utopian state in which rebirth becomes no longer necessary

Buddhism

Buddhism has around 500 million adherents, mostly in Asia. It emerged in India. **Buddhism** resembles Hinduism in many ways, but its origin can be found in the life of an individual, Siddhārtha Gautama, who was born in 563

BC in a high-caste Indian family. He taught that his life of meditation and travel led him to Bodhi (enlightenment), which is available to anyone who pursues it. He subsequently became known as the "Buddha."

The beliefs of Buddhism are based almost entirely on the teachings of the Buddha. These teachings are called **The Dhamma**. They include

1. All existence is **suffering** (joy is fruitless).
2. **Vegetarianism** (for many Buddhists).
3. **Materialism** is a barrier to development.
4. **Reincarnation** until full enlightenment has been attained.
5. **Karma**—All acts have spiritual consequences, even the killing of an insect.
6. **Nirvana**—In Buddhism, an enlightened state in which the fires of greed, hatred, and ignorance have been quenched. The ethic that leads to Nirvana involves cultivating loving-kindness, compassion, and sympathy.

Confucianism

Estimates of the number of followers of **Confucianism** from 6 million to over 350 million, depending upon whether one means "dedicated followers" or those who adhere to elements of Confucianism as "traditional Chinese religion." It was an ecclesia in China from 200 BC until the early twentieth century, when the patriarchal family was criticized. The Communist revolution of 1949 forbade Confucianism as reactionary and old fashioned. It has managed to survive in a weakened form through the centuries.

Confucianism was founded by a man named **K'ungFu-tzu** in 520 BC. It has been characterized as being more like a philosophy than a religion. It emphasizes concern for suffering and social problems. Personal salvation can be attained by moral behavior. Confucianism is closely entwined with Chinese culture and has not been spread very widely throughout the world.

A major feature of Confucianism is called "Jen," roughly translated into English as "humaneness." A few tenets of Jen are as follows:

1. Strong group conformity ethic
2. Family loyalty
3. Devotion to studying the past
4. Little emphasis upon the "sacred"

Judaism

The Western wall or Wailing wall is the holiest place to Judaism in the old city of Jerusalem, Israel.

Judaism claims about 15 million adherents worldwide. The majority lives in North America. The remainder are in Europe and the Middle East. **Judaism** emphasizes the importance of certain Hebrew patriarchs, such as Abraham, Jacob, Moses, David, Solomon, and the Old Testament prophets. The Jews have suffered slavery under the Egyptians and others. Central to Judaism is the belief that a transcendent God created the universe and continues providentially to govern it. The same God who created the world revealed Himself to the Israelites at Mount Sinai. The content of that revelation is the **Torah** (revealed instruction), God's will for humankind expressed in commandments. The Torah is read liturgically each **Sabbath**, the seventh day of the week, which is spent in prayer, rest, and family feasting. In the course of a year, the entire Torah will be read on Sabbath and festival days. The Jewish year includes five major festivals—Passover, Rosh Hashanah, Shebuoth, Sukkot, and Yom Kippur; and two minor festivals—Hanukkah and Purim.

A second major concept in Judaism is that of the **Covenant**, or contract-like agreement between god and the Jewish people. They would acknowledge God, agreeing to obey His laws; God, in turn, would acknowledge Israel as his particular people.

There are three major divisions with Judaism:

1. The orientation of **Reform** Judaism is general liberal and nonauthoritarian.
2. The **Conservative** movement respects traditional Jewish law and practice while advocating a flexible approach.
3. **Orthodox** Judaism tends to be extremely traditionalist.

Antisemitism refers to prejudice and/or discrimination against Jews. The **Holocaust** was almost the complete destruction of European Jews by Nazi Germany. When the Nazi regime came to power in Germany in 1933, it began to take systematic measures against Jews. The Nazi party, government agencies, banks, and business enterprises made concerted efforts to eliminate Jews from economic life, and from German life in general.

In 1938, following the assassination of a German diplomat in Paris by a young Jew, all **synagogues** (Jewish places of worship) in Germany were set on fire, windows of Jewish shops were smashed, and thousands of Jews were arrested. Auschwitz, near Krakow, Poland, was the location of the largest Nazi concentration camp, with inmates from all over Europe. Many Jewish and nonJewish inmates performed industrial labor. The Nazis subjected some prisoners to medical experiments and gassed Jews and Gypsies. They also shot thousands of inmates, while others died from starvation or disease. Large crematories were constructed to incinerate bodies. By the end of the war, in 1945, millions of Jews—as well as Slavs, Gypsies, homosexuals, Jehovah's Witnesses, communists, and others targeted by the Nazis—had been killed or had died in the Holocaust.

Name _____   Date _____

Chapter 14   The Sociology of Religion

Chapter Exercise

(This assignment is to be carefully torn out and completed at the direction of the instructor. The answers are to be legibly handwritten directly on the sheets. *Do not* photocopy these pages, as such action would constitute a blatant violation of the copyright laws of the United States. Thoroughly read the assigned text before attempting to complete a tear-out assignment. It is obvious when a student has tried to fill-in an assignment without reading the background material.)

The Bible makes the outright claim that Jesus Christ is the only way to Heaven. How would you explain this in terms that would be as nonconfrontational to other religions as possible?

_____

_____

_____

_____

_____

_____

_____

_____

_____

_____

_____

_____

_____

_____

Chapter 15

Demography

Demographics, The United States

Demography (or demographics) is a branch of sociology, which explains the quantitative aspects of human populations. It uses birth and death rates and other statistics to characterize a population. In the United States, the **Bureau of the Census** is the fact-gathering agency of the government. The census has been conducted once every 10 years since 1790, when the population was 3,929,000 (Easterling, 1999).

The United States is the third most populous nation in the world with a 2010 population of 308,745,538, 51% of which are female and 49% are male (Bureau of the Census, 2010). In comparison, China has the largest population, with 1,373,541,278 people, followed by India with a population of 1,266,883,598.

Vital Statistics

The **birth rate** in the United States is 12.4 births per 1,000 population per year (Bureau of the Census, 2010). This figure is higher than in Western Europe and Canada, but the lowest it has ever been in U.S. history. The U.S. birth rate in 1990 was 15.48.

The **mortality rate** (death rate) is 8.2 deaths per 1,000 population per year, about the same as in other industrialized nations. These factors combine with the **net migration rate** (15.94 immigrants per 1,000 population per year) to produce a **population growth rate** for the United States of 0.8% per year (Bureau of the Census, 2010).

The average U.S. resident can expect to live from birth to age 78.8. The **life expectancy** for males is 76.2 and females can expect a life that is 81.2 years. The average age for Americans is 37.8 years. Age of about 22.9% are under 18 and 13% are 65 or over (Bureau of the Census, 2010).

The U.S. **infant mortality rate** is 5.8 infant deaths per 1,000 live births per year (Bureau of the Census, 2010). This figure is favorable in comparison to third world countries and is down from 8.36 in 1990. The infant mortality rate for Afghanistan is 112.8 and for Canada, it is 4.6.

Native Americans

A prehistoric Native American rock carving in Albuquerque, New Mexico.

The U.S. population is composed of many racial and ethnic groups. Native Americans make up 0.8% of the population of the United States. They include American Indians and Alaska Natives. According to the 2010 Census, 5.2 million people in the United States were identified as American Indians and Alaska Natives, either alone or in combination with one or more other races. Out of this total, 2.9 million people were identified as American Indians and Alaska Natives (Bureau of the Census, 2010). About half of the 2.9 million Native Americans live on or near reservations. There are 300 such reservations located primarily in South Dakota, New Mexico, Arizona, Utah, Washington, and Montana. Those who live outside the reservation sites reside primarily in urban areas of the western and central states. The largest concentration of Native Americans in an urban area is in Tulsa, Oklahoma (Easterling, 1999).

Largest Native American Groups

Tribe/Nation	Population 2010
Navajo	308,013
Cherokee	285,476
Sioux	131,048
Chippewa	115,859
Choctaw	88,913
Lumbee	66,872
Apache	64,869
Pueblo	59,337
Inupiat (Inuit)	57,137
Iroquois	48,365
Creek	44,085

Source: Bureau of the Census (2010).

Alaska's indigenous people, who are categorized by the federal government as "Alaska Natives," can be divided into five major groupings, based largely on their spoken languages: Aleuts, Northern Eskimos (Inuit), Southern Eskimos (Yuit), Interior Indians (Athabascans), and Southeast Coastal Indians (Tlingit and Haida). **Eskimos** are racially distinct from American Indians and are most closely related to the Mongolian peoples of eastern Asia. Eskimos consider themselves to be "Inuit" (The People).

African Americans

African Americans (non-Hispanic blacks), most of whom are descendants of slaves, comprise 12.1% of the U.S. population, or 37,144,530 (Bureau of the Census, 2010). More than half live in the southern states. The others are concentrated in urban areas throughout the country. The most recent migration pattern for African Americans has been a movement away from northern industrial centers to the large cities of the south and west. Though New York City still has more African Americans, Atlanta replaced Chicago in 2010 as having the second largest concentration of African Americans (Bureau of the Census, 2010).

Hispanic Americans

Persons of **Hispanic origin** are those who classify themselves in one of the specific Hispanic categories listed on the Census Bureau questionnaire. They may identify themselves on the form in the following ways:

Are you of Hispanic, Latino, or Spanish origin?

If yes:

Yes, Mexican, Mexican American, Chicano

Yes, Puerto Rican

Yes, Cuban

Yes, another Hispanic, Latino, or Spanish origin for example,

Argentinean, Colombian, Dominican, Nicaraguan, Salvadoran, Spaniard, and so on.

A person choosing the "another" category may self-identify with Central or South America or Spain. The Hispanic population was 55 million in the 1990 census, or 17%. It increased by more than 50% in the decade of the 1980s, due to large numbers of both legal and illegal immigrants. The Hispanic population increased by 15.2 million between 2000 and 2010 and accounted for more than half of the total U.S. population increase of 27.3 million (Bureau of the Census, 2010).

Mexican Americans comprise 64% of the U.S. Hispanic population and 11% of the U.S. population (Bureau of the Census, 2010). Hispanics live primarily in Texas, New Mexico, Arizona, and Southern California. Among U.S. cities, New York City and Miami have large numbers of Puerto Ricans and Cubans.

Asian Americans

Asian Americans are those who classify themselves in one of the specific Hispanic categories listed on the Census Bureau questionnaire. They may identify themselves on the form in the following ways:

Asian Indian
Chinese
Filipino
Japanese
Korean
Vietnamese
"Other Asian"

The Asian American population in 1990 was 7,273,662. This was 2.9% of the U.S. population (Easterling, 1999). Asian Americans were, at that time, the fastest growing minority, having increased by more than 107% between 1980 and 1990. The Asian American label covers more than a dozen ethnic groups with diverse national origins, histories, religions, languages, and customs.

According to the 2010 U.S. Census, Asian Americans represent 4.8% of the total U.S. population, totaling 14.7 million. When including those who claim that they are Asian in addition to another ethnicity, the total is 17.3 million, or 5.6 of the U.S. population (Bureau of the Census, 2010). The largest ethnic groups represented in the census were Chinese (3.79 million), Filipino (3.41 million), Indian (3.18 million), Vietnamese (1.73 million), Korean (1.7 million), and Japanese (1.3 million).

Asians represent more than 50% of the population in Hawaii, but New York City has the largest Asian population among cities. Among the metropolitan statistical areas with the largest Asian populations, Chinese was the largest detailed Asian group in six of the metro areas (New York, Los Angeles, San Francisco, San Jose, Boston, and Seattle). The Asian Indian population was the largest Asian group in six of the metro areas (Chicago, Washington, Dallas-Fort Worth, Philadelphia, Atlanta, and Detroit). Filipinos were the largest in five of the metro areas (San Diego, Riverside, Las Vegas, Sacramento, and Phoenix), followed by Japanese in Honolulu, the Hmong in Minneapolis-St. Paul, and Vietnamese in Houston (Bureau of the Census, 2010).

European Americans

The vast majority of people in the United States are descended from Europe. Large numbers were attracted to the United States by political and religious freedom as well as by the hope of economic opportunity. Before 1860, most immigrants were from England, Ireland, and Germany, though the Spaniards were the first Europeans to establish permanent settlements in North America. Between 1860 and 1920, the majority of immigrants came from Russia, Poland, the Balkans, and Italy. Thirteen percent of all immigrants to the United States have come from Germany, 9.9% from Italy, 9.5% from Great Britain, 8.8% from Ireland, and 6.4% came from Russia (Easterling, 1999).

Distribution

In 2010, 80.1% of Americans lived in metropolitan areas, up from 79.5% in 2000. Fifty-four percent live in one of the metropolitan areas with 1 million or more population (Bureau of the Census, 2010). The largest cities are as follows:

Largest U.S. Cities

1	New York, New York	8,405,837
2	Los Angeles, California	3,884,307
3	Chicago, Illinois	2,718,782
4	Houston, Texas	2,195,914
5	Philadelphia, Pennsylvania	1,553,165
6	Phoenix, Arizona	1,513,367
7	San Antonio, Texas	1,409,019
8	San Diego, California	1,355,896
9	Dallas, Texas	1,257,676
10	San Jose, California	998,537

Source: Bureau of the Census (2010).

The most populous states in descending order are California, Texas, New York, Florida, Pennsylvania, and Illinois. The states with the smallest populations are Wyoming, Alaska, Vermont, Delaware, and North Dakota.

The fastest growing states are Nevada, Arizona, and Utah. Sixty percent of the U.S. population lives in the Southern and Western sections of the country. U.S. cities are home to 62.7% of the U.S. population, but comprise just 3.5% of the land area (Bureau of the Census, 2010).

In terms of density, the most populated areas are the District of Columbia, with 9,883 persons per square mile, New Jersey, with 1,042 persons per square mile, and Rhode Island, which has 960 persons per square mile. The least dense state is Alaska, with only one person per square mile. Wyoming has 4.7 and Montana has 5.5 persons per square mile, respectively. The population center of the United States is near Plato, Missouri, in the south-central area of the state (Bureau of the Census, 2010).

Religion

Former President Bill Clinton with Evangelist Billy Graham at a crusade in Flushing, New York.

There are more than thousand denominations, sects, and cults in the United States. National surveys indicate that 87% of the adult population express a belief in God and 69% report that they attend church, mosque, or synagogue. The U.S. population has great variation in religious affiliation.

United States Religious Affiliation

Protestant	46.5%
Roman Catholic	20.8%
Mormon	1.6%
Jehovah's Witness	0.8%
Other Christian	0.9%
Jewish	1.9%
Muslim	0.9%
Buddhist	0.7%
Hindu	0.7%
"Other"	1.8%
Unaffiliated	22.8%
Don't Know/Refused	0.6%

Source: CIA Factbook (2014).

Eighty-seven percent identify themselves as Christian. The largest Christian organization is the Roman Catholic Church, with about 64 million members in the United States. The largest Protestant denomination is the Southern Baptist Convention, which has 15 million members (Pipes, 2016), followed by the United Methodist Church, with a declining membership of 7 million (UMData, 2017). Since the 1960s, there has been a shift in membership away from the liberal mainstream denominations toward evangelical and charismatic churches, whose members are "born again" and highly committed to their faiths.

Education

Eighty-six percent of Americans can read and write at age 15 and over. Eighty-five percent of persons are high school graduates at age 25 or over. The percentage with at least a bachelor's degree from a college or university is 32. Sixty percent of all college students in the United States are female. An average of $10,700 is spent annually per pupil for public elementary and secondary schooling (Bureau of the Census, 2010).

The Economy and Labor

Fifteen percent of Americans are below the federal poverty level ($28,290) for a family of four (Bureau of the Census, 2010). In 1992, the poverty level was

$14,335 per year for a family of four (Easterling, 1999). The percentage of African Americans living below the poverty level is 33.3%. For Hispanics, the figure is 29.3%, for whites, 11.6%. Numerically, however, there are more poor whites than any other category.

About 70% of men and 58% of women were in the labor force in 2010, compared with 76% of men and 60% of women in 1990 (Bureau of the Census, 2010). The U-3 unemployment rate in the United States is 4.8%. The U-6 rate (9.6% in January 2017) is a broader definition of unemployment than the "official unemployment rate" (U-3). The U-3 is the rate most often reported in the media. In the U-3 rate, the Bureau of Labor Statistics only counts those who have looked for a job in the past 4 weeks as unemployed! This is, by any definition, a major lack of integrity on the part of the U.S. government designed to make the unemployment situation seem less serious than it really is.

> *The U-6 rate adds those who are marginally attached and discouraged. It also includes part-time workers who would prefer full-time jobs. For that reason, it is almost double the U-3 report. The Bureau of Labor Statistics issues both in each month's jobs report. Surprisingly, there is not as much media attention paid to the real unemployment rate. But even Federal Reserve Chair Janet Yellen said it paints a clearer picture of true U.S. unemployment.*
>
> *The U-3 rate only counts people without jobs who are in the labor force. These people have looked for a job in the last four weeks. The BLS categorizes people who have looked for work in the last year but not the last four weeks as marginally attached. For more, see Labor Force Participation Rate.*
>
> *Among the marginally attached are the discouraged workers, who have given up looking for work altogether. They could have gone back to school, gotten pregnant or become disabled. They may or may not return to the labor force, depending on their circumstances. Once they haven't looked for a job in 12 months, they're no longer counted as marginally attached.*
>
> (Amadeo, 2017)

Projections for the Future

By the middle of the twenty-first century, non-Hispanic whites will no longer be in the numerical majority in the United States. The U.S. population will reach half a billion by the end of the century. These predictions and many others like them are being made by social demographers who project current trends into the future. The actual direction of the future depends, of course, upon many factors. Sociologists were predicting with some certainty that there will be more women than men in the labor force in the United States by the year 2015 or 2020, but this does not appear to be likely, after all. One certain fact, however, is that the United States will continue to be a nation of great diversity and change.

Demographics, Canada

In Canada, **Statistics Canada** is the fact-gathering agency of the government. The census has been conducted once every 10 years since 1851, when the population was 2,440,000 (Easterling, 1999).

Canada is the second largest nation in the world (after Russia) in terms of area. It is the 38th largest in terms of the number of people, with a 2017 population of 36,503,097, 51% of which are female and 49% are male (Statistics Canada, 2017). This is up from a 1991 population of 28,114,000.

Vital Statistics

The birth rate in Canada is 10.3 births per 1,000 population per year (14.48 in 1991). This figure is lower than that of the United States, though Canada has traditionally had a higher birth rate. The death rate is 4.8 deaths per 1,000 population per year, lower than in most other industrialized nations (Statistics Canada, 2017). These factors combine with the net migration rate

(6.9 immigrants per 1,000 population per year) to produce a population growth rate for the Dominion of Canada of 0.9% per year, down from 1.25% in 1991. At the time of marriage, the average female is aged 28 and the average male is 31 (Statistics Canada, 2017).

The average Canadian resident can expect to live from birth to age 79. The life expectancy for males is 79 and females can expect a life that is 83 years (Statistics Canada, 2017). The average age for Canadians is 41 years, up from 31.6 in 1991. Age of about 15.4% are under 15 and 12% are 65 or over (Statistics Canada, 2017).

The Canadian infant mortality rate is 4.9 infant deaths per 1,000 live births per year, down from 7.0 in 1991 (Statistics Canada, 2017). This figure is among the lowest in the world, even when compared with the infant mortality rates of other industrialized nations.

Native Canadians

The Canadian population is composed of many racial and ethnic groups. Native Canadians ("aboriginal peoples") make up 4.3% of the population of the Dominion of Canada (Statistics Canada, 2017). They include indigenous Indians and Inuit who had lived in the area for thousands of years before the Europeans arrived. The Inuit are sometimes referred to as "Eskimos." These groups represent a small minority of the Canadian population as a whole, but are a major element in the northern regions. They make up the majority of residents in the Northwest Territories and are a very significant proportion of the population in the Yukon.

There are 10 major tribes or "nations" to which the most of Canada's Indians belong. These are the Algonquian, the Athapaskan, the Haida, the Iroquois, the Salishan, the Sioux, the Tlingit, the Kootenayan, the Tsimshian, and the Wakashan. The majority of Indians in Canada live within reservations called "reserves." There are 2,250 of these reserves throughout the nation. Their average standard of living is substantially lower than that of the non-Indian population (Easterling, 1999).

European Canadians

Approximately 40% of Canada's population have British, Scotch, or Irish ancestry. Twenty-six percent have descended from French colonists and another 25% immigrated from other nations in Europe. Quebec is the only province not populated by predominantly British, Scotch, or Irish persons.

About 5 million of the 6.5 million Canadians of French ancestry live in Quebec. Repeated attempts have been made by French-speaking groups to establish Quebec as a separate independent nation. Each of the referendums has failed, the latest in 1995 (Easterling, 1999).

Large numbers of Europeans have been attracted to Canada by political and religious freedom as well as by the hope of economic opportunity. About 4% of Canadians are of German descent, 3% hail from Italy, and 2% are Ukrainian in origin. In addition, there are sizable numbers of persons from the Netherlands, Hungary, Poland, Greece, Norway, Sweden, and Portugal.

Other Canadians

About 16.3% of the population of British Columbia are of Asian ancestry (Statistics Canada, 2017). Vancouver has, in recent years, accepted numbers of Chinese from Hong Kong, which reverted to the control of the mainland Chinese government in 1997. Toronto has fairly large numbers of Asian Indians, Chinese, and a contingent from the West Indies. Blacks comprise less than 1% (0.8%) of the Canadian population. The majority of these are West Indians, including Haitians (Statistics Canada, 2017).

Distribution

Seventy-seven percent of Canadians live in metropolitan areas. Twenty-three percent live in rural areas. Eighty percent live within 100 miles of the border with the United States to the south. The most populous province is Ontario, with 38.26% of the Canadian population. Quebec has 23.23%, followed by British Columbia, which has 13.22% of the people of Canada. The provinces or territories with the smallest populations are the Yukon Territory and the Northwest Territories, each with less than two-tenths of 1% of the Canadian population. Prince Edward Island has about four-tenths of 1% (Statistics Canada, 2017).

Provincial Populations of Canada

Canadian Province or Territory	Population 2016	Percentage of Canadian Population
Alberta	4,067,175	11.57%
British Columbia	4,648,055	13.22%
Manitoba	1,278,365	3.64%
New Brunswick	747,101	2.13%

Canadian Province or Territory	Population 2016	Percentage of Canadian Population
Newfoundland and Labrador	519,716	1.48%
Northwest Territories	41,786	0.12%
Nova Scotia	923,598	2.63%
Nunavut	35,944	0.10%
Ontario	13,448,494	38.26%
Prince Edward Island	142,907	0.41%
Quebec	8,164,361	23.23%
Saskatchewan	1,098,352	3.12%
Yukon	35,874	0.10%

Source: Statistics Canada (2017).

Ontario is the most urbanized province, with 80% of its population living in cities. The least urbanized province is Prince Edward Island, which is only 40% urban. The largest urban area in Canada is Toronto, Ontario, with a population of 2,731,571, followed by Montreal, Quebec, with 1,704,694, and Calgary, Alberta, with 1,239,220 (Statistics Canada, 2017).

In terms of **density**, the most populated areas are Prince Edward Island, with 59 persons per square mile, Nova Scotia, with 34.4 persons per square mile, and New Brunswick, which has 21 persons per square mile. The least dense area is the Northwest Territories, with only 0.017 persons per square mile. Yukon Territory has 0.07 and Manitoba has 3.67 persons per square mile. Canada, as a whole, has a population density of only 7 persons per square mile, the lowest in the world (Statistics Canada, 2017).

Religion

There are numerous denominations, sects, and cults in Canada. Statistics Canada's Household Survey indicates that 67.3% of the population identify themselves as Christians (Statistics Canada, 2017). Roman Catholics are 38.7%. Protestants are 27% (of these, 6.1% are in the United Church of Canada, and 5% are Anglican/Episcopalian, and there are substantial numbers of Presbyterians, Lutherans, Baptists, Pentecostals, and Charismatics). Orthodox adherents (1.7%), Jewish (1%), Muslims (3.2%), Hindu (1.5%), Sikh (1.4%), Buddhist (1.1%), and report having no religious identity whatsoever (23.9%) (Statistics Canada, 2017).

Education

Ninety-seven percent of Canadians can read and write at age 15 and over (Statistics Canada, 2017). The percentage of females with at least a bachelor's degree from a college or university is 64.8. The percentage of all males who have completed four or more years of postsecondary education is 64.7% (Statistics Canada, 2017). Public schooling is available for the entire population. In some provinces, Catholic and Protestant schools are publicly funded. Canada has 69 colleges and universities, some of which teach entirely in the English language, some in French, and some are bilingual. Canada is the only developed country without a system of accreditation.

The Economy and Labor

About 91% of men and 82% of women are in the Canadian labor force (Statistics Canada, 2017). The unemployed comprise 6.5% of the working age population. It is estimated that 9.4% of Canadian families are below the poverty level, but Canada does not have an "official poverty line." Statistics Canada considers a family as being in the low income category if it must spend more than 58.8% of its income on the basic needs of food, clothing, and shelter. The poverty level for rural households is about 25% lower than for urban households. About 19% of officially defined poor families live in rural settings.

Projections for the Future

Given the current birth, death, and immigration rates, the Canadian population will continue to age far into the next century. The French-speaking separatists in Quebec may yet achieve secession from Canada. These predictions, and many others like them, are being made by social demographers who project current trends into the future. The actual direction of the future depends, of course, upon many factors. It is certain that Canada will remain a world power with great natural resources and human potential.

Name _____ Date _____

Chapter 15   Demography

Chapter Exercise

(This assignment is to be carefully torn out and completed at the direction of the instructor. The answers are to be legibly handwritten directly on the sheets. *Do not* photocopy these pages, as such action would constitute a blatant violation of the copyright laws of the United States. Thoroughly read the assigned text before attempting to complete a tear-out assignment. It is obvious when a student has tried to fill-in an assignment without reading the background material.)

Explain the importance of accurate demographic information when studying the elements of society.

_____

_____

_____

_____

_____

_____

_____

_____

_____

_____

_____

_____

_____

_____

_____

References

Akmajian, A., Demers, R., & Harnish, R. (1984). *Linguistics: An introduction to language and communication*. Cambridge, MA: MIT Press.

Amadeo, K. (2017, June 2). What is the real unemployment rate? Does the government lie about unemployment? *The Balance*. Retrieved from https://www.thebalance.com/what-is-the-real-unemployment-rate-3306198

Aquinas, S. T. (1273/1948). *Summa theologica*. New York, NY: Benziger Bros.

Asch, S. (1952). *Social psychology*. Englewood Cliffs, NJ: Prentice-Hall.

Atkin, C., & Gibson, W. (1978). *Children's nutrition learning from television advertising*. East Lansing: Michigan State University.

Bartholomew, K. (2007). *Workplace wellness* (p. 145). Old Saybrook, CT: Business and Legal Reports. 145.

Berlin, B., & Kay, P. (1969). *Basic color terms: Their universality and evolution*. Berkeley, CA: University of California Press.

Biesanz, J., & Biesanz, M. (1969). *Introduction to sociology*. Englewood Cliffs, NJ: Prentice Hall.

Buber, M. (1955). *Between man and man*. Boston, MA: Beacon Press.

Bureau of the Census, United States. (2010). Retrieved from https://www.census.gov/prod/2011pubs/12statab/vitstat.pdf

Bureau of the Census, United States Department of Commerce. (1990). *Money income and poverty status of families and persons in the United States*. Washington, DC: United States Government Printing Office.

Bureau of Labor Statistics. (2017). Retrieved from https://www.bls.gov/

Camus, A. (1942). *The stranger*. New York, NY: Alfred A. Knopf.

Camus, A. (1969). *The rebel*. New York, NY: Alfred A. Knopf.

Centers for Disease Control. (2010). QuickStats: Number of deaths from 10 leading causes—National vital statistics system. United States. *MMWR, 62* (8), 155.

Chast, R. (1990). Why oil spills are good. *The New Yorker Magazine* .

CIA—United States Central Intelligence Agency. (2014). *Factbook*. Retrieved from https://www.cia.gov/library/publications/the-world-factbook

Cole, K. C. (1985). *Sympathetic vibrations*. New York, NY: William Morrow.

Comte, A. (1830). *System of positive philosophy*. Paris: Bachelier.

Comte, A. (1851). *Treatise on sociology*. London: Burt Franklin.

Comte, A. (1854). *The positive philosophy of Auguste Comte* (H. Martineau, Trans.). London: Bell and Sons.

Cooley, C. H. (1909). *Social organization*. New York, NY: Shocken Books.

Coser, L. A. (1977). *Masters of sociological thought: Ideas in historical and social context*. San Diego, CA: Harcourt Brace Jovanovich.

Covey, S. (1990). *Seven habits of highly effective people*. New York, NY: Simon & Schuster.

Craib, I. (1976). *Existentialism and sociology: A study of Jean-Paul Sartre*. London: Cambridge University Press.

Dahrendorf, R. (1959). *Class and conflict in industrial society*. Stanford, CA: Stanford University Press.

Davis, K. (1940). Extreme social isolation of a child. *American Journal of Sociology, 45* (4), 554–565.

Davis, K. (1941/1980). *Thorstein Veblen's social theory*. New York, NY: Arno Press.

Davis, K. (1947, March). Final note on a case of extreme isolation. *American Journal of Sociology, 52* (5), 432–437, 554.

Davis, K., & Moore, W. E. (1945, April). Some principles of stratification. *American Sociological Review, 10* (2), 242–249.

Death Penalty Information Center. (2016). https://deathpenaltyinfo.org/states-and-without-death-penalty

Deegan, M. J. (1991). *Women in sociology: A bio-bibliographical sourcebook*. New York, NY: Greenwood Press.

Delisi, M. (2006). Zeroing in on early arrest onset: Results from a population of extreme career criminals. *Journal of Criminal Justice, 34*, 17–26.

Dente, L. A. (1977). *Veblen's theory of social change*. New York, NY: Arno Press.

Dodgen, L. I., & Rapp, A. M. (2006). *Sociology: Looking through the window of the world* (7th ed., p. 79). Kendall Hunt Textbook.

Dorfman, J. (1934/1972). *Thorstein Veblen and his America*. Clifton, NJ: A. M. Kelley.

Duggins, J. (1978). *Bard of savagery: Thorstein Veblen and modern social theory*. New York, NY: Seabury Press.

Durkheim, E. (1893). *The division of labor in society*. New York, NY: Macmillan.

Durkheim, E. (1895). *The rules of sociological method*. London: Macmillan.

Durkheim, E. (1897). *Suicide*. New York, NY: Free Press.

Durkheim, E. (1912). *The elementary forms of religious life*. London: Allen and Unwin.

Durkheim, E. (1925). *L'education morale*. Paris: Presses Universitaires de France.

Easterling, C. H. (1994). *Introduction to the sociological perspective*. New York, NY: Whittier Publications.

Easterling, C. H. (1999). *The sociological enterprise*. Acton, MA: Copley Publishing Group.

Edison, T. (1932, September). Spoken statement (c. 1903). *Harper's Monthly* .

Ember, C., & Ember, M. (1993). *Cultural anthropology*. Englewood Cliffs, NJ: Prentice Hall.

FBI Crime Index. (2016). *Uniform crime reports*.

Feagin, J. R., & Feagin, C. B. (1990). *Social problems: A critical power-conflict perspective*. Englewood Cliffs, NJ: Prentice-Hall.

Foster, G. (1962). *Traditional cultures and the impact of technological change*. New York, NY: Harper and Row.

Foucault, M. (1963). *The birth of the clinic: Archaeology of medical perception.* New York, NY: Vintage Books.

Foucault, M. (1973). *The order of things.* New York, NY: Vintage Books.

Foucault, M. (1977). *Discipline and punish: The birth of the prison.* New York, NY: Pantheon Books.

Frankl, V. E. (1962). *Man's search for meaning: An introduction to logotherapy.* Boston, MA: Beacon Press.

Fromm, E. (1941). *Escape from freedom.* New York, NY: Holt, Rinehart, and Winston.

Gans, H. J. (1971, July–August). The uses of poverty: The poor pay all. *Social Policy,* pp. 20–24.

Glassner, B., & Freedman, J. A. (1979). *Clinical sociology.* New York, NY: Longman.

Glueck, S., & Glueck, E. (1950). *Unraveling juvenile delinquency.* New York, NY: Commonwealth Fund.

Goffman, E. (1959). *The presentation of self in everyday life.* New York, NY: Doubleday.

Hahn, E. (1971, April 24). Chimpanzees and language. *New Yorker.*

Hamilton, C. J. (1893). *Women writers.* London: Warwick House.

Harlow, H. F. (1962). Development of affection in primates. In E. L. Bliss (Ed.), *Roots of behavior* (pp. 157–166). New York, NY: Harper.

Harrington, A. (1969). *The immortalist.* New York, NY: Avon Books.

Heidegger, M. (1927). *Being and time.* Tubingen, Germany: Halle.

Hemfelt, R., Minirth, F., & Meier, P. (1989). *Love is a choice.* Nashville: Nelson.

Hobson, J. A. (1936/1971). *Veblen.* New York, NY: A. M. Kelley.

Hosea. (751 B.C.) Northern Kingdom of Israel.

Hudson, C. E. (1935). *Preface to a Christian sociology.* London: George Allen & Unwin Publishers.

Janis, I. (1989). *Crucial decisions: Leadership in policymaking and crisis management.* New York, NY: Free Press.

Kafka, F. (1957). *The trial.* New York, NY: Alfred A. Knopf.

Kahn, J. (1974). *The political economy of Thorstein Veblen and John Kenneth Galbraith.* Stanford: Humanities Honors Program.

Kierkegaard, S. (1961). The sickness unto death. In R. Bretall (Ed.), *A Kierkegaard anthology.* New York, NY: Modern Library.

Krill, D. F. (1978). *Existential social work.* New York, NY: Free Press.

Krishnamurti, J. J. (1971). *Flight of the eagle.* New York, NY: Harper and Row.

Kurzweil, R. (2012). *How to create a mind: The secret of human thought revealed.* New York, NY: Viking Press.

Laing, R. D. (1967). *The politics of experience.* Baltimore, MA: Penguin.

Lancer, D. (2015). *Codependency for dummies* (2nd ed.). Hoboken, NJ: John Wylie.

Lemert, E. M. (1951). *Social pathology: A systematic approach to the theory of sociopathic behavior.* New York, NY: McGraw-Hill.

Levi-Strauss, C. (1947/1969). *The elementary structures of kinship.* New York, NY: Basic Books.

Lewis, C.S. (1946). *The great divorce* (p. 75). San Francisco, CA: Harper.

Little, P. E. (1968). *Know why you believe*. Downers Grove, IL: InterVarsity Press.

Locke, J. (1690/1986). *The second treatise on civil government*. Amherst, NY: Prometheus Books.

Lombroso, C. (1876/2006). *Criminal man*. Durham, NC: Duke University Press Books.

Lyotard, J.-F. (1984). *The post-modern condition: A report on knowledge* (G. Bennington & B. Massumi, Trans.). Minneapolis, MN: The University of Minnesota Press.

Machiavelli, N. (1513/1985). *The prince* (H. Mansfield, Trans.). Chicago, IL: University of Chicago Press.

Macionis, J. J. (1992). *Society: The basics*. Englewood Cliffs, NJ: Prentice-Hall.

Macionis, J. J. (2016). *Intro to sociology* (p. 6). Boston, MA: Pearson Learning Systems.

Martineau, H. (1983a). *Harriet Martineau's autobiography* (Vol. 1). London: Virago Press.

Martineau, H. (1983b). Introduction. In E. A. Arbuckle (Ed.), *Harriet Martineau's letters to Fanny Wedgewood*. Stanford, CA: Stanford University Press.

Marx, K. (1867). *Das kapital* (Vol. I). New York, NY: Penguin Books.

Marx, K., & Engels, F. (1848). In D. Ryazanoff (Ed.), Chapter II. Proletarians and Communists *Manifesto of the communist party*. New York, NY: Russell and Russell.

Maslow, A. H. (1954). *Motivation and personality*. New York, NY: Harper and Row.

Mather, M. (2016). *Fact sheet: Aging in the United States*. Washington, DC: Population Reference Bureau.

May, R. (1953). *Man's search for himself*. New York, NY: W. W. Norton.

May, R. (1961). *Existential psychology*. New York, NY: Random House.

Mead, G. H. (1934). Social psychology and behaviorism. In C. W. Morris (Ed.), *Mind, self, and society*. Chicago, IL: University of Chicago Press.

Menninger, K. (1973). *Whatever became of sin?* New York, NY: Hawthorn Books.

Merton, R. K. (1949). *Social theory and social structure*. New York, NY: Free Press.

Michels, R. (1911). *Political parties*. Glencoe, IL: Free Press.

Milgram, S. (1965, February). Some conditions of obedience and disobedience to authority. *Human Relations, 18,* 57–76.

Miller, F. F. (1985). *Famous women: Harriet Martineau*. Boston, MA: Roberts Brothers.

Mills, C. W. (1943). The professional ideology of social pathologists. *American Journal of Sociology, 49,* 165–180.

Müller, R. (2016). *Archives. International Sociological Association.* Retrieved from https://isaforum2016.wordpress.com/2015/04/20/persecution-and-exile-of-austrian-sociological-authors-during-fascism/

Murdock, G. (1945). *Social structure*. New York, NY: Macmillan.

Myrdal, G. (1944). *An American dilemma*. New York, NY: Harper & Bros.

National Center for Health Statistics. (2014). Retrieved from https://www.cdc.gov/nchs/fastats/marriage-divorce.htm

Niebuhr, H. R. (1951). *Christ and culture*. New York, NY: Harper and Row.

Nietzsche, F. W. (1954). On ethics. In W. Kauffman (Ed.), *The portable Nietzsche*. New York, NY: Viking Press.

Nisbet, R. (1990). *The quest for community: A study in the ethics of order and freedom* (p. 29). San Francisco, CA: ICS Press.

Olien, J. (2013, August 23). Loneliness is deadly. *Slate Magazine*. Retrieved from http://www.slate.com/articles/health_and_science/medical_examiner/2013/08/dangers_of_loneliness_social_isolation_is_deadlier_than_obesity.html

Papst, C. (2017, May 22). Who's at fault? District responds to 6 city schools with zero proficiency. *KBFF TV Fox 45 News*.

Parsons, T. (1937). *The structure of social action*. New York, NY: Free Press.

Parsons, T. (1951). *The social system*. Glencoe, IL: Free Press.

Parsons, T. (1953). Illness and the role of the physician: A sociological perspective. In C. Kluckhohn & H. A. Murray (Eds.), *Personality in nature, society, and culture* (pp. 609–617). New York, NY: Knopf.

Parsons, T. (1967). *Sociological theory and modern society*. New York, NY: Free Press.

Parsons, T. (1975). The sick role and the role of the physician reconsidered. *Milbank Memorial Fund Quarterly: Health and Society, 53* (Summer), 257–278.

Parsons, T. (1977). *Social systems and the evolution of action theory*. New York, NY: Free Press.

Parsons, T., & Platt, G. M. (1973). *The American university*. Cambridge, MA: Harvard University Press.

Paul, S. (65 A.D.). *The first epistle to Timothy*. Macedonia.

Peterson-Wilthorn, C. (2016, October). Forbes 400: The full list of the richest people in America 2016. *Forbes Magazine*.

Pew Research Center. (2017). *Religious landscape study*. Retrieved from http://www.pewforum.org/religious-landscape-study/

Piaget, J. (1969). *The psychology of the child* (2nd ed.). New York, NY: Basic Books.

Pichanick, V. K. (1980). *Harriet Martineau: The woman and her work, 1802–76*. Ann Arbor, MI: The University of Michigan Press.

Pipes, C. (2016, June 7). ACP: More churches reported; baptisms decline. Southern Baptist Convention. *Baptist Press* .

Ramirez, E. (2014). *Self-regulation in the alcohol industry*. Washington, DC: Federal Trade Commission.

Rand, A. (1944, January). The only path to tomorrow. *Reader's Digest*. p. 8.

Reckless, W., & Dinitz, S. (1968). *The prevention of juvenile delinquency*. New York, NY: Little, Brown and Company.

Reiman, J. H. (1979). *The rich get richer and the poor get prison*. New York, NY: John Wiley & Sons.

Riesman, D. (1953). *Thorstein Veblen: A critical interpretation*. New York, NY: Seabury Press.

Ritzer, G. (1988). *Sociological theory*. New York, NY: Alfred A. Knopf.

Rorty, R. (1984, April). Habermas and Lyotard on post-modernity. *Praxis International, 4* (1), 32–44.

Sansom, W. (1956). *A contest of ladies* (pp. 230–231). London: Hogarth.

Sapir, E. (1961). *Selected writings of Edward Sapir in language, culture, and personality.* Berkeley, CA: University of California Press.

Sartre, J.-P. (1943/1956). *Being and nothingness.* New York, NY: Philosophical Library.

Sartre, J.-P. (1945). *Existentialism and humanism.* London: Methuen.

Seckler, D. W. (1975). *Thorstein Veblen and the institutionalists: A study in the social philosophy of economics.* Boulder, CO: Colorado Associated University Press.

Sifferlin, A. (2016, November 2). Most Americans want to live to 100. *Time Magazine.*

Sheldon, W., Hartl, M., & MacDermott, E. (1949). *Varieties of delinquent youth.* New York, NY: Harper.

Simmel, G. (1908). *Soziologie. Untersuchungen uber die formen der vergesellschaftung.* Berlin: Duncker and Humbolt.

Simmel, G. (1914). *The conflict of modern culture.* New York, NY: Teacher College Press.

Simmel, G. (1950). On the significance of numbers for social life. In K. Wolff (Ed.), *The sociology of Georg Simmel.* New York, NY: Free Press.

Simmel, G. (1956). *Conflict and the web of group affiliation.* Glencoe, IL: Free Press.

Simmel, G. (1978). *The philosophy of money.* Boston, MA: Routledge and Kegan Paul.

Skousen, C. (2014). *The naked communist: Exposing communism and restoring freedom.* Salt Lake City, UT: Izzard Ink.

Smith, A. (1776/1937). *An inquiry into the nature and causes of the wealth of nations.* New York, NY: The Modern Library.

Spencer, H. (1862). *First principles.* New York, NY: A. C. Burt.

Spencer, H. (1867). *The principles of biology.* New York, NY: D. Appleton.

Spencer, H. (1898). *The principles of sociology.* New York, NY: D. Appleton and Company.

Statistics Canada. (2017). http://www.statcan.gc.ca/tables-tableaux/sum-som/l01/cst01/demo02a-eng.htm

Sutherland, E. H. (1949). *White collar crime.* New York, NY: Holt, Rinehart & Winston.

Thoreau, H. D. (1849). *Civil disobedience.* Pamphlet. First paragraph.

Tillich, P. (1952). *The courage to be.* New Haven, CT: Yale University Press.

Tolstoy, L. 1931 (1869). *War and peace.* New York, NY: The Modern Library.

Turner, J. (1985). *Herbert Spencer: Toward a renewed appreciation.* Beverly Hills, CA: Sage Publications.

U.S. Department of Human Services (2014). https://www.samhsa.gov/data/sites/default/files/NSDUHresultsPDFWHTML2013/Web/NSDUHresults2013.pdf

U.S. Department of Justice (2014). https://www.bjs.gov/content/pub/ascii/fjs1314.txt

UMData. (2017). *United methodist church.* Retrieved from http://www.umdata.org/UMFactsHome

UNAIDS (2016).

Unamuno, M. (1931). *San Manuel Bueno, martyr*. Madrid: Castalia.

Veblen, T. B. (1899). *The theory of the leisure class: An economic study of institutions.* New York, NY: New American Library.

Veblen, T. B. (1919). *The vested interests and the common man*. New York, NY: New American Library.

Walzer, M. (2000). *Just and unjust wars*. New York, NY: Basic Books.

Washington, G. (1790, January 8). Address to the second session of the first congress. Retrieved from http://www.presidency.ucsb.edu/ws/?pid=29431

Weber, M. (1920). *The Protestant ethic and the spirit of capitalism* (T. Parsons, Trans.). New York, NY: Scribner's.

Weber, M. (1921a). Intellectual orientations. In H. H. Gerth & C. W. Mills (Eds.), *Essays in sociology*. New York, NY: Oxford University Press.

Weber, M. (1921b). *The religion of India: The sociology of Hinduism and Buddhism*. Tubingen: Mohr Siebeck.

Weber, M. (1922). *Economy and society*. Yubingen: Mohr Siebeck.

Wheelis, A. (1958). *The quest for identity*. New York, NY: W. W. Norton.

Whorf, B. (1956). The relation of habitual thought and behavior to language. In *Language, thought, and reality*. Cambridge, MA: MIT Press.

Williams, R. (1964). *American society: A sociological interpretation*. New York, NY: Alfred A. Knopf.

Wurmbrand, R. (1986). *Marx and satan*. Westchester, IL: Crossway Books.

Index